Redundant Masculinities:

ANTIPODE BOOK SERIES

General Editor:
Noel Castree, Reader in Geography, University of Manchester, UK
Like its parent journal, the Antipode Book series reflects distinctive new developments in radical geography. It publishes books in a variety of formats – from reference books to works of broad explication to titles that develop and extend the scholarly research base – but the commitment is always the same: to contribute to the praxis of a new and more just society.

Published

Space, Place and the New Labour Internationalism
Jane Wills and Peter Waterman

Redundant Masculinities? Employment Change and White Working Class Youth
Linda McDowell

Forthcoming

Spaces of Neoliberalism
Neil Brenner

David Harvey: A Critical Reader
Edited by Noel Castree and Derek Gregory

Redundant Masculinities?

Employment Change and White Working Class Youth

Linda McDowell

Blackwell
Publishing

350 Main Street, Malden, MA 02148–5020, USA
108 Cowley Road, Oxford OX4 1JF, UK
550 Swanston Street, Carlton, Victoria 3053, Australia

First published 2003 by Blackwell Publishing Ltd

Library of Congress Cataloging-in-Publication Data

McDowell, Linda, 1949–
    Redundant masculinities? : employment change and white working class youth / Linda McDowell.
            p. cm. – (Antipode book series ; 2)
        ISBN 1-4051-0585-2 (hardback : alk. paper) – ISBN 1-4051-0586-0 (pbk. : alk. paper)
    1. Young men–Employment–United States. 2. White men–Employment–United States. 3. Minorities–Employment–United States. 4. High school dropouts–Employment–United States. 5. White men–United States–Psychology. 6. Masculinity–United States. I. Title. II. Series.

    HD6273.M396 2003
    305.242'0973–dc21

                                                                            2002152560

A catalogue record for this title is available from the British Library.

Set in Sabon 10.5/12.5 by Kolam Information Services Pvt. Ltd, Pondicherry, India
Printed and bound in the United Kingdom
by MPG Books Ltd, Bodmin, Cornwall

For further information on
Blackwell Publishing, visit our website:
http://www.blackwellpublishing.com

Contents

Plates

Tables

Preface

Boys will be boys. (World-wide proverb)

For many years now, I have written, worked and organized around issues of gender inequality. One of my strongest beliefs is in the necessity for equal opportunities policies, and for a long time I took it for granted that women should be the main beneficiaries. This belief was strengthened not only by statistical surveys and historical analyses but in part by my own experiences as I grew up in the late 1950s and 1960s, going to university in 1968 as the new left but also second wave feminism were influential social movements. When I became a university teacher in the 1970s, I found an academy dominated by men. My earlier life, before entering the labour market, however, had not totally resonated with my practical knowledge of men's superiority. As a girl I had grown up with only sisters as siblings and a strong mother who made most of the day-to-day decisions. I had attended an all-girls school and all-women's college. As a consequence, manhood and masculinity was a mystery to me in almost all practical senses. The ideas and values about masculinity that I internalized as a girl were from novels and music rather than 'real life' in the mid-1960s when gender relations were far more dichotomous than they are now. All that was on offer to girls and young women was the wholesome 'I want to be Bobbie's girl' or a version of rebellion to girlfriends of the 'leader of the pack'. In those years there seemed to be few opportunities for autonomy for girls: autonomy was a correlate of youthful masculinity. Boys and young men were the dominant sex, whether in the workplace or in other arenas.

At the start of the twenty-first century, this widespread taken for granted assumption of masculine superiority has been challenged as a 'problem with boys' has been identified. In 1999, the then Labour Home Secretary Jack Straw was reported as saying that one of the major social problems facing Britain was the behaviour of young men. By that time I was the mother of a teenage son, and Straw's statement had some resonance with my experiences. As my son went through his secondary school years between 1992 and 1999, it had become clear to me that the discourse of female disadvantage was unrecognizable to him and his peers. In his school it was the girls who were tough, independent and successful and the boys who were failing in growing numbers. Between the ages of 16 and 18, while many of the young women in his peer group achieved good results in school- leaving exams, too many of his male friends lost their commitment to academic success and left school to look for work in a local labour market increasingly dominated by low-paid service-sector jobs. This same pattern was evident across the country and a worrying problem about growing numbers of young men, apparently failing at school and increasingly troublesome in public spaces – on street corners and on the football terraces – began to be widely debated.

My son and his friends are becoming men as transformations in society, and particularly in the economy, are reducing the options of many young men, especially those who are least successful at school. Achieving adult independence and a decent standard of living through their labour market participation – the correlate of masculinity – seems increasingly problematic for working class young men. At the same time, by a sad irony and a seemingly wilful misunderstanding of the consequences of manufacturing decline and economic restructuring, waged work has become valorized as *the* route to adulthood and its virtue is enshrined in the so-called New Deal policies of New Labour: workfare by another name.

This book brings these two issues together: the transformation of work in advanced industrial societies and the 'problem of boys'. It unites my long-term research interests in social and economic restructuring and feminist theory and scholarship with my personal life as a mother of a son. It has been perhaps the most personal, the most difficult but also the most enjoyable book I have written so far. Many people – too numerous to name – have helped me in its production. I should like to acknowledge, however, the particular help of a small number of them. Thanks, as always, to Chris, Hugh and Sarah McDowell: the mainstays of my household. Sarah and Patrick Kilkelly, a frequent visitor, have shared with me their experiences of bottom-end jobs during their 'gap' year. Hugh and

Sarah and also Kelsey Boast deserve thanks for transcribing most of the interviews and for their astute criticisms of my interviewing style: I think I improved over the year's fieldwork thanks to you all. The Joseph Rowntree Foundation funded the fieldwork under their Youth Programme and I gratefully acknowledge its support as well as that of the steering group, especially Bob Coles, Rob MacDonald, Peter Jackson and Tessa Mitchell. Jo Casebourne was an excellent assistant and minute-taker at these meetings. Thanks too to colleagues in the Geography Departments at Cambridge University, LSE and UCL where I began and finished this work and to all those in other departments and in other places who commented on talks I have given based on this work. At the LSE, in particular, the seminars on young people run by the Gender Institute were a useful stimulus to this work, as were the many conversations about working with children and young people that I had with Ginny Morrow on the train to Kings Cross. Thanks too to Ann Phoenix, now at the Open University, for numerous, often rushed but always useful, conversations at conferences and meetings in various places and to Paula Meth, now at Sheffield Hallam University, for all those drinks at the Station Bar.

My tutorial students at UCL over the last two years and Tara Duncan, a graduate student working with me, probably heard more than enough about this research but always offered cheerful and astute criticism: so thanks to you all too. I am enormously grateful to the heads, the year 11 teachers and the secretarial staff of Fenland Community College and Park Edge School. I cannot name you, as I promised anonymity for the participants, but you know who you are and how much I owe to your co-operation in the middle of a busy school year. My greatest thanks, of course, must go to 24 young men, 10 in Cambridge and 14 in Sheffield, most of whom were prepared to talk to me not just once but three times in 1999–2000. I hope that you might read this book and find something of interest in the ways in which I have represented your lives as you left school and became workers.

Some of the chapters draw on earlier versions of my published papers, revised to varying degrees here. I should like to acknowledge the permission of the journal editors and publishers to reprint, in revised versions, parts of 'Learning to Serve? Young men's labour market aspirations in an era of economic restructuring', *Gender, Place and Culture*, 7 (2000), 389–416; 'Masculine discourses and dissonances: Strutting "lads", protest masculinity and domestic respectability', *Environment and Planning D: Society and Space*, 20 (2002), 97–119; and 'Transitions to work: Masculine identities, youth inequality and labour market change', *Gender Place and Culture*, 9 (2002), 39–59 (http://www.tandf.co.uk).

1

Introduction: Young, White, Male and Working Class

There is a virtual invisibility of the voices and concerns of adolescents and young adults in academic debates. (*Signs* editorial 1998: 575)

This book is a study of gender as a social, cultural and economic force but also of individual young men and their lives in particular places. It is about 'the way particular men created their manhood within the limits of their time and place' (Rotundo 1993: x) and about meaning, power and the construction of identity at a particularly significant moment in the lives of young men: as they finish compulsory schooling and start to think about their future working lives. As Connell (1994: 14) has argued, 'masculinities and femininities are actively constructed, not simply received'. Similarly, people are not just at the mercy of the social and economic transformations that have restructured the labour markets of British towns and cities in the last two decades or so. While these transformations may have affected the life chances of individuals, often for the worse, and changed the set of opportunities that are open to young people at the beginning their working lives, individuals and social groups are also agents in their own construction and in their responses to altered circumstances. My aim is to challenge the too-common assumptions in the media and also in social policy that working class young men, adversely affected by economic change, are idlers, layabouts or 'yobs'. I want to show instead the often admirable efforts made by many young men on the verge of adulthood, and with few educational or social advantages, to acquire and hold down a job and to construct lives imbued with the values of domestic respectability, while negotiating the complex and often contradictory expectations associated with working class masculinity.

In the chapters that follow, the interrelationships between different forms of social inequalities and the ways in which they are lived out in local areas in different towns are investigated through the lens of a year in the lives of 24 young men who finished their compulsory schooling in the summer of 1999. For young people leaving school this is the beginning of a period of transition in their lives as they decide on their next steps. It is also a key moment when inequalities between young people begin to become particularly significant. Despite the huge class inequalities that are evident in the British school system (Adonis and Pollard 1998; Mortimore and Whitty 1997; Rutter 1979; Sparkes and Glennester 2002), until the age of 16, all children, theoretically at least, must attend full-time education and all of them sit the same set of school-leaving examinations. At 16, however, while most young people remain in the educational sector, a minority of young people, predominantly from working class families, leave school and begin to search for work. Twenty-five years ago, when Paul Willis (1977) investigated the lives of a group of young men living in a Midlands town, a majority of 16 year olds left school as soon as they could. In 1977, less than 25 per cent of the age group continued their full-time education, whereas at the end of the century, almost two-thirds of all 16 year olds stayed in full-time education, and many others were involved in some form of training. What was once the start of a transition into the labour market for most young people has now become exceptional, as the majority stay in full-time education and strive to attain the credentials that are increasingly important in gaining access to well-paid and permanent employment.

At the same time as the educational participation patterns of 16-year-olds changed, the labour market had also been transformed by the shift from manufacturing employment to the dominance of service-sector occupations. The types of work that most of Willis's lads had walked into in 1977 – unskilled manufacturing work with relatively good rates of pay and some prospect of security – had virtually disappeared by 1999. For most 16-year-olds now, casual and insecure jobs in the service sector – in fast-food outlets, in shops and restaurants, as waiters, in bars, as cleaners – are what is widely advertised. This type of service-sector employment that increasingly dominates the labour market of most British towns and cities, provides fewer opportunities for steady and reasonably well-paid work for men than the manufacturing sector used to. Indeed, in a paper less often quoted than the 1977 book, Willis

(1984) himself had noted that the prolonged period of unemployment in the early 1980s in Britain was affecting the traditional transition from school to the labour market, particularly for working class young men. He argued that in the early 1980s young men without a steady job were becoming less attractive to increasingly independent young women, and so not only was the transition into work disrupted but so too was the usual path into heterosexual relationships, marriage and family life: the correlates of the dominant version of masculine adulthood. His prescient arguments were, however, not to become common currency for a further two decades when the anxieties about young men's successful attainment of heterosexual masculinity had become widespread. As I shall demonstrate later, in the UK, in contrast to the USA where race and ethnicity is a key part of the *fin de siècle* crisis of masculinity, these anxieties focused in particular on young white working class men who were portrayed as a social problem in school, at work and in urban public spaces.

The increasing dominance of service employment in contemporary Britain and, indeed, in the advanced industrial nations of the world in general, has been recognized as significant for more than poorly educated young men looking for work. A set of new debates about the changing expectations of employment and the impact of new working patterns on personal identity now dominate the academic and policy literature. These debates emphasize the growth of risk, uncertainty and insecurity in the labour market (Allen and Henry 1997; Bauman 1998; Beck 1992; Elliott and Atkinson 1999; Giddens 1991), even the potential corrosion of character in contemporary workplace relations (Sennett 1998), rather than the achievement of the status and respect that was traditionally associated with waged employment, especially for men. Waged employment, identified as a core element in the social construction of a masculine identity (Connell 1995), has altered in its nature and form and, in particular, in its associations with masculinity. Service-sector work, especially at the bottom end, demands care, deference and docility as key attributes of a desirable workplace identity – characteristics that are more commonly identified as feminine than masculine traits and it seems that women rather than men are now preferred employees (Bradley, Erickson, Stephenson and Williams 2000; Duster 1995; Leidner 1991, 1993). Indeed, for many men, and especially young men at the beginning of the twenty-first century, there seems to be growing evidence of a reversal of long-standing relationships between gender and achievement, as girls' rates of achievement at school and at university improve, and between gender and employment chances that previously positioned girls and young women as the underachieving and disadvantaged group (Arnot,

David and Weiner 1999). Men, it is claimed, are the new disadvantaged, trapped in relationships of dominance and aggression that penalize them in the public and the private spheres. Disadvantaged in the service sector, rejected as marriage partners as rates of divorce rise and women remain single longer, even biologically redundant as new technologies alter the social relations of reproduction, it is small wonder that growing numbers of men feel out of place in the new millennium. For young men in particular it is a difficult time to negotiate the transitions to adulthood and pathways to employment when traditional ways of becoming a man are increasingly less available.

In this book I investigate the ways in which the coincidence of these changing material circumstances and theoretical debates about new relationships between employment and gendered identities are affecting the attitudes and aspirations of young men in two British cities as they contemplate their transition from school to labour market participation. The particular group of men that I focus on is white English 15- to 16-year-olds with low educational achievement. There are several reasons for this focus. This group has perhaps been particularly adversely affected by economic change, but they are also currently neglected – indeed discriminated against – by social policy-makers. Young people's eligibility for welfare benefits such as income support and housing benefit has been eliminated and they are also excluded from the new workfare programme introduced in the United Kingdom in 1998 – the so-called New Deal – which requires 18- to 24-year-olds to participate in workfare schemes in return for income support. A further reason for the focus on young men is the spread of debates about masculinity from arcane theoretical papers into the popular imagination. Since 1997 or so, there has been a consistent argument in the media that young men are facing a crisis of confidence. The popular and broadsheet press concur in their view that young men are a 'lost generation', caught, according to a comment in a Sunday broadsheet, 'between the Nineties New Man and New Lad' (Ardlidge 1999: 13). The comments are repeated elsewhere in the media (Hill 1997; McInnes 1997) and are the topic of popular books about masculinity in the USA, from Robert Bly's *Iron John* (1990) to Susan Faludi's *Stiffed* (2000); in Stephen Biddulph's *Manhood* (1994) in Australia; and in the UK, where the radio psychiatrist Anthony Clare (2000) weighed in with his book *On Men: Masculinity in Crisis*. The arguments about crisis are variously supported by statistics about the rising rate of suicide among young men and, especially, by figures that demonstrate the relative successes of young women both in school-leaving examinations and in access to higher education. Boys and young men also truant more, offend more and are both more violent themselves and more at risk of violence than young women. While these latter differences are not new, the opening gender gap in educational performance at the age of 16 certainly is. Combined with the rapid rise in feminized service-sector employment opportunities in the majority of British towns and cities, masculinity is coming to be seen as a disadvantage rather than an advantage in labour market entry.

At the centre of the book are the voices of two groups of young men, whom I interviewed three times in the 12 months after they left school. One group lived in the northern deindustrializing town of Sheffield, the second in the expanding science-based and service-sector market town of Cambridge in East Anglia. As the comment at the chapter head suggests, there has been a perhaps surprising absence of the voices and opinions of young people themselves in these debates about gender and crisis, whether in press stories or in the work of social scientists. This absence persists despite the recent expansion of studies of childhood, school life and the transition to adult status (see e.g. Ashton, Maguire and Spilsbury 1990; Furlong 1992; Irwin 1995; Krahn and Lowe 1991; Lowe and Krahn 2000; Raffe 1988). It has been partially countered, however, by two recent British school-based studies of young men in secondary schooling (Frosh, Phoenix and Pattman 2002; O'Donnell and Sharpe 2000), and a third study by Stephen Ball, Meg Maguire and Sheila Macrae (2000) following school leavers born in 1979 and 1980 into the labour market. In all three cases the research was undertaken in London. This latter book is similar in its aims to my work, although the so-called crisis of masculinity was not an explicit focus and the participants, of both sexes, came from a range of class backgrounds. In the other two studies, both of which focused explicitly on the social construction of masculinity during the transitional years of adolescence, the boys who were interviewed had not then left school. The boys interviewed by Stephen Frosh and his colleagues were aged between 11 and 13. The 44 boys whom Mike O'Donnell and Sue Sharpe interviewed were in year 11, and so aged 15 and 16, the same age as the boys in this book were when I first talked to them. O'Donnell and Sharpe asked their participants about work prospects, although in neither of these studies were the young men followed into the labour market, nor did they address geographical differences between local labour markets. All three of these excellent empirical studies provide a useful comparative basis for the work reported here.

It is now a common theme in recent 'transition' studies that childhood is a social construction that is historically and geographically specific (Aitken 1994; Aries 1962; Coffield, Borrill and Marshall 1986; Jones 1995; Jones and Wallace 1992; Katz 1991, 1993; Matthews and Limb

1999; Ruddick 1996; Valentine 1996, 2000; Winchester and Costello 1995). Further, it is recognized that in complex post-industrial societies the notion of transition itself is increasingly inappropriate as individuals pursue multiple and complex paths, sometimes concurrently (Coles 2000; Furlong and Cartmel 1997; Irwin 1995; James, Jenks and Prout 1998; MacDonald 1997, 1998), in times when the risks of failure are great, but chances of individual success are also correspondingly greater, less tramelled by conventional social markers such as class position or ethnicity (Beck 1992, 2000). In comparing the lives of young men in two cities I want to explore how these ideas of complexity and risk take different forms in particular places as individual choices are made in the context of geographically specific and differentiated sets of opportunities in the labour and the housing market. For young working class men, however, the risk society is not one in which more optimistic debates about individualization (Giddens 1991) or about new forms of aestheticized workplace performances (Bauman 1998) have much relevance. Rather, the structural constraints of economic transformation seem ever more likely to limit their options to poor work and membership of the expanding numbers of the working poor.

These young men were born in 1982 and 1983 when the Thatcherite 'revolution' that had such an impact on the lives of the working class in Britain was at its height. During the 1980s and early 1990s, as these boys moved through primary school into their secondary education, the impact of authoritarian populism and the New Right (Hall 1988; Hall and Martin 1983), of neo-liberal social and economic policies (Gamble 1994) and the deregulation of capital, restructured the social, economic and political landscapes of Britain (Hutton 1996). Welfare spending was cut, directly affecting many of the families in which these boys grew up, growing school choice adversely affected schools in poorer localities, and devolved budgets from the local education authority directly to schools made it harder for many schools to balance their budgets (Gamble and Kelly 1996). In the labour market the decline of employment in the manufacturing sector was marked and its impact felt most severely by men in northern towns such as Sheffield (Turok and Edge 1999). But in all cities, the gap between the poorest inhabitants and those with the greatest income and wealth and opportunities grew, affecting the boys growing up in Cambridge as well as those in Sheffield (Gregg and Wadsworth 1999; Hills, Le Grand and Paichaud 2002). One consequence of this growing polarization was an increase in the number of children living in poverty. In 1992–3, when these boys were 10, a third of all children in the UK were poor (Oppenheim 1998), including among them some of the boys whom I interviewed. This combination of economic transformation, labour market changes, welfare state restructuring and growing inequalities means that 'young people now grow up in social, economic and political conditions radically different to those encountered by their parents' generation in the post-war years of relative prosperity and social cohesion' (MacDonald 1997: 20).

A general culture of individualism and an economic policy based on the supposed superiority of individual effort was a marked feature of the Thatcher years, perhaps best summed up in her claim that 'there is no such thing as society'. Throughout the 1980s and into the 1990s, then, at a time of growing risks and uncertainty, people increasingly were held to be accountable for their own futures (Giddens 1991; Beck 1992). As these working class boys began to approach the end of their school lives, new Labour gained power but, despite the introduction of a number of innovative policies to improve the living standards of the poorest members of society, including the right to a minimum wage, the notion of individual effort continued to dominate economic and social policy, accompanied by a strong belief in the moral superiority of labour market participation for the largest possible number of people (McDowell 2001b; Peck 2001). At the same time, consumerism became an increasingly significant part of the social construction of identity, increasing the disadvantages of poor working class teenagers for whom many of the iconic goods of contemporary style were out of easy financial reach. In circumstances in which access to employment and consumption – key elements of the social construction of masculine identity – became increasingly uncertain for young men such as the ones whose lives are the focus here, questions about the pathways from school into early adulthood and the associations between employment, consumption and gendered identities gain increasing salience.

Theorizing Gender, Ethnicity and Class: Difference and Inequality

In recent years, questions about social identity have been at the forefront of the social sciences in exciting new theoretical work about the construction of difference. The notion of 'difference' and its significance in distinguishing 'self' from various culturally defined 'others' has dominated debates in many disciplines. In this work – loosely grouped under the heading of 'postmodern' or 'post-structuralist' – earlier notions of a stable, immutable sense of identity, typically rooted in social class position, have been disrupted. The significance of other dimensions of identity, especially gender and ethnicity, and their interconnections, has been recognized, as well as the provisional, tentative nature of identity which is theorized as an ongoing performance, variable in space and time, albeit regulated by social norms and cultural expectations (Butler 1990; Evans 1997; Friedman 1998). This approach to identity is sometimes termed a 'relational perspective' in which identity is theorized as a contingently defined social process, as a discursively constituted social relation, articulated through complex narratives. Thus as Somers (1994: 635) has argued:

> Narrative identities are constituted by a person's temporally and spatially variable place in culturally constructed stories composed of (breakable) rules, (variable) practices, binding (and unbinding) institutions, and the multiple plots of family, nation or economic life. More importantly, however, narratives are not incorporated into the self in any direct way; rather, they are mediated through the enormous spectrum of social and political institutions and practices that constitute our social world.

This quotation nicely captures the connections between material structures and social practices, as well as the complex and variable ways in which identities are plural and dynamic. Somers also insists on the significance of place – a recognition that has been of great significance for geographical understandings of social identity. Identity is constructed through social interactions in specific locations which themselves both reflect and affect the construction and performance of particular identities. For young men on the verge of leaving school, their sense of themselves as masculine, and increasingly as independent, is constructed through the intersection of institutional rules and acceptable (or unacceptable) behaviours in the school, the local streets, their homes and potential workplaces that construct and constrain them in their everyday lives as classed, gendered and raced subjects.

In the following sections I explore in more detail approaches to understanding gender, class and ethnicity as relational processes, endeavouring to spell out the interconnections between masculinity, class position and whiteness that construct the young men in this book as a complex and hybrid group whose ethnicity and gender – as white men – endows privilege in certain spheres, but whose age and class position – as working class adolescents – locates them as subordinate. Although class, gender and ethnicity are mutually constituted, for conceptual clarity and ease of presentation, I first address the burgeoning literature on masculinity.

Theorizing masculinity

For some years now there has been a recognition that masculinity, as well as femininity, deserves theoretical scrutiny. A large, and still rapidly expanding, literature has accepted the challenge, laid down initially in feminist theorizing, of defining and mapping the multiple ways of being a man. This literature has begun to explore from a range of theoretical perspectives the complex dynamics of power and identity and the relationships between class, ethnicity, age and other social characteristics that situate men in relationships of power and inequality with women and with other men in different ways in particular places and in different historical circumstances (Whitehead [2002] provides a useful summary of the different perspectives). In the early work on gender, especially in psychoanalytic approaches, femininity and masculinity were theorized as binary opposites – woman is what man is not, even absence or lack – and so women are defined as emotional compared to the rationality of men, the inferior other to the dominant masculine One. This binary construction, albeit reversed, still distinguishes some of the recent popular texts on masculinity (including Biddulph 1994; Bly 1990; A. Clare 2000) where the problems of men are analysed in terms of their inability to tap into their emotions, compared to women's intuitive sensitivity to their own and others' emotional needs.

In recent scholarly works, however, a more complex notion of masculinity is common. As Martain Mac an Ghaill (1996b) has documented in his survey of work in the area during the 1980s and 1990s, a wide range of literature about masculinity was published, drawing on sex roles, psychoanalysis and power theories, in disciplines including sociology, criminology, social psychology, psychoanalysis, anthropology, history and cultural studies (see e.g. Brittan 1989; Brod and Kaufman 1994; Clatterbaugh 1990; Connell 1987; Craig 1992; Dollimore 1991; Edley and Weatherell 1995; Edwards 1994; Hearn 1992; Jefferson 1994; Middleton 1992; Sedgwick 1994; Segal 1990; Sinfield 1998; Tolson 1977; Weeks 1991, 1989). Within this literature there was a common focus on the relationship between structure and agency, or society and the individual, as well as on the interconnections within and between gender, sexuality, class, 'race', ethnicity, nation, age. The 'starting point [was] that masculinities are problematic, negotiated and contested within frameworks at the individual, organizational, cultural and societal levels' (Mac an Ghaill 1996b: 2). In a forward-looking conclusion Mac an Ghaill suggested that the agenda for future research should include unpacking the complex links between masculinities, sexualities and power; analysing the cultural production of masculinities within local institutional sites; exploring the contextual contingencies, confusions and contradictions of contemporary forms of masculinity; and, in particular, making problematic dominant forms of heterosexuality in a male-dominated society. Building on his agenda, recent analyses, many of which have adopted an ethnographic approach, have addressed the complex constitution of masculinities in a wide range of different sites and locations (see e.g. Barrett 1996; Collinson and Hearn 1994; Connell 2000; Craig 1992; Edwards 1994; Kerfoot 1999; Massey 1995; McDowell 2001a; Middleton 1992; Nardi 1999; Poynting, Noble and Tabar 1998; Segal 2000; Sweetman 1997; Walker 1998; see also the useful surveys in Whitehead 2002; and Whitehead and Barrett 2001).

The focus on multiple masculinities and their specificity owes a great deal to the pioneering work of the sociologist Bob Connell who has been a key theorist here, as well as producing a whole range of stimulating empirical work about a range of masculinities. In a recent book (Connell 2000), pulling together not only his own work over a decade and a half but also summarizing the field more generally, Connell suggests that the new social research on masculinity is defined by a set of key propositions or arguments that emphasize both the variations, across time and space, in the construction of masculinities as well as evidence of hierarchical social relations, not only between men and women, but within and between groups of men. The first of his propositions is that masculinities take multiple forms, constructed differently across cultures and in different time periods as well as across a range of spatial scales. Thus there are both large- and small-scale, relatively enduring as well as more flexible, differences in what it means to be a man. As Connell (2000: 10) notes, there are 'different ways of enacting manhood, different ways of learning to be a man, different conceptions of the self and different ways of using a male body'. For young men, this emphasis on learning how to be a man is a key part of the transition from childhood to adult manhood. Differences between social constructions of masculinity not only vary between nations – as Gilmore (1993) has illustrated in a cross-cultural review of manhood, in some non-western societies generosity, selflessness and nurturing are masculine attributes – but also between and within particular spaces and social settings. Research on schools (Ball, Maguire and Macrae 2000; Connell 1989, 1994; Dixon 1997; Frosh, Phoenix and Pattman 2002; O'Donnell and Sharpe 2000; Segal 2000), for example, has shown not only how young men from different ethnic backgrounds or social classes enact masculinity in different ways, but also how boys at school act differently there from their behaviour in public arenas or in their own homes.

The second of the set of propositions is that masculinities may be ordered in relations based on hierarchy and dominance. This is perhaps where Connell's own work has been of greatest significance. As he has documented, there are distinctive social relations of power that position men in a hierarchy, opening up a theoretical space for the analysis of power relations between men, as well as men's domination of women. Thus, he has suggested, particular versions of dominant or hegemonic masculinity characterize gender regimes at different historical periods. And further, these hegemonic definitions of masculinity are 'constructed in relation to various subordinated masculinities as well as in relation to women' (Connell 1987: 183). While the construction of masculinity as differentiated from and superior to femininity – the masculine, disembodied rational One to women's embodied inferior Other – has long been accepted (see e.g. De Beauvoir 1972) as the most significant feature of gender relations, it is now clear that masculinities too are not only multiply constructed but may also be ranked in a hierarchy of dominance. The idealized embodied masculinity of working class men, for example, both differentiates them from the rational cerebral masculinity of middle class men, but also constructs them as inferior. And so:

> To recognize diversity in masculinity is not enough. We must also recognize the *relations* between the different kinds of masculinity: relations of alliance, dominance and subordination. These relationships are constructed through practices that exclude and include, that intimidate and exploit, and so on. There is a gender politics within masculinity. (Connell 1995: 37; original emphasis)

This gender politics is based on relations between men based on hegemony, subordination and complicity. Hegemonic masculinity (that which is most respected, desired or dominant within a society) captures power relations between men. In contemporary western societies – as the research on media representations (Chapman and Rutherford 1988; Dyer 1997; Simpson 1994) or workplace cultures (Collinson and Hearn 1994; Kanter 1977; Lewis 1989; McDowell 1997a, 2001a; Wright 1994) has made clear – this encompasses men who are economically successful, racially superior and visibly heterosexual. Dominant versions of masculinity are constructed by 'othering' masculinities that are differentiated, and regarded as inferior on the basis of, for example, ethnicity or sexuality, and on the basis of class position. Thus young white men, the subjects of this book, may be ascribed masculine privileges as white men, but as working class men they are a subordinated

masculinity, subject to constant surveillance in public arenas, as well as
to condescension at school (Charlesworth 2000). As Connell (1987,
1989) found in his own empirical study of young Australian men, the
impoverished urban environments in which working class youths grew
up, combined with their taste for risk, produced what he termed a
'protest masculinity'. This form of masculinity contrasts with the hegemonic masculinity that is inculcated in the middle class pupils of elite
Australian schools where boys are trained to be rational and expert –
traits that are then played out and reinforced in professional and man-
agerial careers in hierarchically organized workplaces, where these men
have authority over other men (and women).

Thus class and ethnicity, as I shall illustrate, are widely acknowledged
as major factors in the social construction of masculinities, interacting
with gender and generation to produce varied and unequally valued
positionalities, which in themselves are both complex and fluid. Class
position for the middle class not only brings with it the privileges based
on social and cultural capital accumulated through, for example, elite
schooling and familial resources, but is marked on the body (Bourdieu
1984; Young 1990) and is evident in accent, weight and height and in the
very ways in which the body occupies space. Thus the subordinate
'protest' masculinity described by Connell is often portrayed through
an aggressive 'macho' stance in which the positioning of the working
class male body in space is used to threaten and challenge perceived
'others'. Further, as I argue later, the particular construction of a
'threatening' working class masculine embodiment is one way in which
young men from working class backgrounds may disqualify themselves
from many of the service-sector jobs that increasingly are the only
options for early school leavers in British towns and cities.

The third proposition insists that masculinities are more than individual characteristics but that, as the examples above have suggested, they
are constructed, defined and maintained in discourse and culture and
sustained through institutional practices. Masculinities are, in other
words, collective social practices. In capitalist societies the construction
of masculinities occurs in a range of institutions from the family to the
school and the workplace. The significance of particular institutions
varies in different historical circumstances. Connell (2000: 11) suggests,
for example, that 'the institutions of competitive sport seem peculiarly
important for contemporary western masculinities'. The current emphasis on sporting prowess makes abundantly clear the claim that the
body is a key element in social construction of masculinities. Men's (and
women's) bodies are surfaces that are inscribed with, defined by and

disciplined through social norms and conventions about gendered appearances, in size, weight and deportment as well as through decoration and clothing (Bordo 1993; Foucault 1977; Grosz 1994). Thus, through bodily performances as well as in all social interactions, masculinities are constantly being actively constructed, maintained or challenged. For working class men in particular, embodiment is a crucial part of their masculinity, both in the workplace and in leisure arenas, as the disembodied rationality of idealized hegemonic masculinity is contrasted to the strength, agility or sporting prowess that are the advantages of subordinate masculinities, forms of embodied social capital that, of course, depreciate with age, whether in the workplace or in sporting arenas.

Finally, this emphasis on active construction and performance, on 'doing gender' (West and Zimmerman 1987) as an everyday act (Butler 1990; Kondo 1990), combined with the recognition of multiple ways of being a man, makes it clear that masculinities are complex and often contradictory, riven with conflicting desires and ambivalences. As Mac an Ghaill (1994, 1996a, 1996b) has noted, hegemonic masculinity itself is 'constituted by cultural elements which consist of contradictory forms of compulsory heterosexuality, misogyny and homophobia. These are marked by ambivalence and contingency' (1996b: 133). In his work with young men, Mac an Ghaill has suggested that 'what emerges as of particular salience is the way in which heterosexual young men are involved in a double relationship: of disparaging the "other", including women and gays (external relations), and at the same time expelling femininity and homosexuality from within themselves (internal relations)' (1996a: 133).

Numerous studies of schools (Griffin and Lees 1997; Haywood and Mac an Ghaill 1995; Holland, Ramazanoglu, Sharpe and Thomson 1998; Kehily and Nayak 1997; Thorne 1993; Valentine 2000; Woods and Hammersley 1993) have reinforced these conclusions, showing how boys disparage their female peers as well as women teachers, but also assert their own superiority through labelling less powerful boys as 'cissies', 'big girls', 'poofters' and other sexualized insults. Dominant versions of masculinity in schools value aggression, repression, conflict and control in the school environment. Fears of being soft, of feminine characteristics, and so their derogation, are part of the development of a hegemonic masculinity. Through ethnographic research, there is also now greater knowledge of the complex ways in which gendered identities in schools are constructed in multiple settings. Discourses in school, but also in the home, in workplaces, streets and other places of leisure and pleasure offer a range of ways of being male and female, despite privileging some as superior or 'normal'. For young men and women on the cusp of leaving school, their identities typically tend to be marked by anxiety about their sense of self and uncertainties about their future place in the world as they begin to negotiate the transition to adulthood.

Ethnicity and whiteness: the abject white working class

The connections between masculinity and ethnicity are a key element in the recognition and definition of multiple masculinities. As I noted above, the concept of hegemonic masculinity, with its emphasis in most western nations on middle class, majority group, heterosexual men, constructs men from minority groups as the Other, in ways that have parallels with women's Otherness and subordination. A range of studies, often drawing on the insights of postcolonial theory, have demonstrated the ways in which men of colour are positioned as subordinate or complicit by the hegemonic discourse. In both the USA and the UK, men of African or African Caribbean origins, for example, are constructed both as a threat and as enviable, or as objects of desire, confined to their bodies by a rhetoric of rampant sexuality, of naturalized athleticism or of degradation and dirt (Dyer 1997; hooks 1992; McClintock 1995; Segal 1990). For men of Asian origins, on the other hand, more commonly a stereotypical feminized identity is conferred upon them by the majority discourses and practices (Alexander 2000; Frosh, Phoenix and Pattman 2002). What has been missing, however, in this work, at least until relatively recently, is the theorization of 'whiteness'.

Whiteness has tended to remain invisible and unexamined: 'unqualified, essential, homogeneous, seemingly self-fashioned and apparently unmarked by history' (Frankenberg 1997: 1), locating white men (and, in some circumstances, women [Ware 1992]) in a sphere of unexamined privilege. But like skin 'colour', whiteness is a socially constructed marker, the meaning of which is also socially variable across time and space. Whiteness too should be understood 'as ensembles of local phenomena complexly embedded in socioeconomic, sociocultural and psychic interrelations' (Frankenberg 1997: 1). Thus whiteness is a historically specific and variable social formation, a process rather than a categorical attribute, shaped within a racialized problematic (Bonnett 1997, 2000; Jackson 1998; Kobayashi and Peake 1994). Critical attention to whiteness offers a way of examining not only its multiple construction and the position of groups who might be categorized as white 'others' (working class men might be so categorized in certain circumstances as well as white immigrant groups such as the Irish in mainland

Great Britain [Walter 2001]), but also provides a different way into the examination of the foundation of all cultural constructions of 'race' and ethnicity. This claim should dispel the fears of critics of intellectual work on whiteness who argue that it might recentre rather than displace whiteness from its current central position in social theory. Examining views of the 'Other' among, for example, young white men leaving school in British cities, adds to an understanding of their own and other groups' developing sense of themselves as masculine and white/ 'raced' and the ways in which it is co-constructed.

While the initial analyses and theorizations of whiteness tended to be within the humanities, in film and cultural studies, for example, as well as in literary theory (Dyer 1997; Morrison 1992; Young 1996) there are a growing number of studies that address the social and economic advantages that accrue to white groups because of their whiteness. In the USA, for example, the economist Roediger (1994), in a magnificent analysis of the relationships between emerging nationhood and the labour process in the nineteenth century, has shown how some ethnic groups, European immigrants, for example, accepted what he terms the 'wages of whiteness' to distinguish themselves from and as superior to African Americans. Roediger also documented the interconnections between 'race', class and masculinity, showing how constructions of whiteness were interwoven with particular ideas about masculinity and femininity. From the 1950s onwards in Britain, Cohen (1992) examined what he has termed the 'habitus of race' – its embodiment in variable forms as black and white labour and the associated social constructions of the male body – to explain the cultures of racism often found among white male manual workers. He illustrates his arguments through ethnographic work in the East End at the time when the London Docklands were being re-developed, as well as through work with young white men, both at school and at play, as football supporters, for example (Cohen 1992, 1997a, 1997b). Cohen deftly reveals the ways in which a white racist discourse among these different groups of men was connected to the simultaneous class and ethnic restructuring of the East End in the 1970s and 1980s.

In the UK, today still a predominantly white country, male manual workers are, of course, the group currently most threatened by deindustrialization, economic change and the growing dominance of the service sector. Rates of unemployment are consistently higher for men in old manufacturing districts and during periods of economic retrenchment, and, as I explore in more detail in the next chapter, the least skilled members of the labour force are disproportionately disadvantaged. In a provocative analysis of the intersection of economic restructuring with the growing emphasis of welfare policies on labour market participation, also to be discussed in more detail in chapter 2, Haylett (2001) recently has argued that the discursive construction of the white working class poor in Britain as 'socially excluded' is achieved through their racialization as a backward, unprogressive group in a modern, multicultural society. As well as, or even instead of, earlier emphases in poverty programmes on the inner city, where the majority of Britain's non-white population lives, recent Government policies to address inequality and area-based deprivations have focused on working class areas of mass housing, often local authority estates on the peripheries of towns and cities. In these places, the white working class occupants are represented as impoverished not only by their economic circumstances but also because of their cultural attitudes. They are portrayed both in the quality press and in policy discourses as abject, white and racist, 'symbols of backwardness and specifically of a culturally burdensome whiteness' (Haylett 2001: 351). Consequently, they are constructed as out of place in the new dominant discourse of 'multicultural modernization'. To support his contention, Haylett quotes Peter Mandelson's astonishing statement when launching the Government's new Social Exclusion Unit in 1997 that the problem of social exclusion was about 'more than poverty and unemployment. It is about being cut off from what the rest of us regard as normal life' (quoted in Haylett: 352).

Haylett suggests that the discursive construction of the socially excluded members of the white working class as unmodern or backward is best conceptualized as a form of 'class racism'. Class racism is a term with its origins in Bourdieu's (1984, 1999) assessment of the ways in which accent and comportment mark out working class people as inferior to the middle classes, which as I have already noted, is also a key part of the social construction of masculinity. Drawing on Bourdieu in their recent work with working class women in Britain, both Diane Reay (1997, 1998) and Beverley Skeggs (1997) have argued that British society is imbued with a class contempt for the working class, based on moral judgements of superiority that stigmatize the less privileged as undeserving rather than economically less fortunate. Like gender, class identity is a lived reality constituted in and marked on the intimate locale of the body, the home and the locality, identifying its bearers as subordinate and inferior. Young white working class men, as I shall demonstrate in greater detail in chapter 3, are explicitly positioned within these discourses as morally inferior, excluded from hegemonic versions of masculinity, and portrayed as a threat to the norms and values of middle class England: the 'normal life' taken for granted by British politician Peter Mandelson. However, whether their positioning also constructs them as actively racist, blaming the 'Other', whether minority groups or women, for their growing relative disadvantage in the labour market, is an empirical question that will be addressed in later chapters. In their work with a slightly older group of young white working class men (in the main between 18 and 24 years old) in deindustrializing towns in the USA, Fine, Weiss, Addelstone and Maruzsa (1997) found that a rhetoric of blame was developed by these men as a compensatory mechanism for their inadequate understanding that employment change and economic restructuring was responsible for their declining fortunes. Instead, they preferred the explanation that people of colour and women had 'stolen' their jobs.

In his work with young people on urban multiculturalism and racism in Greater London, Les Back (1996) found a more complex situation, neither blaming the other, nor full acceptance nor complete rejection of the contemporary discourses of multiculturalism, identified by Haylett as influencing Government policies and also dominant in the influential work of key cultural studies theorists, including Hall (1991, 1992) Gilroy (1987, 1993), Bhabha (1990) and hooks (1992). Back argued instead that there are 'complex combinations of racist and non-racist sentiment evident in the lives of young whites' (1996: 3) in which the interrelations between class, gender and ethnic differences, as well as local and translocal processes affecting identity formation, position young white people in complex ways, rather than in simple binary constructions. As Back (1996: 7) notes 'forms of social exclusion and inclusion work through notions of belonging and entitlement in particular times and places' and 'urban vernacular cultures possess incommensurable impulses that allow racism and transculturalism to be simultaneously proximate and symptomatic of what it means to grow up in post-imperial cities'. These incommensurable impulses are also evident in contemporary official discourses of belonging. As well as the 'modern' multicultural discourse identified by Haylett, a form of cultural racism that has its origins in growing uncertainties about Britain's role in the world and about the definition of 'Englishness' has also been evident from the late 1980s and early 1990s (Barker 1981; Gilroy 1987; Hall 1978). Thus in 1990 Lord Tebbitt, appearing on the BBC programme *Newsnight*, said that 'many youngsters leave school totally confused about their origins and their culture' (quoted in Back 1996: 9).

A similar sentiment was resurrected in 2001 with debates about the 'mongrel'-ization of Britain: a term used in a speech in April by right-wing Conservative MP John Townend, in defence of a mythical way of British/English life in the face of threats from outside (whether from

Asians, refugees, or asylum seekers). While the new Labour Government attempted to diffuse such claims by defining and supporting a new kind of cultural politics and sense of national identity that is both 'black' and British (see e.g. the report of the Runnymede Commission 2000), its own White Paper on Nationality and Immigration *Secure Borders, Safe Haven*, issued in February 2002, undermined its position. David Blunkett, then Home Secretary, in introducing the proposed legislation, reasserted the significance of a singular notion of Britishness, insisting that new occupants of the British homeland conform to its customs and common practices, as well as requiring an English language competency and the selection of marriage partners from within the UK. Discussions about asylum seekers and economic migrants reinforced these notions. Later in the same year, in a speech noticeable for its incautious use of language, Blunkett suggested that if in-migration were not controlled, then public services, such as schools and doctors surgeries in certain areas of British cities, might become 'swamped' by non-English speakers, thus linking contemporary debates and policies to the racist language of earlier Conservative Governments' policies. For the young men in this book, growing up on peripheral estates in Cambridge and Sheffield in the context of these conflicting national sympathies and sentiments, and in labour markets differentially transformed by restructuring, ideas about their white identity will take different forms in particular encounters and spaces, from the home to the streets and clubs of the urban landscapes, as well as in schools where, as I demonstrate in chapter 3, particular ideas about black style and image play a part in the construction of masculinity.

Material structures and discursive practices

The relational approach to understanding social identities provides a way both of theorizing the multiple constitution of gender, class and ethnicity and also of a way of recognizing that gender is not only a social structure, produced within a matrix of power relations, but is also a lived identity in which the social relations that constitute gender, ethnicity and class are more complex and contradictory, more fragmented, shifting and ambivalent than public definitions of these categories suggest. Thus in investigations of the changing position of different groups of workers in labour markets, structured by the flows of global capital as well as locally specific needs for different categories of workers, an approach that brings together materialist and discursive analyses, combining the insights of political economy with a cultural studies perspective, has the greatest explanatory reach. As feminist scholars have long argued, and theorists of masculinity now accept, work in a range of different settings and locales, in the home or the factory, waged, unwaged, formal and informal, plays a central role in shaping people's place in the world and in informing their identities. But so too do people's everyday lives – their routines, desires and aspirations as gendered social beings affect their commitment to work and their sense of self as labourers (Bradley 1999; Freeman 2000; Pringle 1998; Wajcman 1998). In this book I try, as in my earlier work with merchant bankers (McDowell 1997a), to bring culture and economy into a productive conversation in an attempt to understand the changing relationships between gender, employment and identity that are evident in contemporary Britain.

The theoretical recognition of the hybrid and performative nature of gender identity and the intersectionality of its construction, as well as the extent of variations across space and through time has been extremely productive. However, it is also important not to lose sight of the relative fixity in definitions of masculinity and femininity and the ways in which they are constituted through social relations of power and inequality. Dominant notions of masculinity, for example, continue to be based on their differentiation from an inferior 'Other'. For men, women are the classic Other and to be masculine is to be not feminine, not a woman. Further, idealized, highly valued versions of both femininity and masculinity are also constructed through comparison with a range of other 'Others' – ethnic or sexual minorities, for example. In contemporary western societies, as I noted earlier, hegemonic versions of both masculinity and femininity that stress whiteness, heterosexuality, good complexion, weight and height continue to define men and women with different attributes as less valued (Young 1990). Consequently, despite the growing theoretical recognition of cultural difference, there remain significant and relatively enduring inequalities in the social structures and social relations that constitute, maintain and reinforce such differences. As Tilly (1999) has noted, what he terms 'categorical differences', among which gender is significant, continue to structure unequal social relations in western societies. While fully accepting the arguments outlined above, that gender, as well as ethnicity and class, is a process rather than a category in its construction, it is clear that a set of binary distinctions based on 'distinctly bounded pairs such as male/female, aristocrat/plebeian, citizen/foreigner, and more complex classifications based on religious affiliation, ethnic origin, or race' (1999: 6) remain central to analyses of inequality. These bounded categories, according to Tilly, 'deserve special attention because they provide clear evidence for the operation of durable inequality, their boundaries do crucial organizational work, and because categorical differences actually account for much of what ordinary observers take to be the results of variation in individual talent or effort' (1999: 6). Like other analysts of contemporary economic change, I insist that both 'cultural diversity' and structural inequalities must be theorized in tandem (Bradley and Fenton 1999; Fraser 1997; Freeman 2000; Phillips 1999; Ray and Sayer 1999).

Despite the durable nature of these divisions, the social attributes associated with categorical differences do change. As Connell (2000) has argued, there are key moments in the collective process of gender construction, when the social dynamics in which masculinities (and femininities) are formed are particularly clear. At such moments, he suggests, the formation of the person and of social institutions is simultaneously at issue. I believe that the current time, just after the turn of the millennium, is such a moment: the dominant version of white working class masculinity, which (relatively) advantaged men both at school and in the labour market (at least in comparison with working class women), is being challenged by girls' growing success in both institutional spheres. Their success is related to, if not the cause of, growing uncertainty among young men about their place in the world and their ability to fulfil traditional notions of masculine responsibilities, based on workplace achievement and the provision of support for dependants. These contemporary uncertainties among young men are more fully explored in chapter 3. Both dominant, or hegemonic, and subordinate versions of masculinity are neither static nor unchanging, but subject to challenge and to periodic change, especially in times of crisis (see Berger, Wallis and Watson 1995; Connell 1991, 1993; Cornwall and Lindisfarne 1994; Hearn 1992; Jackson 1990; Jackson 1991; Nilan 1995).

The long, and partial, transformation from a Fordist to a post-Fordist economy in advanced industrial societies that has been documented by economists and geographers is commonly designated a crisis or sea change (Harvey 1989), and its association with a more general transformation in the dominant gender regime (McDowell 1991) has begun to be explored. A range of theorists whose work will be the subject of the following chapter have noted changes in gender relations associated with economic restructuring, even, optimistically, the decline of patriarchy (Castells 1997). Alternatively, it might be argued that, in these changing times, in a period that seems to be associated with deep anxieties about gender identities and gender relations, deepened by traditional *fin de siècle* anxieties (Showalter 1990), the hegemonic version of a masculinity that is misogynistic as well as deeply ambivalent about race and sexuality might, in fact, be strengthening its hold, cementing both divisions between men and women and between men. It may be that young men, without fully understanding the nature and consequences of recent economic changes, exacerbate their disadvantaged labour market position by exaggerating the very attributes of working class masculinity that currently disbar them from many of the expanding jobs in the service sector that dominate most British local labour markets. Further, their exaggerated masculinity, and their relative labour market disadvantage, might also construct them as less desirable lifetime partners for young women whose own gendered identities are changing. These are some of the issues to be explored in the rest of this book through the lens of a year in the life of 16-year-old male school leavers.

The Argument, Chapter by Chapter

In the pair of chapters that follow this introduction the connections between labour market transformations and gendered identities are explored. In the first of the two, I lay out the major dimensions of the changing nature of employment in Britain as well as explore the contradictions between the uncertainty faced by growing numbers of working people of securing an adequate income from employment and Government policies that increasingly place waged work at the centre of its programme for reducing inequality, while reducing non-work based benefits. Being outside the labour market has become a less legitimate way of surviving at the start of the twenty-first century, not only in the UK, but also in the USA and, albeit to a lesser extent, in many countries in continental Europe. This growing emphasis on the centrality of work is paradoxical as employment itself becomes increasingly uncertain and insecure for growing numbers of people in Britain. This insecurity has led, according to a number of key theorists of employment change, to a decline in the significance of employment in the social construction of identity, leading variously to new forms of identities, constructed through consumption or in defensive attachments to locality and an exclusive version of community. As employment has long been recognized as a major element in the social construction of masculine identities, new forms of work and transformations in gendered identities are interconnected.

In the second of this pair of chapters, chapter 3, recent debates about the construction of identity and the connection between class-based, gendered and racialized identities are critically assessed and their connection with debates about work are explored, in the specific context of the changing position of young white men. New debates about the relative failure of young men at school are connected to older, as well as contemporary, debates about working class youth as folk devils and hooligans, showing how working class masculinity has re-emerged as an urgent social problem. Here the key theoretical debates of the book are developed as the arguments briefly outlined above, about connecting material and discursive approaches in theorizing identities as relational, are expanded in the specific empirical context of understanding the position of young white working class men today. The ways in which a white ethnic identity based on ideas of Britishness is constructed in opposition to ideas about a stereotypical black masculinity are explored, showing how boys from African Caribbean backgrounds are both role models and the focus of resentment for white working class boys. Idealized versions of both white and black masculinities are articulated with class and gender in ways that often emphasize the more aggressive aspects of working class young men's sense of themselves and their behaviour at school and in the streets.

In chapter 4 the focus and scale of the argument shifts to an assessment of the extent of geographical variation in labour market inequality and in the options open to 16-year-olds entering the labour market, as well as an analysis of their experiences during their final year of compulsory schooling. Despite the national coverage of schemes for the education and training of young people, there are clear spatial differences in the set of opportunities facing early school leavers: in a very real sense, geography matters. In a second paradox, rates of educational attainment and continuing participation are lowest in areas where rates of youth and general unemployment are highest and where the negative impacts of manufacturing decline are most severe. Labour markets are deeply affected by the histories and cultures of locally specific industrial patterns. The particular mix of industry and employment in a locality is connected to the development over time of the central institutions of daily social life – the family, churches, schools, clubs and sports teams – that take a geographically distinct shape. As Storper and Walker (1989: 12) have noted, 'the result is a fabric of distinctive, lasting local communities and cultures woven into the landscape of labour'. One of the most significant differences in the labour landscapes in Britain is the North–South divide (Allen and Henry 1997; Ball, Gray and McDowell 1989; Hudson and Williams 1995; Martin and Townroe 1992; Mohan 1999; Philo 1995). Reflecting the nineteenth century pattern of industrialization and the late twentieth century pattern of decline, the northern regions of the country have been most severely affected by the loss of manufacturing employment and the slower growth of service-sector employment, especially in high-paying occupations in south-east England.

To capture this large-scale differentiation, I chose a deindustrializing northern city (Sheffield) and an affluent service-dominated southern city (Cambridge) as case studies. But spatial differentiation and geographical inequality is also marked within cities as well as between them. While the inner areas of the largest urban conurbations typically have high rates of deprivation, peripheral estates in both small and large cities are also areas that have above average rates of unemployment and are home to households with below average incomes (Fainstein, Gordon and Harloe 1992; Jarvis, Pratt and Wu 2001; Turok and Edge 1999). As Cambridge has nothing paralleling the inner area deprivation of large cities, I chose to work on a peripheral estate in each city in order to identify young men living in similar circumstances. And as Haylett (2001) noted, it is here that the 'abject' white working class is concentrated. In chapter 4 the similarities and differences between the two cities and the lives of young men therein are identified. Here (and in appendix 1) I also address some of the practical and ethical issues that arise in working with young men in an attempt to explore how they make sense of their lives and their view of themselves as men in a period of rapid economic and social change.

In the second part of chapter 4, and in chapters 5, 6 and 7 the voices of the 24 young men to whom I talked are at the centre of the analysis. The authoritative voice, or commentary, deliberately becomes less audible in these chapters, although it is undeniable that the selection of the material to foreground remains an authorial responsibility. At the end of chapter 4 the attitudes and behaviour of boys then on the edge of leaving school are the focus. As earlier studies of working class boys at school have demonstrated, in a whole variety of ways, a hegemonic version of a working class masculinity that emphasizes fooling around, having a laugh as preferable to academic achievement, and inconsistent attendance, constructs these boys as disruptive, even uneducable, and so labels them as low achievers. Here, I explore the extent to which boys in their final months at school understand the institutional and demographic changes that are reshaping gender relations. As I show, there is the same sort of 'cultural lag' among white boys in both Cambridge and Sheffield as O'Donnell and Sharpe (2000) found among boys in London schools, and Lowe and Krahn (2000) among Canadian school leavers. Young people in all these locations seemed to be relatively unaware of how the opportunities open to men and women from different classes on leaving school are being reshaped. And as well as demonstrating a limited knowledge of the changing structure of the labour market, the young men to whom I talked also had little awareness of the changing aspirations of many young women. They held conservative views about sex and marriage, and about sharing (or rather not sharing) family and domestic responsibilities. They expected to be able to reproduce the same gendered patterns of responsibility that their parents and grandparents had relied on before them. And, despite their general awareness of the growing significance of credentials in the uncertain and flexible labour market of the twenty-first century, these school leavers were also confident that they would always be able to find work.

The core of gender inequality lies in the gender division of labour in both paid and unpaid work, but, as I argued in the first two chapters, the ideological and material underpinnings of this division are eroding. Young people on the edge of adulthood can no longer rely on the old moral certainties that constructed men as breadwinners, whose identities were constructed in the main in the workplace, and women as primary carers of dependants in the home. The changes in the institutions of the education system and the workplace have transformed women's opportunities and enhanced their prospects of self-sufficiency and independence. Similarly, more diverse and fluid personal relationships have both given women more choice about the circumstances in which they become mothers and less certainty about male support if they do. In the succeeding three chapters (5, 6 and 7) young men's contemporary experiences in the labour market are explored in detail, documenting the consequences of the growth of a service-dominated economy. In the first of this trio of chapters the overall strategies of the boys in the summer during which they left school are examined, documenting the ways in which they searched for work, the jobs that they accepted, as well as the decisions of some of them to combine employment and further study. In the second two chapters the focus is on detailed case studies of different pathways, focusing on differences between the young men in their orientation to employment and to further education and training as they look for and start work in a range of jobs. Chapter 6 focuses on relative success stories, while in chapter 7 less successful transitions are examined.

During the course of three interviews with each of the participants I collected a great deal more information than is included in the pages of these three chapters. All the interviews were transcribed and analysed and reanalysed around a series of emerging themes. For this book, with its key focus on the connections between employment and masculinity, I have presented the material in the form of what Ball, Maguire and Macrae

(2000: 17) termed 'analytic sets' of young people, that blend 'fairly detailed narratives with a degree of conceptual focus'. The sets presented here are organized around young men's attitudes to the labour market and to employment participation. The stories in each case are neither complete nor exhaustive but are presented to allow comparisons between the sets to be easily made and points of similarity and difference identified. While each set or category highlights specific life opportunities and experiences, it is important to emphasize that the groupings are not mutually exclusive nor watertight and that the young men may move between these categories in the coming years. However, while notions of fluidity change and instability are currently a key part of theories of identity, I also want to emphasize the relatively limited options of these men and the key and continuing significance of their class position in structuring their possible options. In each case the narrative may also be compared to the more general stories told about the future of work that were outlined in chapter 2. My aim is to challenge both theoretical models of greater choice and individualization in the world of work, as well as the idea, embedded in current official policies, that human capital models of labour endowment are a sufficient basis for increasing participation rates and enhancing the opportunities of current and potential employees.

In the final substantive chapter (chapter 8) I counterpose this material about workplace-based identities to discussions about other arenas of these boys' lives as they negotiate the transition from adolescent schoolboy to independent youth in order to assess contemporary notions and dimensions of multiple masculine identities. Here I suggest that the typical strategies that are emphasized in the current literatures about the 'making of a man' tend to focus on the macho, energetic, anti-authority attributes of young masculinities, the protest masculinity outlined by Connell, to the neglect of alternative versions, including what I define here as domestic masculinity. In this and the final chapter I examine the ways in which young men adhere to a gendered version of respectability that is often used to distinguish 'rough' from 'respectable' members of the working class. In chapter 9 the connections between class and gender are discussed and the continuing salience of class position in the lives of young white men is emphasized. Finally, the specifics of youth policies are discussed, critically examining the continuing reliance of labour supply measures to the neglect of measures to increase the availability of work for the less skilled and to improve the conditions under which they labour.

2

The Rise of Poor Work: Employment Restructuring and Changing Class and Gender Identities

Difficulty in selling labour has consequences of a different order of harm-fulness from those associated with difficulty in buying labour. A person who has difficulty in buying the labour that he wants suffers inconveni-ence or reduction of profits. A person who cannot sell his labour is in effect told that he is no use. The first difficulty causes annoyance or loss. The other is a personal catastrophe. (Beveridge 1944: 3)

The social deconstruction of men as the male breadwinner amongst the poorest groups of society is proceeding apace. (Rubery 1996: 26)

Since some time 'around 1972', as David Harvey (1989) noted in his classic text on the condition of postmodernity, there has been a sea change in the structure of advanced industrial economies, in the nature of employment and in its distribution across space and between social groups. A series of transformations, perhaps captured in a number of all-encompassing terms including 'globalization', 'feminization' and 'casua-lization', has profoundly affected the lives and life chances of working class people, with particular consequences in the old industrial areas in the core economies in the USA and in Western Europe. In Britain, as a long geographical tradition of studying industrial decline has revealed, the economies of towns and cities in the north of England, Scotland and

Wales have been devastated by the loss of relatively well-paid and stable manufacturing employment. These losses have redistributed employment opportunities, as unskilled male workers who lost their jobs found it hard to secure employment in the new service industries that have expanded in these places and, indeed, in the economy as a whole. The service sector seeks to employ workers with quite different social attributes and sets of skills than manufacturing industries.

The shift to a service dominated economy has undoubtedly been the most significant change in the labour market in the final quarter of the twentieth century (Castells 1996; Macdonald and Sirianni 1996; Poynter 2000). Two out of every three British workers are now employed in the service sector, and in these industries, new organizational structures, new employment practices, the introduction of information and communication technologies, and new production systems and management techniques, have fundamentally altered the nature of work and the social characteristics of workers. While for some service workers their employment brings with it the advantages of white-collar middle class employment, with good conditions and reasonable wages, many service firms have taken advantage of the deregulation of the labour market that has dominated British neo-liberal economic policy in the last two decades and more to enforce ever more casual, often part-time, 'flexible' working practices, which have radically changed ordinary people's experience of work and with it their way of viewing their lives. For growing numbers of workers, employment is an increasingly uncertain prospect (although the extent of casualization should not be exaggerated [see Doogan 2001]), based on temporary contracts and often less than full-time employment. The expectation of lifetime employment by a single employer has also diminished. And what is increasingly clear is that in the British economy at the beginning of the twenty-first century, for the majority of people, their working lives are now overwhelmingly shaped by the experience of delivering a service of some form or other (Allen and du Gay 1994; Sturdy, Grugulis and Willmott 2001).

The Attributes of Service-sector Employment

Service delivery has been associated with the so-called feminization of the economy, in terms both of working practices and women's growing labour market participation rates. Since the 1970s in the UK and other West European nations, for example, there has been a steady rise in the numbers of women employed, paralleled by a noticeable decline in men's workforce participation rates. In 1975 more than 92 per cent of men of working age had a job, compared with only 80 per cent by the end of the 1990s. Over the same 20 years for women, participation rates rose from 59 to almost 70 per cent. Thus by the start of the new millennium, women's participation rates were only 10 per cent below those men. One of the most interesting features of recent changes in women's labour market participation is that since 1991 the particular life cycle pattern that distinguished women's working lives from men's participation has virtually disappeared (Gregg and Wadsworth 1999). Until approximately 1992, a graph of women's participation rates by age was different from that of men's. It was marked by two peaks of high participation – among young women until their mid-twenties, after which rates declined but then rose to a peak again by about the age of 40. At the present time, however, this line is now almost flat, paralleling the pattern for men, with no distinction by age or status between women except for a decline after age 50. Thus the pattern now mirrors that of men's participation, but about 10 per cent below it. Women are now a key part of the contemporary labour force and the most significant change in women's participation, which has been evident since 1975, but especially noticeable since 1991, has been for women in their thirties with dependent children. The majority of women, including mothers, are now employed throughout almost all their working lives, and their incomes are a key component of total household incomes. As Rubery, Smith and Fagan (1999: 1) have argued, 'women's employment, far from constituting a marginal segment of European labour markets, has come to be a key force in the restructuring of work and employment within Europe'.

There is, however, still a marked gender difference in the number of hours worked by men and women. Over half of the female workforce is employed part-time compared with less than 10 per cent of all male workers. There is also evidence of a continuing and significant gender differential in male and female average earnings, whether women are employed on a full-time or a part-time basis. Among full-time workers, women earn 18 per cent less per hour than men, whereas for women employed on a part-time basis their hourly earnings are 41 per cent less than for men employed full-time. Clearly, these differences between men and women – in rates of pay and hours worked – affect the degree of economic independence and standard of living that women living on their own rather than in a household unit are able to maintain. Despite these continuing inequalities, the increase in women's labour market participation has been associated with a series of social changes including decreases in marriage rates, rises in the rate of divorce, and declines in fertility rates and in average household size (Crompton 1999). One important corollary of the rise in women's labour market participation has been a decline in the dominance of single-wage households (Beatson 1995; Rodgers and Rodgers 1990; Watson 1994). Together these changes are proving a potent challenge to traditional notions of men's place as the key breadwinner (Bradley, Erickson, Stephenson and Williams 2000) and to the significance of employment as the key indicator of masculine status and social worth (Sennett 1998), unsettling traditional associations between masculine identity and employment participation. These arguments will be explored in more detail in the second part of this chapter.

Interactive skills and emotional work

Key areas of recent growth in employment in Britain have been in female-dominated sectors such as health, retail, catering, education, financial services and clerical work. In these sectors it has been argued that many of the skills and qualities sought by employers are those stereotypically associated with women, or rather with traditional notions of femininity, so that men are disadvantaged in seeking work in certain arenas (Alvesson and Billing 1997; McDowell 1997a). Service-sector work typically involves the exchange of intangibles, such as knowledge and information, rather than material artefacts, and is crucially dependent upon a social relationship between the producer and consumer of a service. This is a particularly significant aspect of exchange relationships involving direct face-to-face or voice-to-voice contact with customers and clients: what Leidner (1991, 1993) and others (e.g. Fenkel, Tam, Korczynski and Shire 1999; Macdonald and Sirianni 1996) have termed 'interactive service work'.

In many kinds of interactive service work employees' identities are not incidental to the job but are an integral part of it. Interactive jobs make use of workers' looks, personalities and emotions, as well as their physical and intellectual capacities, sometimes forcing them to manipulate their identities more self-consciously than do workers in other kinds of jobs (Leidner 1991: 578–9). Thus, as Lash and Urry (1994) have emphasized, in interactive service work the embodied performance of the provider or employee is effectively part of the 'product' that is 'sold' to the customer. Similarly, Walkowitz (2002) has argued that what she terms 'body work' is becoming increasingly significant in the British economy. Almost 20 years earlier Hochschild (1983), in a series of case studies of different types of interactive work in the USA, had argued that 'emotional labour' was a growing part of the labour process in contemporary capitalist economies. Hochschild suggested that this emotional labour required that employees were expected to display emotions that they did not necessarily feel as part of their paid work, creating the appearance that they loved the job, so distinguishing this type of service work from older forms of labouring in which employees were not required to 'act'. Hochschild distinguished 'surface acting' from 'deep acting'. In the former case, workers pretend to feel the requisite emotions, whereas in the latter the feelings are 'real', based on self-induced emotions, which, nevertheless, employers are able to exploit as a resource. Whether real or false, however, the emotional labour and feeling performance required by service occupations distinguishes them from other forms of labour. As Macdonald and Sirianni (1996: 4) have astutely noted (despite their implicit assumption that workers are male):

> The assembly-line worker could openly hate his job, despise his supervisor, and even dislike his co-workers, and while this might be an unpleasant state of affairs, if he completed his assigned tasks efficiently, his attitude was his own problem. For the service worker, inhabiting the job means, at the very least, pretending to like it, actually bringing his whole self into the job, liking it, and genuinely caring about the people with whom he interacts.

Such manipulation of emotion and the emphasis on the bodily attributes of employees has also led some commentators to designate this type of work 'aesthetic labour' (Nickson, Warhurst, Witz and Cullen 2001). This identification is part of a wider claim that in post-scarcity, postmodern societies, an aestheticized performance (Bauman 1998) is a key prerequisite of successful participation in the arenas of both production and consumption. In advanced capitalist economies the possession of social skills and personal attributes, including a particular embodied appearance and looks, is an increasingly important part of social success. In the selection of appropriate workers for interactive service occupations it seems clear that women have the advantage in terms of their 'natural' skills in the performance of emotional labour, where traits such as sensitivity, tact and caring are regarded as part of the social construction of femininity. Thus as Bradley, Erickson, Stephenson and Williams (2000: 78) have noted, 'Women are seen "innately" to possess skills considered valuable in the new service economy; "feminine" qualities of caring, communicating and making people feel good are important employment assets.' In addition, care and attention to personal appearance and a pleasing bodily image is regarded as an explicitly feminine attribute (Bordo 1993), although in recent years men too have become preoccupied with surface appearance (Simpson 1994).

High-tech, high-touch and regional differentiation

It is, however, important to distinguish between different types of service-sector employment in assessing the gendered consequences of economic restructuring. It is increasingly recognized that service dominated economies tend to exhibit greater polarization than earlier manufacturing-dominated economies (Castells 1996, 1998; Sassen 1991). As many commentators on economic and social restructuring have noted, service industries typically consist of 'two kinds of jobs: large numbers of low-skill, low-paid jobs and a smaller number of high-skill, high-income jobs, with very few jobs that could be classified in the middle' (Macdonald and Sirianni 1996: 11). In recent years it has been the former category – the bottom end, casualized and poorly rewarded jobs – that has expanded fastest (Crompton 1999; Ehrenreich 2001; Gallie, White, Cheng and Tomlinson 1998; Greg and Wadsworth 2000; Lash and Urry 1994). These jobs are often referred to in derogatory terms, as 'junk jobs' (Lash and Urry 1994) or 'donkey work' (Warhurst and Thompson 1998). They include a range of jobs, such as cleaning, fast-food and bar work in which the work is often highly routinized, standardized, and subject to control and surveillance, where employees often have to learn and repeat standardized scripts in the interaction with customers. Analysts of the workplace performances in the fast-food industry have argued that this work has more in common with the Taylorist or Fordist forms of workplace organization in the manufacturing sector than is often acknowledged. The work process is routinized rather than flexible (Gabriel 1988; Schlosser 2001), although the use of labour may be flexible, as employees often have variable hours depending on demand for the products that they sell. As Ritzer (1998) has argued, this bottom-end service-sector work is increasingly 'McDonaldized' in that technology is used to 'control workers and reduce them to robot-like actions' performing 'McJobs' where initiative, responsibility and autonomy are not valued workplace characteristics.

These routinized jobs might be further distinguished from jobs based on less-scripted and controlled interpersonal interactions in the expanding care sector, what Brush (1999) has termed the 'high-touch' jobs of the service sector to distinguish them from the high-status 'high-tech' occupations. These 'touchy' jobs include care of the elderly, general nursing, and work in counselling services, which are somewhat better paid, and certainly more socially valued than the 'trash' jobs just described, as well as the less reputable end of the care sector, including, for example, lap dancing, massage parlours and prostitution. There is no doubt, however, that both these types of work, what I have termed elsewhere 'servicing' occupations (McDowell 1997a) as distinct from service employment, are an increasingly important part of overall employment growth in industrial economies such as the UK and the USA. Their expansion is also the major explanation for the growth of income inequality that is an associated attribute of contemporary economic change in these societies. As Castells (2000: 18) has argued, in new service economies those workers who are most highly valued, and so well remunerated, are what he terms 'self-programmable or networked labour', educated, mobile and prepared to retrain, compared to less valued, and low-paid, generic labour: workers with few skills who all too easily may become non-labour.

Castells noted the socio-spatial division that has opened between these two forms of labour: 'There is a sharp divide between valuable and non-valuable people and locales' (Castells 1998: 161). For some, the expansion of the service sector has been linked to social mobility and access to a middle class lifestyle. A higher percentage of people with degree-level qualifications, compared with those workers with no qualifications, for example, are employed in the service sector in the UK, and almost a third of these graduates work in the financial and business services sector, where rates of pay are high (Erdem and Glyn 2001). But at the bottom end, prospects for mobility and security are minimal. Thus, for example, the services such as retailing, which do employ large numbers of workers with few or no educational qualifications, are dominated by poorly paid jobs. Further, the spatial distribution of these low-paid jobs tends to be uneven. In the northern regions of Britain, most severely affected by manufacturing decline, at present not only do individual sectors employ a higher proportion of unqualified workers than in the economy as a whole, but the regional structure itself is also slightly biased towards those sectors employing a high proportion of the less qualified (Erdem and Glyn 2001: 38). Thus low-skilled workers in deindustrialized local labour markets in the peripheral parts of Britain are at a disadvantage, not only compared with highly skilled labour in the core of the British economy, which, as Allen (1992) has argued, is increasingly dominated by Greater London and the outer South-East, but also in comparison to less skilled workers in the South-East. But even in the South-East, increasing inequalities in the wages paid to networked and generic labour mean that workers with poor educational qualifications and no specialist skills work for poverty wages and so are unable to maintain a decent standard of living in high-cost localities.

Hutton (1996) has suggested that Britain has become what he terms a 40:30:30 society in which a fortunate 40 per cent of employees are in full-time tenured employment or secure self-employment, 30 per cent work on an involuntary part-time or casual basis and 30 per cent work for poverty level wages or are unemployed. Although during the 1990s rates of unemployment fell across the country and regional differences declined (Jackman and Savouri 1999), as I suggested above, a significant North–South divide in labour market structure and opportunities continues to be evident. Access to well-paid employment opportunities, especially for the least qualified, is more difficult in certain parts of the country than others. This difficulty is reflected not only in spatially variable rates of unemployment but also in inactivity rates: the numbers of those of working age who are not seeking employment. Lack of opportunities in the older industrial areas is a major problem not only for those nearing the end of their working lives, some of whom may be unfit or disabled because of their earlier working lives in dangerous or demanding industries, but also for younger workers with fewer qualifications in these regions (Erdem and Glyn 2001). In addition, in these same regions there is a higher than average proportion of young people with few educational qualifications, with lower rates of post-compulsory schooling and lower than average participation in higher education.

Regional differences

In the labour force as a whole since 1977 there has been an astonishing decline in proportion of the population with no educational qualifications and credentials. In 1979, for example, 47 per cent of adult men (aged 25–64) and 61 per cent of adult women were without any qualifications; by 1999 the proportions had declined to 15 per cent and 21 per cent respectively (Erdem and Glyn 2001). In addition, the expansion of university places by 154 per cent since 1977 has increased participation rates among 18-year-olds to over a third of the age cohort. However, the benefits of this increase have accrued, in the main, to middle class students (Aldridge 2001), further exacerbating the barriers excluding working class young people from high-status service occupations, where the possession of a degree is a prerequisite for entry. The prospects of upward career mobility, through 'working one's way up', have declined in postwar Britain, a trend that was especially noticeable from

1990 onwards. Although Britain is now a more middle class society, the prospects of sons (longitudinal occupational mobility data for women are unreliable) of working class fathers moving into the middle class have actually declined in recent decades (Aldridge 2001; Walker 2001; Webb 1996). For the least qualified, regional variations both in unemployment and especially in activity rates have remained persistent. Lone parents and the long-term sick in northern regions, for example, are most likely to be without work, and overall non-employment rates among those with no qualifications varied from 30 per cent in the South-East to 60 per cent in Merseyside in 1999. Furthermore, in the most disadvantaged regions there are also higher proportions of the working age population who are without qualifications or who have only minimum levels. Thus of the age group who was in the final year of compulsory education in 1996/7, in the North-East (Tyne and Wear and the rest of the North) 12 per cent left with no GCSEs; 34 per cent achieved 'good' results (five GCSEs at C or above) and 20 per cent two A levels. This compares with 8 per cent, 46 per cent and 32 per cent respectively in the South-East (Regional Trends 1999). Basic literacy and numeracy are crucial attributes in contemporary labour markets (Bynner and Parsons 1997), as are the possession of minimum school-leaving credentials (Dolton and O'Neil 1996; Sparkes and Glennester 2002) as less than half of all jobs are open to those with only entry-level skills. Labour market difficulties associated with poor skills emerge right from the start of working lives. By the age of 21, for example, poorly qualified male school leavers are more likely to be unemployed and to have experienced twice as many months of unemployment as their counterparts with only average skills (Ekinsymth and Bynner 1994). Further, in the current economy mathematical attainment is of particular significance in terms of maintaining employment (Bynner and Parsons 1997), and the overall importance of educational qualifications is increasing over time (Robinson and Oppenheim 1998).

Although in the early 1990s there was rising unemployment in service industries and in the South, and unemployment and inactivity rates remain higher than average in Inner London, the most widespread problems at the beginning of the new century were still in the northern regions (Green and Owen 1998). Indeed, regional variations in non-employment rates for the least educated quartile of the labour force are higher than they were at the beginning of the 1990s. These regional variations in unemployment and inactivity rates clearly reflect the older industrial heritage. It might be assumed that they are predominantly the consequence of deindustrialization and heavy job losses among older workers, especially men, in the recessions of the early 1980s and 1990s. The differentials should, therefore, decrease as these older workers reach retirement age and are no longer counted in unemployment and inactivity figures. Moreover, despite the regional differences just outlined, there is no doubt that younger workers, even in these regions, are far better educated than their fathers' generation, which should also reduce regional differentials. However, Erdem and Glyn (2001) have argued that optimism is misplaced. The regional range in average non-employment rates remains wide not only for 55- to 64-year-olds (even though many have taken early retirement) but also for 16- to 24-year-olds (although many, of course, are still in some form of further education rather than being without work). But, as Erdem and Glyn (2001: 37) insist, 'lack of work for the less qualified is being reproduced throughout the labour force in low employment regions, representing a major problem for younger workers with few qualifications and not just for those with no qualifications nearing the end of their working lives'. This is especially a problem for men, and the sons of these men, who traditionally have tended to look to employment in the manufacturing industries rather than for jobs in services. As Dickens, Wadsworth and Gregg (2001) have shown, for all the least qualified workers, rates of unemployment declined more slowly in the 1990s expansion in the 'low employment' peripheral regions (Tyne and Wear, South Yorkshire, Merseyside and Strathclyde) than in the more prosperous, tighter labour markets of the 'high-employment regions' (the South-East [excluding London] and East Anglia). However, there was a noticeable gender differential in prospects and in patterns of employment participation. Even in these peripheral regions, women's employment prospects, including women with few or no qualifications, were significantly better than for men, with the exception of single mothers. Thus in the late 1990s and into the new millennium, labour market prospects for those young men who leave school as soon as they are officially permitted to do so, with low levels of exam success, look bleak, even in southern cities such as Cambridge, but especially in cities in the peripheral regions, including Sheffield. Low-status 'servicing' work, in which the attributes typically associated with femininity are most highly valued, seems to be their main prospect.

Growing income inequality

The pattern of uneven opportunities is mirrored in earnings. Poorly qualified workers in the tight labour markets of the South-East, for example, had higher weekly earnings than in the North and also experienced a higher rate of increase in the late 1990s, although interestingly there was also a marked gender differential in this pattern. Unqualified men in tight markets did poorly over the last seven years of the 1990s, whereas women workers in all regions benefited from wage increases. This gender differential is often, as I argue in the later part of this chapter, ignored in some of the larger-scale claims about changes in the nature of the labour markets and their consequences for workers' identity. But even for women the wage increases in bottom-end service jobs were inadequate, increasing at a much lower rate than for qualified workers. In general, the increasing stratification of opportunities and living standards in a service-based economy is associated with growing income inequality.

Throughout the 1980s there was a particularly marked increase in the extent of income inequality in Britain (Walker and Walker 1997). During the Thatcher era, for example, analyses by the Institute for Fiscal Studies showed that the income of the poorest 10 per cent of the population fell from £79 a week in 1979 to £61 in real terms in 1991 (Gosling, Johnson, McCrae and Paull 1997; Hutton 1996). Based on the European Union's definition of poverty (i.e. the number of people living on half, or less, of the average wage) the numbers of poor people increased from 5 million in 1979 to 13 million in 1990. While the rise in inequality declined slightly in the early 1990s, recent figures from the Office of National Statistics show that the gap between the richest and poorest households began to increase again in the second half of the decade, despite the election victory of New Labour in 1997, and the introduction during its first term of government of a series of measures to alleviate extremely low rates of pay, including a national minimum wage. In 2001, 1.3 million adults and 140,000 18- to 21-year-olds in the UK earned the minimum wage (the rate was increased to £4.10 for over 21-year-olds and £3.50 for 18- to 21-year-olds in October of that year), of whom 70 per cent were women. Among the lowest paid full-time employees in the UK are bar workers, who on average receive slightly more than the minimum. Other occupations with very low rates of pay include cleaners, kitchen porters, waiters and hairdressers. These occupations are typically among the poorest paid in other industrial economies, and, as Ehrenreich (2001) has vividly documented in her own personal participation in a range of types of 'poor work', it is almost impossible to maintain an independent life on these wages. Poverty wages are also more common in some labour markets than in others. According to the Low Pay Unit, in England the right to a basic minimum wage affects only 60,000 workers in Greater London but 210,000 in the North-West region.

One of the corollaries, then, of the continuing expansion of the low-wage economy, or rather, a service economy dominated by both low and high pay, is growing income inequality between individuals and households. By 2000 inequality had risen again, to the greatest level for 10 years, in part because of a decision that year to raise additional revenue though rises in indirect taxes and excise duty on petrol, cigarettes and alcohol which have a disproportionate impact on the poorest households. Over the same 10-year period, changes in the system of direct taxation reduced the burden of the high paid by an astonishing 34 per cent. Consequently, in the financial year 1999/2000 households in the top 10 per cent of the income distribution had an average annual income of £54,000 in 2000, compared with only £2,800 for the lowest 10 per cent. For these households, largely dependent on state support, changes in the welfare system including privatization, and the relative decline in the value of benefits, which were uncoupled from rises in wages or inflation, exacerbated the growing inequality and increasing poverty among the least well off. For the poorest members of society, access to state benefits and pensions has become increasingly difficult at the same time as their relative values have fallen. Despite New Labour's decision to increase the rates of basic state benefits in its second term, their real value remains below 1977 levels. For example, the weekly benefit entitlement of a single unemployed adult claimant was £53.05 in 2002 but would have been £87 if it had risen in line with average earnings. Over the same period the numbers of individuals living on incomes below the official poverty line had increased from 9 per cent to 25 per cent of the population. Many of these poor households, especially where the wage earners are forced to depend on irregular or insecure work or on state benefits, contain dependent children. The number of children living in poverty in Britain at the start of the new century was 3.5 million, a savage indictment of a supposedly affluent society. Two in five children are born into poor[1] households and almost a quarter of these children will themselves spend their lifetimes in poverty.

The rise of the new workfare state

At the same time as working lives have been transformed by economic restructuring, and as incomes have become less reliable and more inadequate for growing numbers of the British population, the Government has chosen to place a growing emphasis on employment both as a source of financial support and as an indicator of social esteem, respect and self-worth. Since 1997, when the first New Labour Government was elected, there has been an emphasis on increasing the total level of labour force participation in Great Britain. This is to be achieved through the combination of a series of new labour market policies to increase the 'work-readiness' of unemployed individuals and others who are outside the labour market, and reforms of the benefit system to tie it more closely to the labour market. These policies are not unique to Britain. Indeed, since the 1970s, especially following the 1973 and 1979 oil crises, there has been a movement in the USA, as well as in several European countries, towards neo-liberal social welfare regimes. These regimes, united by a common belief that the availability of universal welfare benefits at a reasonable level prices people out of work, emphasize market-led provision, deregulation and the reduction of universal benefits (Musterd and Ostendorf 1998; Peck 1998a, 1998b, 2001; Peck and Tickell 2002). This comment from an editorial in *The Economist* provides a useful summary of the main lines of the argument:

> Europe has priced much of its labour force out of employment, compensating it with welfare payments. Only a thoroughgoing reversal of that strategy can do much to get Europe's unemployed off the park bench and back into work. Encouraging the kind of dynamic economy in which lots of jobs are created will mean hacking away at policies that have long operated in favour of rigid work rules, high social costs, subsidies and protectionism. (*Economist*, 30 July 1994: quoted in Musterd and Ostendorf 1998: 6)

In its efforts to facilitate a flexible labour market and to 'hack at' universal welfare entitlements, the British Government looked, in particular, to the USA for examples of policy innovation (House of Commons 1998). In 1996, through the Personal Responsibility and Work Reconciliation Act, the Clinton Government scrapped the federal entitlement status of welfare, and introduced time limited benefits, capped spending, and introduced mandatory labour market participation (Peck 1998a, 1998b, 1999). Marked similarities in the discourses and practices of welfare reforms proposed and introduced by the new Labour administration have been identified by social policy commentators (Deacon 2000; Dolowitz 1997, 1998; Gray 1998; Jones 1996; Theodore 1998; R. Walker 1998), continuing a trend established earlier in the decade (King 1995; Willetts 1998). Thus since 1997 there has been a distinct shift in the UK away from a universal system of needs-based benefits as of right, towards compulsion, selectivity and a requirement of labour market participation or, at least, an assessment of fitness for work (Peck 1999, 2001).

In these policy shifts it seems that the Labour Government, unlike either the Democratic or Republican Parties in the USA, continues to accept the structural foundations of social inequality and lack of work. It is clear that Blair recognizes the worst excesses of US rhetoric, preferring, for example, to speak of the workless class rather than the underclass, and of social exclusion rather than poverty. Even so the critique of welfare dependency is pervasive and there is an overriding emphasis on the responsibility of individuals to ensure their labour market participation. In recent debates ideas about family dysfunctionality and poor work ethics, as well as claims that the poor are unskilled and unprepared for work, have dominated official statements. At its crudest, in this scenario, the unemployed are characterized as work-shy layabouts rather than, for example, the victims of poor schooling, of regional inequality or at the mercy of the vagaries of a labour market increasingly dominated by low pay and casualized work in its lowest ranks. Thus an ideology of 'blaming the victim' rather awkwardly coexists with a more structural understanding of the causes of inequality and social exclusion.

Whatever the ideological underpinnings of recent policy, however, the emphasis on labour market participation means that reliance on welfare benefits is recast as a strategy of last resort, thus residualizing the welfare system and stigmatizing claimants. It also means that the focus of the welfare system has moved to an emphasis on transitions – on facilitating the movement from welfare to work, emphasizing job search programmes, and training and skills with penalties for non-compliance and attendance – rather than the provision of a secure and basic minimum income for all to ensure daily reproduction. As Theodore and Peck (1998: 4) have pointed out, the aim in both the UK and the USA is to use welfare reform to 'transform regulatory norms in the lower reaches of the labour market... to articulate a regulatory strategy concerned *to make flexible labour markets work*' (original emphasis) rather than to ensure social security (and see Peck and Theodore 2000). Those who chose not to be included in the labour market would have no rights or claim on society. As Alastair Darling explained in a radio interview (on Radio 4 *World at One* on 24 November 1997), when he commented on the new proposals outlined in the State Opening of Parliament in 1997, the new welfare reforms would finally end 'the something for nothing culture' in Britain. In its second term, the Government's insistence on labour market participation was extended to include not only lone parents but also disabled people and claimants of sickness benefit in an extension of the Jobcentre Plus scheme (combining the jobcentre and benefit functions), which includes compulsory regular assessment meetings to ensure 'job readiness'. In echoes of the earlier programme, the rhetorical presentation of the programme in a speech by the Prime Minister emphasized his desire to end the 'the sick note culture' (Ahmed and Hinsliff 2002: 4) and to initiate a new 'contract' between the citizen and society.

In the new Britain of New Labour, then, the workless and unemployed are no longer to be compensated for their lack of work by the state, but instead, wherever possible, they are to be retrained and made ready to enter the labour market, ensuring that they take individual responsibility for their own lives. The major policy to implement this shift is the New Deal (welfare to work) programme, with the echoes in its name of an earlier US programme, introduced initially to retrain 18- to 24-year-olds and young single parents, and later extended to include older workers. Participation in this programme is compulsory (Millar 2000). In the launch of the New Deal programme in 1998 (DSS 1998: 19) the Government spelt out its thinking on what was identified as a 'third way' for welfare reform:

> The welfare state now faces a choice of futures. A privatized future, with the welfare state becoming a residual safety net for the poorest and most marginalized; the *status quo*, but with more generous benefits; or the Government's third way – promoting opportunity instead of dependence, with a welfare state providing for the mass of the people, but in new ways to fit the modern world. . . . We propose . . . a modern form of welfare that believes in empowerment not dependency. We believe that work is the best route out of poverty for those who can work. We believe in ensuring dignity and security for those who are unable to work because of disability or because of caring responsibilities, as well as those who have retired. This system is about combining public and private provision in a new partnership for the age.

So, in a paradoxical combination of neoliberal individualist economic beliefs and communitarian social beliefs (a modern flexible competitive economy combined with large-scale but targeted social intervention), the postwar ideal of a society based on universal state benefits was jettisoned. The postwar compact, based on economic planning and a universal welfare state, underpinned by full, lifetime employment for men who would share their income with dependants, has been replaced by the notion of flexible employment for all those who are physically fit, regardless of their other responsibilities, including the care of children. This is a remarkable and largely unremarked (Carnoy 2000; McDowell 2001b) shift in the nature of family responsibilities and one that has not, so far, been facilitated by the provision of accessible and affordable childcare services for all families with children. In addition, it is a change of ideals that is not yet reflected in the realities of labour market provision, in wage rates and in a wide range of social policies that continue to reflect the notion of a male breadwinner income, complemented by the earnings of secondary workers. As Rubery (1996: 31) has argued, there remains in the UK an important set of organizational and institutional arrangements that constructs certain categories of the potential workforce as cheap labour:

> These include the continuation of the male breadwinner system of social organization, thereby providing employers with a large supply of cheap female part-time labour; the social security system which, by topping up wages through the family credit system, provides the basis for those with household dependants to enter low wage or part-time jobs; the education system which has expanded the supply of young people available to work for 'top-up' wages; early retirement schemes and redundancy pay-offs which have provided a supply of older workers for part-time or self-employment; the tax and social security system which has encouraged the growth of self-employment as an easier route to tax avoidance than direct employment; the introduction of youth training schemes paying low allowances which has provided the basis for adjustment downwards of all youth wage levels to match the new institutions.

Her comment remains as valid now as in 1996.

Welfare, tax and labour market institutions continue to facilitate and maintain a segmented labour market with a wide range of employment systems and practices, making it virtually impossible for the growing proportion of the labour force in low wage service-dominated jobs to achieve independent living on an individual basis. As I shall show in the next part of this chapter, this undermines theoretical claims, recently outlined by a range of key contemporary social theorists including Ulrich Beck and Anthony Giddens, about the growing individualization of advanced industrial economies. Instead, it seems that among the disadvantaged and the working poor there is a 'reterritorialization' (Adkins 2000) of traditional gender relations, with the major difference that in the twenty-first century increasing numbers of working class young men, as well as women, are disadvantaged. Further, as I shall demonstrate in chapter 3, the category of youth has been extended in Britain, through both longer periods of educational participation but also policy decisions (such as the failure to include young workers aged 16 and 17 in the New Deal programme, and the introduction of a lower, young workers' rate for the National Minimum Wage). This extension has exacerbated parental and familial responsibilities for young people as they struggle to establish themselves as independent adults. One of the problems faced by these young people, especially early school leavers with few educational advantages, is that the jobs they are likely to be able to find offer little security, training or prospects for promotion and are also poorly paid.

An important question so far remains unanswered in the literature about economic and welfare restructuring: for the holders of these low-income insecure bottom-end jobs – often dubbed 'poor' work – does participation in the labour market provide greater security or greater self-respect than dependence on some form of a social wage? Rather than address this specific question now, however, I want to turn instead to an assessment of recent theoretical debates that have focused more generally on the connections between economic change, the growth of the service sector and 'flexible' working practices and notions of social identity. What does it mean to be a worker in this new economy? How has the growth of women's participation and the policy focus on individual responsibility affected the attachments between workers as men and as women, as members of a particular class stratum or residents of a particular part of the country? These and other questions have been at the centre of a number of provocative analyses of the future of work but, as I shall argue, their assessment of current trends fails to illuminate both the specific position of working class young men and gender relations more generally.

New Debates about Identity and Employment

The connections between the changing characteristics of employment in advanced industrial economies and the transformation of individual and group identities have been captured in a series of highly influential theoretical debates about the nature of work in 'post-industrial/postmodern' societies. Unsurprisingly, the key commentators on these trends differ significantly in their interpretations but, interestingly, there is a common insistence on the declining importance of the occupational 'order' in structuring wider social relations. Thus, for example, there is a new and rapidly expanding literature about the significance of consumption in contemporary societies. Bauman (1982, 1998), Beck (1992), Gorz (1999), Offe (1985) and Rifkin (2000) have all written about the decline of the 'work society': a perhaps surprising focus in the light of current increases in labour market participation rates in almost all industrial societies. In assessing the nature of these debates and their implications for the changing social relations between men and women, but especially young people, it is useful to distinguish between a more pessimistic and a more optimistic school, as Beck (2000) has suggested in his recent summary of the 'brave new world of work'. The writing of sociologists Richard Sennett (1998) and Zygmunt Bauman (1998) might be seen as representative of the former perspective, whereas Ulrich Beck (2000) and Andre Gorz (1999) are representatives of the latter. The arguments of the first two of these commentators might be characterized as narratives of loss (McRobbie 2002), whereas the latter two explore the risks but also the potential opportunities of the changing world of work.

Deciding to focus on the work of these four authors as important contributions to debates about the significance of economic restructuring, means ignoring the parallel, but largely separate, debate about the rise of the so-called 'new' economy (Quah 1996, 1999). Often termed an informational or network society in this literature (Castells 2000), the focus is on the positive implications of the introduction of new technologies for employment at the top end of the labour market: the high-tech workers 'living on thin air' (Leadbeater 1999), whose attachment to grounded localities may have become irrelevant, although the evidence is disputable. I have also largely ignored the growing body of work on the new cultural industries where a risk-taking, highly mobile workforce is highly dependent on attributes of cultural capital and highly individualized social networks (McRobbie 2002). Instead, as the focus here is on working class youth, analysts who address the changing redistribution of work in general, and its social consequences for the 'old' as well as the 'new' working class, have been chosen for examination. I conclude this assessment of recent debates about work and the relationship to workers' sense of their identities in the late twentieth and early twenty-first centuries with a brief comment on the 'crisis of masculinity' and a potential transformation in gender relations in the future lives of young workers: topics which are then dealt with in detail in the succeeding chapter.

Narratives of loss

Bauman and Sennett are pessimistic about current trends in the labour market. They argue that the decline of manufacturing employment and the increase in casualized and impermanent attachments to employment, associated with the growth of the service sector, as outlined earlier, have resulted in a labour force whose commitment to work is limited. In consequence, these employees' central identity as a worker, according to Sennett, is becoming 'corroded'. The central message of both authors is regret for the loss of the Protestant ethic that previously endowed all forms of waged work with meaning and value. Sennett (1998), in his elegiac and nostalgic book *The Corrosion of Character*, suggests that the idea of long-term commitment has been destroyed by new institutional and labour market practices. The short term is what matters (both for profits and employment), which is destroying the ideas of character and self-worth, which workers used to build up through loyalty to an employer, and the mutual long-term commitment of workers and bosses. Thus, he argues, the sense of linear time and cumulative achievement that marked the lives of the 'decent' working class in previous (postwar) decades have been disrupted and replaced by uncertainty, in which the ability to reinvent oneself as an employee is crucial. This has led to a destructive corrosion of self-worth, as well as the loss of trust and integrity, valued by earlier generations. The key significance of labour in the construction of self has been replaced by the rise of new urban identities increasingly rooted in the neighbourhood rather than in the workplace and in a conservative attachment to locality. Instead of the cosmopolitanism of an ideal urban realm, explored by Sennett (1996) in detail in an earlier book, strangers and urban 'Others' are now seen as a threat to be guarded against and to be excluded from the neighbourhood.

Sennett accepts that the old Fordist division of labour imposed heavy costs on its predominantly male workforce, in terms of the pain and boredom experienced by many industrial workers: it was 'claustrophobic in outlook; its terms of self-organization were rigid' (1996: 57). However, he disputes the purported advantages of the new regime of flexible post-Fordism celebrated by theorists and policy-makers alike. 'Flexibility' is a misnomer for the key characteristics of this new industrial order, according to Sennett. Instead, like the earlier regime, the new economy is also claustrophobic, regulated by invisible surveillance mechanisms. However, where it differs is that this new order is 'illegible' in ways in which the old regime was not. It is hard for employees to read its rules and understand power structures in organizations where bureaucratic structures have been replaced by individual and team work, and rewards and promotion are frequently on the basis of individualized performance targets. Thus he suggests that the old solidarity of the industrial working class has been replaced by fluid networks of highly individualized workers, acting largely on the basis of self-interest. Increasing uncertainty, combined with greater mobility, both occupational and geographical, also loosens ties to firms, neighbourhoods and localities. Thus for Sennett a key issue is how workers might recapture or reconstruct a coherent life history and life narrative 'in a capitalism which disposes us to drift' (1996: 117).

Sennett's analysis has much to recommend it, but his outline of current trends seems to me to be more relevant to the top end of the service sector, in large organizations such as merchant banks or legal firms where individual effort is rewarded and mobility is important rather than to the bottom-end 'servicing' jobs described earlier in this chapter. But more significantly, what Sennett completely fails to recognize, however, is the way in which the new order has disrupted the older narrative of a gender order based on *male* responsibility through employment and *female* fulfilment in the home, proving a significant challenge to the ability of young men to step into older versions of masculinity. Although Sennett does not entirely ignore women's growing labour market participation, he restricts his analysis to the suggestion that 'flextime arose from a new influx of women into the world of work' (1996: 57): a simplistic assumption that has the relationship the wrong way round. The lack of reflection on gender relations is partly a reflection of the limited empirical content of his work. It includes just one case study of female employment (and several of men's work). But there is also another reason why his analysis may have limited purchase of future trends, and why the text is pervaded by a sense of something lost rather than gained. His workers are middle aged and elderly. The sole woman who is interviewed tries, in her middle age, to move from bar work to advertising but finds herself excluded by her age and dowdy appearance in an industry in which presentation is almost everything. As McRobbie (2002: 102) has also noted:

> The men and women Sennett writes about are not young. Even in early middle age they already feel used up and depleted. They have been buffeted by a range of forces beyond their control: from the need to relocate again and again, with the lack of rootedness which avails such mobility, to being excluded from the youthful socializing and networking by age and appearance.

What is invaluable, however, in Sennett's analysis is his emphasis on the ways in which attachments to the local neighbourhood among an older working class were based on the symbiotic relationships between employment and place, creating what the critic Raymond Williams termed a 'structure of feeling' in a locality. This place-based connection between employment and residence provided the meaning and narrative whose loss Sennett mourns. Sennett's emphasis on the middle aged thus leaves open a question about whether young workers entering labour markets in which service employment has largely replaced manufacturing also feel this loss of a rooted identity. For the sons of working class men, often now reduced to looking for work in multinational retail chains or in fast-food outlets, the same sense of attachment to workplace and locality perhaps seems unlikely. As Sennett's analysis seems to indicate, their sense of identity, both in the labour market and in the neighbourhood, may be constructed on the basis of fear and dislike of a range of 'Others', including women or members of other ethnic groups. This parallels suggestions from empirical studies of economic change in deindustrializing cities in the USA (Fine and Weiss 1998; Fine, Weiss, Addelstone and Marusza 1997) and provides scope for a comparative investigation of attitudes in British cities. As I document in chapter 8, the idea of loss and threat to urban neighbourhoods is an important part of young men's narrative about place.

For Bauman (1998), the second representative of pessimistic analyses of contemporary labour market changes, economic restructuring and new forms of employment also bring in their wake loss of identity. Like Sennett, Bauman links changes in the workplace to wider social relations, but rather than focusing on place-based attachments, as his book's title *Work, Consumerism and the New Poor* indicates, Bauman explicitly examines the relationships between employment and the growing dominance of consumerism as an arena for the construction of social meaning and the growth of new forms of inequality. He suggests that in recent years identity is constructed, in the main, through the consumption of an ever wider range of goods and services as well as, or even rather than, through workplace participation. For the newly affluent, employed in the high-status end of the service sector, access to consumption goods and services both permits and demands the performance of an aestheticized identity in which the body is a key indicator of social status. In the workplace and in leisure arenas, activities and space, which are increasingly interdependent in high-status employment (Budd and Whimster 1992; du Gay and Pryke 2002), an aestheticized body is an essential attribute. As Leidner (1993) and Walkowitz (1999 have argued, the body is an inalienable part of workplace performance in both high-tech and high-touch jobs. However, the continual production of the desirable attributes of a slim, burnished, and well-presented body, through participation in a range of leisure activities and stylish dressing, is largely restricted to the former employees (McDowell 1997a; Negus

2002). For less affluent workers in, for example, the retail sector, maintaining and performing an acceptable workplace identity involves considerable ingenuity (du Gay 1996; Ehrenreich 2001) when time and money are short, and for young people leaving school and entering low-paid employment the desire for iconic goods often creates anxieties. Thus, while high-status workers are both valued producers and consumers in contemporary economies, the value of the working poor and the urban unemployed, for whom the acquisition of valued goods and services is more difficult or even impossible on their low incomes, is reduced to that of 'flawed' consumers.

At both ends of the labour market, then, according to Bauman and to Sennett, the old ideals of the 'Protestant work ethic', in which workers took pride in their job and employers took responsibility for their workforces, have been abandoned. The centrality of employment in the construction of individual identities, in notions of self-worth and in the development of social cohesion is reduced. As Bauman (1998: 65) notes:

> the apotheosis of work as simultaneously the highest human duty, the condition of moral duty, the guarantee of law and order and the cure for the plague of poverty, chimed in once with the labour intensive industry which clamoured for more human hands in order to increase its product. The present day streamlined, downsized, capital – and knowledge-intensive industry casts labour as a constraint on the rise of productivity.

Global corporations often do not need more workers to increase their profits or, if they do, they are able to find them elsewhere and employ them on more favourable conditions, for capital if not for the workers, than in the core regions of the old industrial economies (Dicken 1998; Panitch and Leys 2000). In the bottom-end service-sector jobs that are expanding in these societies, disposability is also often a dominant consideration in employment policies. The 'McJobs' in global cities go to the young and mobile, who move on as soon as they become bored or dismayed by their conditions of employment and low wages, producing the high rates of turnover that characterize industries such as fast food and the retail sector (Shlosser 2001). And yet, as I noted above, the work ethic has again come to dominate public debate about employment through the dominance of welfare-to-work initiatives, associated with an assumption that workers themselves are responsible for their own circumstances at the same time as income inequality has widened and rates of social mobility have stalled (Aldridge 2001). Further, as Bauman and other commentators (see e.g. Sunley, Martin and Nativel 2001; Peck 2001) have argued, these programmes will prove not to be sustainable in periods of recession as their focus on the characteristics of labour does nothing to address either the 'jobs deficit' identified by Turok and Edge (1999) in the towns and cities most severely affected by deindustrialization nor to ameliorate the exploitative conditions and extremely low wages in much of the service sector. As Ehrenreich (2001) has shown, the push for 'full employment', identified as a key policy goal in the USA and the UK, has resulted in the growth of poverty-level wages, which will not sustain independent living. The new socially excluded, therefore, in societies such as the USA and the UK which relied heavily on the growth of low-wage employment during the period of economic expansion in the 1990s, consist not only of people completely without waged employment but also the working poor – those who might be termed the 'unexceptional disadvantaged', whose standard of living has fallen over the last decades. Growing numbers of working class young men in British cities, especially those that have been most adversely affected by economic restructuring, will find themselves numbered among the unexceptional disadvantaged. Bauman's book is a powerful plea for society to rethink its moral obligations to the new poor and the socially excluded, and the implications of his arguments for policies to improve their condition will be addressed in the final chapter of this book.

Narratives of risk and opportunity: reflexive modernity and individualization

The work of Ulrich Beck and Andre Gorz is representative of more optimistic analyses of the changing nature of employment in industrial societies, although in both cases perhaps a more accurate label is 'pessimistic optimism'. What is interesting about their work, however, is their willingness to think beyond the world of employment *per se* and to beginning to sketch out the possible emerging outlines of a less exploitative society in which citizens might be able to combine a range of forms of work – waged employment, community work and familial work – over their lifespan, supported by new social arrangements. Their analyses thus provide a way to link emerging debates about the future of work with those about wider social changes including the 'crisis' of masculinity and new forms of gender relations. Unfortunately, neither author appears to be aware of key debates about gender divisions and employment change taking place elsewhere, especially among feminist scholars (see e.g. Adkins 2000; McDowell 2001b; Perrons 2001; Walby 1997). However, their work is provocative, albeit underspecified, and has been extremely influential in recent debates about the nature of late-modern or 'risk' societies and for this reason it is explored below.

Beck (1992, 1994, 2000), writing both individually and with scholars such as Antony Giddens and Scott Lash (Beck, Giddens and Lash 1994), has been one of the most significant contributors to debates about the nature of modern society. These authors have persuasively argued that the key characteristic of contemporary capitalist societies in the period that they refer to as late modernity is their capacity for reflexivity: that is, the ability to reflect on social conditions. Lash (1994) has suggested that two forms or levels of reflexivity are distinguishable: 'structural reflexivity', in which agents or social subjects reflect on the rules and resources of the social structure; and 'self-reflexivity', where subjects reflect on themselves and engage in self-monitoring. Structural reflexivity is associated with modernization, as 'the more societies are modernized, the more agents (subjects) acquire the ability to reflect on the social conditions of their existence and to change them in that way' (Beck 1994: 174). Thus people's capacity to alter the conditions of their existence increasingly lies in their own hands: 'we are, not what we are but what we make of ourselves' (Giddens 1991: 75). Consequently, through self-reflexivity, these theorists suggest that 'agency' is increasingly freed from 'structure' in late modernity.

The conventional restraints of an older industrial order are assumed to diminish in significance. In the economic arena, reflexivity includes not only the growing 'disorganization' and 'deterritorialization' (Lash and Urry 1987) of work as new types of waged work expand and are organized in new ways in a multiplicity of spaces and locations; it also involves the disruption of the old structural constraints of class and gender that restricted people to and channelled them into particular forms of work. Thus Beck (1992), in initial speculations about new forms of social organization, has suggested that in the new knowledge-based economy there is a shift away from the more standardized and exploitative relations of an older form of industrial capitalism, creating the prospect of greater equality and scope for individual improvement and self-realization. Labour market position and occupational success, he suggests, is increasingly constituted not by gender or class location but instead by self-design and individual effort, and, as Bauman and Sennett also noted, through the construction of individualized performances. However, as the older, more organized and standardized world of full employment (for most men) is replaced, these late-modern societies are also being transformed into 'risk societies' (Beck 1992) in which the emphasis on individual credentialization and performance, which may be a passport to major success for some, also entails high risks. The impact of failure is correspondingly greater. For the less well qualified and uncredentialized, who are excluded from the ranks of the professions and from the high-tech and creative industries that dominate the top echelons of the labour market, the expansion of exploitative low-waged forms of service work and their increasing uncertainty provides an unsustainable basis of a decent standard of living.

In a more recent book, *The Brave New World of Work*, Beck (2000) sketched out a number of alternative futures for reflexive economies. He counterposed a nightmare version of a neo-liberal unregulated low-wage economy, dubbed the 'Brazilianization of the west', to a more positive view of what he terms 'an active civil society'. In this latter scenario, communal democracy and civic identity are ensured through participation in a wide range of different forms of work, including self-organized local activities and more equitably distributed work in the home, as well as more formal waged employment. Like Bauman, Beck recognizes that one of the key problems of contemporary economies lies in the inequitable distribution of decent, well-rewarded work and, perhaps reflecting his origins as a European scholar from a state with relatively well-developed forms of social provision (Beck is German), he argues that new forms of state intervention will be required if a fairer society is to emerge from the current transformation of work. New institutional forms and new structures of financial remuneration, as well as new lifetime educational and training opportunities to equip individuals to participate in all spheres of life will be essential. Again I shall return to the implications of these suggestions for youth policy in Britain in the final chapter of this book.

Gorz (1999), whom Beck himself dubs a 'pessimistic optimist' (Beck 2000: 5), also embraces the opportunities that lie in the declining centrality of employment to suggest the outlines of a society in which the expansion of 'free' time provides the impetus for individuals to become more active and creative in the establishment of a low-growth society. He too believes that moving beyond a wage-based society will strengthen the social bonds of responsibility in civil society, resulting in a society of active citizens. Thus he suggests that growing communal involvement to resolve the current crises of the contemporary world, such as the ecological crisis, would be one form of positive outcome from the decline of the centrality of waged work in industrial economies. While Beck and Gorz's work grasps the opportunities, rather than lamenting the problems of new forms of work organization, what is problematic for their claims and utopian belief that new institutional arrangements might be forthcoming is the increasing insistence among western governments of the continuing centrality of an employment-based society. As I documented earlier in this chapter, labour force participation is now regarded as a requirement for almost *all* citizens, except those too old or disqualified by illness or disability, in the USA and the UK, regardless of familial and other responsibilities. The policy changes and new forms of social institutions that would be necessary to facilitate Beck and Gorz's vision of a society beyond one based on the centrality of the wage relation and continuous employment are completely missing from contemporary political agendas, other than perhaps in current European Union policies to facilitate what has been often termed 'work/life balance'. Further, the opportunities that a flexible, knowledge-based, aestheticized economy opens up for the credentialized middle class to take risks, construct portfolio careers and move between tasks in an exciting and creative manner are unlikely to be available to the mass of workers in early twenty-first century societies. Indeed, one of the ironies and unintended consequences of the expansion of the British higher education into a mass system, but one that continues largely to benefit the children of the middle class, is that it has widened the gulf between well-educated young people and early school leavers, cutting off access to employment with promotion prospects and the opportunities to 'learn on the job' that once existed. For the young men, whose lives are at the centre of succeeding chapters, for example, looking for work with the basic minimum school-leaving qualifications, the restrictive structures of class, gender and ethnicity continue to affect their life chances, just as they have done throughout industrial capitalism. Their prospects of even a reliable minimum income, let alone the lifetime of education that would be needed to retrain or to participate fully in the new institutions of civil life envisaged by both Beck and Gorz, seem remote.

In all four narratives too I suggest that the extent of change and transformation in working lives is exaggerated, in part because of the male-biased focus of the analysts. Their arguments are dependent on the contrast between the old Fordist standard industrial workers, supposedly united by workplace-based social ties built up through a lifetime's attachment to a single employer and place of work, and the new world of high-tech global capitalism characterized by risk-taking and individual effort. This narrative neglects the careers or non-careers of a host of other workers throughout the twentieth century – of women, many immigrants and ethnic minorities, of youth – whose attachment to the labour market has long been fragmentary and discontinuous. For these workers, the benefits of the Fordist postwar settlement between capital and labour that accrued to the labour aristocracy in the USA and Western Europe were not a significant element in their living conditions. It might therefore be argued that the construction of a new economy based on individualized risk-taking by the culturally talented and highly educated employees of the cultural and information industries has re-introduced or extended to the more privileged and educated minority the terms and conditions under which the less privileged workers of Fordism always laboured. However, as all the narratives of the future of work recognized, the new economy is dominated not only by the accelerated mobility of its key workers and patterns of capital investment, but also by growing inequality and the decision to link eligibility for state sup-port to an obligation to participate in the labour market participation. In the harsh world of twenty-first century capitalism, individual effort is apparently the key criterion of worth. The old certainties of industrial capitalism have been displaced by new forms of workplace-based and local identities, which has the potential for transforming the meaning of individual worth and group identity. As Pierre Bourdieu presciently argued (1984: 156):

> Whereas the old system tended to produce clearly demarcated social identities which left little room for social fantasy but which were comfort-able and reassuring even in the unconditional renunciation which they demanded, the new system of structural instability in the representation of social identity and its legitimate aspirations tends to shift agents from the terrain of social crisis and critique to the terrain of personal critique and crisis.

This emphasis on personal responsibility and a related rhetoric of crisis has been exacerbated by contemporary changes in the relationship be-tween employment and welfare entitlements. Recent social policies em-phasize the social characteristics of workers, and their individual responsibility to become work ready, albeit with the aid of the personal counsellors and advisors who are a crucial part of both the New Deal programme and the more recently introduced Connexions service for young people (see chapter 9). It seems probable that the identification of a growing crisis of masculinity among men whose labour market pos-ition is uncertain is but one effect of the illegibility and individualization of the world of work and the insistence that young working class men are the agents of their own lives.

The extent to which the growing requirement for each individual to enter into the social relations of waged work, despite the uncertainty of this new world of work, will disrupt 'traditional' gender relations based on networks of familial obligations is unclear. In his analysis of the risk society Beck (1992: 105) argued that 'people are being removed from the constraints of gender... men and women are released from traditional forms and ascribed roles'. In *Brave New World* (2000: 21) he outlines the ways in which reflexive modernization challenges the social relations of the first modernity. In this second modernity, he rather prophetically announces, 'sexual and inter-generational relations between men and women, adults and children are stripped of their basic pseudo natural premise, so that a gradual revolution affects the whole world of the small family with its conceptions of the division of labour, love and home life'.

But what form will this revolution take and what are its implications for young people leaving school? Will young women reject the bonds of marriage and family as they enter the labour market in growing numbers and as their opportunities begin to match those of men in the same class position? Will young working class men resent their inability to fulfil the role of the breadwinner? Writing with Elisabeth Beck-Gernsheim, Beck (1995: 1–2, 14) has suggested that 'the nuclear family, built around gender status, is falling apart on the issues of emancipation and equal rights', predicting that 'we are in for a long and bitter battle; in the coming years there will be a war between men and women'. But an alternative view is perhaps just as plausible as better-educated and more independent young men and women renegotiate familial responsibilities in more equitable ways, reducing the potential for domestic disputes and, through joint labour market participation, increasing their living standards. Among the less well educated and less affluent, however, economic necessity might have a similar effect, tightening familial bonds as a single income is insufficient to reach a decent living standard. But it also seems that without empirical evidence based on detailed investigations of the aspirations and attitudes of young people entering the labour market, the predictions of a gender revolution are mere speculation. As I shall demonstrate in the succeeding chapters, many young British men have a strong adherence to conventional notions of gender divisions and domestic responsibilities. Whether they will have the means and the opportunities to fulfil their aspirations as young women's lives change and as economic restructuring disrupts older ways of making a living is a central issue that interests contemporary analysts of the interconnections between gender relations and economic change, and is at the heart of this investigation.

Conclusions

There is little doubt that economic restructuring since the 1970s, which has transformed the old Fordist relations of employment, has had a huge impact on the life chances of the British population. Waged employment has altered in its form and content as the majority of British employees now work in some form of service-sector occupation. Waged work has also been redistributed across the country, over the working day and week, and between individuals. The majority of working age women are now economically active, whereas men's labour market participation has declined. These social, spatial and temporal shifts in the distribution of employment have been paralleled by the growth of non-standard hours and non-standard contracts as organizations have developed new ways of working. For some, the benefits of growing flexibility have been significant. However, many of the wilder claims about both the extent and benefits of 'flexibility' have been exaggerated (Bradley, Erickson, Stephenson and Williams 2000) and the majority of workers in the post-Fordist era continue to labour in traditional ways at a designated workplace with a contract for standard hours. A large proportion of the so-called non-standard forms of working is a consequence of the rise in female participation rates and are a continuation of the traditional pattern of female employment, usually on a part-time basis to facilitate continuing domestic responsibilities. For many women, as well as a growing number of men, the growth of non-standard work, the conditions under which it is undertaken and the financial rewards are typically exploitative. The rise of low-wage service employment has led to growing inequality and a social 'speed up' in the lives of many individuals and households where multiple labour market participation is now essential to retain a standard of living that once might have been possible based on the wage of a sole, usually a male, breadwinner.

At the same time as employment participation has become an ever increasing economic necessity, social policies introduced by the new Labour Government have the consequence of forcing unemployed people into any available job. As Rubery (1996: 26) has noted, 'all forms of wage employment are being deemed suitable for workers in all types of family circumstances or occupational history'. Despite the introduction of the minimum wage (which, however, remains at an unacceptably low level), in general, state interventions to alleviate poverty have been based on mechanisms to increase labour market participation and to support workers in the lowest-paying jobs through employment related benefits rather than to substantially challenge market-determined poverty wages. Young unskilled workers, however, are excluded from these provisions, ineligible for either the minimum wage or for its subsidization through the benefit system. Thus young workers are constituted both as a cheap labour force but also as less than independent, reliant on their families for continuing support. In the next chapter, I shall explore in greater detail the ways in which young people, but especially working class men, are constituted as dependants and as socially disruptive.

These young people, but also growing numbers of women, older workers and some members of minority communities who have been excluded from the benefits of further and higher education and from the high-paying sectors of the service economy, find that they have to accept jobs designed for second-income earners even though they themselves are in need of full subsistence support in order to establish an independent lifestyle. The growth of these forms of unsustainable work threatens the future security of the economy.

> Stable employment and pay levels are essential not only for the reproduction of skills but also for the whole functioning of, for example, the housing market, the consumer credit system, the pension system, the taxation system and the social production and nurture of children. Stability and transparency are being undermined by the increasing precariousness of jobs, the increase in the number of jobs which do not provide for acceptable living standards, and the increasing opaqueness of the labour market as pay is linked supposedly to organizational and individual performance, but in practice to discretionary decisions at the organizational level. (Rubery 1996: 34)

And, as Bauman, Beck and Gorz so powerfully argued, the flexibility, casualization, fragmentation and precarious work that characterizes advanced industrial economies are not the inevitable and unchallengeable outcome of contemporary economic change, but are instead the result of the interplay between labour market institutions, employers' strategies and broader social and institutional changes in western economies. If the growing income and social inequality that has been documented in the first part of this chapter is to be challenged and reversed, then new ways of thinking about the distribution of employment between individuals and over the life cycle are needed, accompanied by new institutional arrangements to ensure economic security and civic participation for all citizens.

3

The Contemporary Crisis of Masculinity: It's Hard to Be(come) a Man

> Youth is an idea that is used to represent hope, optimism and the possibilities for a future, as well as rebellion and trouble making. (*Signs* editorial 1998: 575)

> Large numbers of youth are now growing up without the expectation of stable employment around which familiar models of working class masculinity were organized. Instead they face intermittent employment and economic marginality...In such conditions, what happens to the making of masculinity? (Connell 1995: 94)

In this chapter the emphasis shifts to a more explicit focus on young men. Here I examine the position of young men, assessing the ways in which the traditional narrative about the transition from adolescence to adulthood has unravelled in recent years. In the story about adolescence – itself a relatively recent one (until the postwar period of relative affluence there were few years between casting off childish things and the assumption of adult responsibilities [Aries 1962; Mitterauer 1992]) – working class young men have been defined in different ways to their more affluent peers. These working class young men are viewed as rebels and rascals, and their adolescence has been constructed as a period of rebellion rather than one of freedom to explore, which has long distinguished middle class youth (Gillis 1981; Kett 1977; Mungham and Pearson 1976; Platt 1969; Ruddick 1996). Thus the dual construction of youth reflected in the quotation above has always been a class-specific one. For all young men, however, the achievement of a mature adulthood in western industrial societies typically is associated with, even defined by, a number of transitions – from the family home to independent living, and from education into the labour market. In addition, the establishment of a successful heterosexual relationship, followed by fatherhood, has also often been seen as a marker of successful adult masculinity. These transitions, and their temporal coincidence, were most evident in the 1960s (Kiernan 1985), when there was relative affluence, full employment, and a supply of cheap rented housing. Since that date the transition has become more complex and extended, and the link between transitional statuses (leaving home, employment and marriage) has become weakened (Jones and Wallace 1992). While complexity and an extended period of transition is now common among all young people, the successful achievement of these three markers of adult status has become particularly problematic for working class young people, and especially for men. As I argued in chapter 2, labour market restructuring has altered the set of opportunities in the labour market and not only have house prices risen in many parts of the country, but the building programme, by both local authorities and private construction firms, has significantly declined, making it increasingly difficult for young people to form new households and to establish independent living arrangements.

Of the three transitions, it is the movement into employment that is the most significant for young men, as work provides the means to establish a home and to support a family. Based on a series of case studies of different types of labour markets in the early 1990s, Roberts (1993) argued that there were really only three main trajectories in the transition to adulthood: (1) a successful trajectory leading to good jobs, (2) less successful trajectories leading to respectable working class jobs, and (3) trajectories resulting in insecure employment, low-level training and bouts of unemployment. Since the beginning of the 1990s, however, the huge expansion of low-paid and insecure jobs, even though overall labour market participation rates have risen, means that the circumstances of the working poor has became a key policy issue. In assessing the relative degree of success of young people in avoiding Roberts's third transitional pathway, it is clear that the first and critical stage is around or before the age of 16, when young people's abilities and aptitudes in education, as well as the type of school they attend and its locality, lead eventually to good, indifferent or poor 16+ qualifications. These results either open or close the door into the second phase of transition to adulthood between 16 and 18. Those who fall into Roberts's third category tend to become trapped in a mixture of training schemes and unemployment followed by more training, or in periods of high employment, low paid and insecure jobs. Some become tempted by other, often illegal, ways of making a living (MacDonald 1994). It is this third group or category who are the focus of the rest of this book.

The successful transition to employment is also, for young men, more than a purely material transition. It is also a key element in the establishment of an acceptable version of adult manhood. As theorists of the social construction of masculinity have argued, it is waged work that is of crucial significance to the construction of a masculine identity. Waged work defines the sort of man young men become. Further, 'the central function of masculine ideology is to motivate men to work' (Connell 1995: 33). The reverse argument also holds: masculinity itself is deeply embedded in the social meaning of work and, as Connell (1995: 29) has shown, 'definitions of masculinity are deeply enmeshed in the history of institutions and economic structures'. A growing number of studies have documented the ways in which work not only affects the construction of masculinity but is also defined and performed in numerous occupations to construct femininity as 'out of place'. However, as I argued in chapter 2, the growth of 'poor work', especially in the service sector has been associated with a shift in the gender division of waged labour and in the gendered associations of employment. What happens to men's sense of themselves as masculine when the sort of work associated with masculinity disappears, as it has in many urban localities? Will young men be prepared to undertake servicing work for low wages in common with increasing numbers of young women, or do they feel it is an affront to their masculine dignity? For some young men reaching maturity at the start of the twenty-first century it has been suggested that the story of transition to adulthood through employment participation has become intertwined with one about a 'crisis of masculinity'.

In this chapter, therefore, I want examine the nature and different dimensions of the current crisis of masculinity and its construction in a range of different discursive arenas. It is apparent that, sometime in the 1990s, the stories of what it means to become a man started to unravel. As well as the exciting, and rapidly expanding, academic work, in the main by sociologists and psychologists, about masculinity that was outlined in chapter 1, the late 1990s also saw the rise of a popular genre of books analysing the apparent crisis of masculinity. In Britain the radio commentator and psychologist Anthony Clare published *On Men: Masculinity in Crisis* in 2000, in which he analysed contemporary male insecurities, suggesting that a growing split between men's personal feelings and desires and their public preoccupations lay at the root of their problems. Threatened by women's success, Clare argued that men are now seen as emotionally crippled and biologically redundant, suggesting that they might reclaim their sense of self and their pride through the establishment of more intimate personal relationships as friends, lovers and fathers. In the USA Susan Faludi, in her book *Stiffed: The Betrayal of Modern Man*, also published in 2000, interviewed a varied group of US men about their fear of failure and told a similar story about men's fear of women's success. A parallel but more particular debate has also developed about young men, about their fear of failure and their sense of themselves as masculine. And, as I shall document, in these debates too, the relative success of girls and young women, as well as feminism *per se*, is often suggested as an explanation for their anxieties.

There is widespread popular and academic agreement in a number of industrial societies, among them Great Britain, France and the USA, that something is troubling this group of men. This trouble takes a variety of forms from 'laddish' and loutish behaviour in public spaces to rising suicide rates among young men. In the media, as well as in contemporary policy debates, urban youth are constructed as a danger to the wider society in which they live as well as a challenge to community life, especially in the inner city and on peripheral estates of state-provided housing. I want therefore to document the emergence and the main features of this crisis of urban youth, questioning both its newness and, indeed, its very nature. Rather than a crisis of masculinity, I shall argue here that something more complicated than a straightforwardly gender-based issue is emerging in western cities. Instead, a fundamental transformation in the relationships between waged work, gender and class is underway and so the arguments in this chapter build on those already laid out in chapter 2 where some of the implications of new forms of work were examined. The changing connections between waged work, gender and class are revealing the new shape of an older pattern: that is, class-based inequalities, in which members of the working class – both male and female – are finding their standards of living threatened in service-based economies. For young men, these inequalities are particularly problematic as they are among what is probably the first generation of men in industrial economies to experience downward intergenerational mobility. In service-dominated economies working class young men are faced by more restricted labour market opportunities than their fathers found in previous decades (Fine and Weiss 1998; Finnegan 1998), whereas working class young women, in comparison with their mothers, seem to have greater job opportunities (Egerton and Savage 2000). At the end of this chapter I connect the debates about the risk society and the growing individualization in the workplace, introduced in the previous chapter, with contemporary debates about the social construction of youth and changes in the transition to adulthood, as well as potential pathways to employment, in risk societies.

The trouble with boys

In the last few years it has become impossible for anyone reading the broadsheets or the relevant academic papers and journals to avoid debates about the trouble with young men. From the mid-to late 1990s onwards, headlines such as 'new lads to new sads' (*Observer*, 14 March 1999), '"laddish ideal" helps drive men to suicide' (*Guardian*, 19 April 2000), masculinity in question' (*Guardian*, 2 October 2000), and 'the truth about the male crisis' (*Independent*, 27 February 2001) have relentlessly examined the trouble caused by, but also the troubles experienced by young men. Young men are, for example, more likely to be arrested than young women, to spend periods on remand or in prison, and in the late twentieth century their mental health was also a cause for concern, as suicide rates rose among their age group in most industrial societies. In France, for example, Government statistics show that the rate of suicides by all men more than doubled between 1970 and 1990 and was the most common cause of death for men aged between 15 and 25. For this same age group in the USA suicide rates have tripled since 1950. In the UK the rate among young men was 70 per cent higher at the beginning of the 1990s than it was 20 years earlier (Miles 1991: 11).

As well as the laddish and loutish behaviour and worse of these youths, recent years have seen a further significant gender differential. A gender gap has opened up in educational performance. In Great Britain, girls are now outperforming boys in school-leaving examinations taken at the end of the period of compulsory schooling. Every August, on the release of the exam results, a parallel set of headlines to those listed above ask why 'boys [are] lagging in class' (*Observer*, 23 September 2001), noting 'The growing divide' (*Daily Mail*, 27 September 2001) or 'the greater divide' (*Times Higher Educational Supplement*, 9 January 2001) between boys and girls, commenting in the former headlines on school results and in the latter on the rapid expansion of young women taking up university places. A recent headline, also in the *Times Higher Education Supplement*, argued that universities must 'bring lost boys back from Neverland' (*Times Higher Educational Supplement*, 26 July 2002), without a single reflection on the long dominance of universities by white men. In this chapter the social construction of the troublesome boy – the lad or yob of newspaper headlines – will be examined, followed by an assessment of boys' changing educational performance and then by the changing nature of the youth labour market. Thus the different arenas or spaces within which a masculine performance is constructed – the streets and other public spaces, schools and the workplace will be addressed in turn. As I argued in the introduction, masculinity is a multiple and fluid construction that varies according the spaces in which it is performed. The type of masculinity that is interrogated in the succeeding sections is that exemplified by the 'rebel' or the outlaw – the young man who is anti-school, anti-work, despises ties, and wants his freedom to enjoy himself unconstrained by the banalities of everyday life – if only at the weekends.

In the long tradition of youth studies across the twentieth century the focus has not only been predominantly on young rebellious men, but it has also addressed the more spectacular aspects of their lives. Thus the literature includes studies of gangs and bikers, dropouts and hobos, beats, mods, rockers and punks, hooligans, muggers, yobs and 'lads'. As is now widely accepted, the social construction of identity, be it as a man, or as a young person, is linked to modernization and, especially, to periods of rapid social change. In these periods of change there is often a moral crisis, and fears of a particular social group, usually some form of underclass or outsider, are common. In the youth literature, for example, as I explore in more detail below, young men are frequently constructed as 'folk devils' (Cohen 1973) and their supposedly rampant sexuality has long been seen as a threat to be tamed. Dick Hebdige (1988) has argued that these troublesome, sexualized, often working class, young men first appeared in the urban and geographical literature in the ethnographic studies undertaken by the Chicago School under the influence of Robert Park from the 1920s onwards. In vivid case studies, usually of inner city areas, the focus was often on the criminal, the gang member or the troublemaker, initiating the long association between inner urban areas and troublesome, even riotous, youth that is still a distinguishable focus in Anglo-American postwar urban policy to the present day. Indeed, as Hebdige (1988: 17–18) has suggested:

> youth is present only when its presence is a problem or regarded as a problem. More precisely the category 'youth' gets mobilized in official documentary discourse, in concerned or outraged editorials and features, or in...the social sciences at those times when young people make their presence felt by going 'out of bounds', by resisting through rituals,

dressing strangely, striking bizarre attitudes, breaking rules, breaking bottles, windows, heads, issuing rhetorical challenges to the law.

It is apparent, however, that the association of youth, and especially male youth, with trouble, has an even longer heritage than the one delimited by Hebdige. In a fascinating documentary survey, Pearson (1983) traced the figure of the hooligan back through British history to the seventeenth century, drawing out the discursive parallels between (going backwards) popular representations of Teds, the hooligans whom Baden-Powell hoped to reclaim through the scouting movement, London street gangs and ruffians, the cads and roughs of the Victorian period, rebellious chartists and unruly apprentices in 'Merrie' England. And in the UK, at the turn of the millennium, a period often dominated by social anxieties about gender and sexuality (Showalter 1990), youth, and in particular young men, as I noted above, have once again become the focus of both policy and academic debates, culminating in proposals by the Home Secretary to address the problems of the 'yob', the Prime Minister to reduce street crime, and the Education Minister to resolve the crisis among non-academic young men who number largest among the school resisters.

Contemporary Representations 1: Young Men in Policy Discourses – the Yob, Vandal and Hooligan

the media is wedded to the image of the yob because it seems to encapsulate the real and imaginary fears of our times. The yob is carrying the weight of masculinity which, for a variety of reasons, middle class society finds increasingly unacceptable, and rhetorically dumps onto the men of lower class. He is the classic scapegoat: lugging around the sins of our culture while the rest of us look sanctimoniously on. . . . There is a growing belief that there is something in masculinity itself which inclines poor young men to anti-social behaviour. In fact, this is a recent twist to an old story. The yob is not a new phenomenon. (Ros Coward quoted in Charlesworth 2000: 156)

The hooligan or the yob is as evident in contemporary policy discourse as his (and it is almost always a male figure) historical predecessor. As Hebdige noted, it is particularly in periods of crisis or civil unrest that the figure of the young male as a symbol of disruption is most evident. In 1981, 1991 and most recently in the spring and summer of 2001, for example, when some of Britain's towns and cities experienced urban unrest and street protest, the media images were predominantly of young, apparently violent men. These images were succeeded by debates about the problems of youth unemployment – high at the beginning of the two earlier decades – but also about the erosion of parental discipline, the 'decline' of the family and the need for 'firm' policing in these areas Throughout the 1990s the figure of young working class men was demonized in the press. In a stinging indictment of press coverage, Ros Coward, a journalist with feminist sympathies, outlined the ways in which young men were represented by the media in that decade:

> 'Yob', once a slang insult, is now a descriptive category used by tabloid and quality newspapers alike ... yob is a species of young white working class male which if the British media is to be believed is more common than ever before. . . . The yob is the bogey of the Nineties, hated and feared with a startling intensity by the British middle class. Janet Daley describes such men as 'drunken Neanderthals', while Jeremy Kingston, also in the *Times*, reckons they are 'crapulous louts'. Simon Heffer of the *Telegraph* claims, like Peter Lilley, that not even women of their own social class can tolerate such ghastly specimens: 'Nobody wants to marry a yob because he is boorish, lazy and unemployable.'

As she noted, these representations of young men would have been regarded as offensive if a different group were being portrayed.

> The language in which such young men are described – lots, scum, beasts – can be heard across the political spectrum. It appears in an extreme form in *Sun* editorials and in a modified version in sombre discussions of youth culture, as well as in some feminist writings on contemporary masculinity. . . . This insistent view of the 'yob' as morally delinquent – idle, criminal, unemployable, and (a very Nineties inflexion, this) unmarriageable – would cause outcry if used to refer to race or women. (Coward 1994: 4; and quoted in Charlesworth 2000: 156)

This hysterical fear and hatred remained evident at the beginning of the new century when debates about the links between revolting youth, inadequate parenting and firm/zero tolerance policing provided a new twist in the representations of urban youth. In new Labour policy, the mindless vandal and disaffected yob made a striking reappearance in the first years of the new decade, especially in debates about street crime, which became one of the most significant issues in the run-up to local elections in May 2002. What has made recent pronouncements so tantalizing, however, is the personal involvement of the Prime Minister and the Home Secretary, whose own sons seemed set to challenge the habitual, but usually implicit, class associations of these stereotypical figures. When lack of parental control was asserted as part of the problem of youth, it surely never crossed the minds of these two ministers that their own parenting would become the focus of press scrutiny. However, when Jack Straw's son William was arrested for suspected drug dealing at Christmas 1997 and Tony Blair's son Euan, for being drunk and incapable in public in summer 2000, their assertion of the connections between family background and irresponsible behaviour surely should have been re-evaluated.

Despite these personal challenges, though, Labour policy pronouncements firmly continued to reflect the view of young *working class* men as out of control. Earlier in the same week in July 2000 in which his son was arrested, Blair had made several policy pronouncements about youth 'justice', in part spurred by the appalling behaviour of British soccer supporters at European cup matches. This policy nicely sums up the approach of new Labour to 'yobbish' behaviour. Thus, in an article in the *Guardian* headed 'Policing Yob Culture' on 3 July, it was reported that 'Tony Blair is on a law and order kick. After his weekend speech urging on the spot fines for drunken, noisy, loutish and antisocial behaviour, he is now proposing new police fines or 48-hour closure orders on rowdy pubs' (Brown 2000: 4), referred to by the Prime Minister as 'thug pubs'. The aim of reducing 'disorderly' behaviour had already been written into a recently announced Home Office Crime Reduction Strategy, and Jack Straw, then Home Secretary, had announced so-called zero-tolerance 'antisocial behaviour orders' under which the courts had new powers to jail anyone who is persistently disorderly but not convicted of a specific crime. As commentator Ros Coward (2000: 20) noted a day later, not only was the rhetoric emotive and Blair's language particularly florid, but it dishonestly conflated delinquent behaviour with more serious problems of violent crime. It is, as Coward suggested, 'bogeyman politics, spinning working class men as hate figures'. In January 2001 this conflation was complete when headlines greeting the new Criminal Justice Bill argued that it gave 'More clout for Police in tackling murders and drunken yobs' (*Guardian*, 20 January 2001) – a rather surprising coincidence of what seem to be problems of a significantly different magnitude (see plate 3.1). Eighteen months later, however, in August 2002 in three experimental areas (the West Midlands, Croydon and Essex), new powers for the police to issue fixed penalty fines for drunken and disorderly behaviour, being drunk and incapable, and using threatening words were introduced.

Earlier in 2002 the debate had taken a somewhat different turn as popular concern about urban crime, especially the soaring rates of street theft (in the main accounted for by the theft of mobile phones by and from school-age children), replaced the more general emphasis on yobbish behaviour. This led to the formation of a street crime action group within the Cabinet that met weekly in early 2002, culminating in a promise by the Prime Minister, Tony Blair, in April 2002 to have brought street crime under control within six months (*Guardian*, 25 April 2002). A wide range of measures to deal with youth crime, truancy, antisocial behaviour, graffiti and parental neglect were placed on the statute book, including community supervision orders, which if not complied with might result in the reduction of Job Seeker's Allowance for unemployed people, antisocial behaviour orders, fines for parents of truants, education supervision orders and parenting orders under which people have to attend classes in managing their children, as well as curfews, tagging and the proposal to hold under-16-year-olds in adult prisons. In an apparently off-the-cuff piece of policy-making, which media commentators compared with the Prime Minister's announcement of on-the-spot fines for 'hooligans', Tony Blair announced in April 2002 that the Cabinet was considering reducing the child benefit payments to parents of young persistent troublemakers. At the same time the Minister for Education, Estelle Morris, announced 'truancy sweeps' of shopping malls and open spaces by the police, and, if head teachers agreed, the attachment of a police officer to schools in one hundred areas most affected by youth crime and misbehaviour. These fears of out-of-control youths were exacerbated by the collapse in April 2002 of the trial of two 16-year-old boys accused of the murder of Damilola Taylor, a 10-year-old who had been stabbed by a broken bottle and left to bleed to death on a 'sink estate' in Peckham in South London. In this area, youth gangs apparently ran riot and press commentary on the case exemplified a 'moral panic', identifying 'feral children who run wild with no fear of the law... roaming in packs', and 'feckless parenting' (*Observer*, 28 April 2002) as the key contributing factors.

These reactions, and the policy proposals of the Government, are reminiscent of what the sociologist Stuart Hall (Hall and Martin 1983) termed the 'authoritarian populism' of the Thatcher Government. The *Guardian*, editorial of 29 April 2002, for example, was headed 'punitive populism'. The social construction of troublesome urban youth as 'muggers' – a definition with no legal status – is also reminiscent of

Criminal justice bill

More clout for police in tackling murderers and drunken yobs
[20.01.2001]

Straw extends youth tagging
[21.11.2000]

Blair wants on-the-spot fines for louts
[1.07.2000]

disaffected young men on council estates

Turn the yobs back into boys
[19.12.2000]

National news

Number of boys held on remand doubles
[02.01.2001]

Police win powers to shut down 'thug bars'
[02.07.2000]

Yob parents blamed for class chaos

Minister attacks 'feckless' adults over child crime
[24.03.2002]

3.1 Yobs, lads and hooligans

Hall's earlier analysis of the links between urban crime and inner city youth. Further, there are clear parallels between current US and UK attempts to redefine eligibility for welfare payments and social benefits. The principles that lie behind the introduction of workfare programmes, linking of the rights to social benefits to the obligation to participate in the labour market, have been extended to youth policy. The various proposals – to cut educational maintenance allowances for 16- to 19-year-olds who do not attend school or college regularly, for example, and to fine parents or to reduce their benefits if their children misbehave, truant or are caught engaging in criminal activities – clearly illustrate a new direction in welfare provision, more familiar in right wing ideologies than ideals of welfare provision previously associated with the left in Great Britain. As well as the administrative issues to be resolved in linking the payment of child benefit, which is at present a universal entitlement, to children's behaviour, it seems a travesty to suggest that youth crime might be resolved by deepening family poverty.

Although this unsympathetic figure of the yob or hooligan – rebellious, dangerous and threatening to 'society' – is not merely a contemporary phenomenon but has a long history, his representation has been more complex than just as an antisocial lout. Indeed, as I shall argue below, in some of the most influential school-based studies published since the early 1970s, he is also represented in a more positive light as an anti-hero, engaged in acts of everyday resistance and rebellion. Latterly, however, the deep vein of romanticism and envy apparent in some of this work (Walker 1986) has been replaced by a more negative concern with an apparently widespread 'crisis of masculinity' in which men are apparently becoming the victims of women's (relative) success. As I also argue below, the failures of working class young men are currently interpreted as if they are the consequence of the gains that young women are making in contemporary Britain. A similar set of issues is evident in other industrial societies – the US educational press, as well as that of Australia and New Zealand, is also concerned about the problem of the educational achievements of boys and young men (Finnegan 1998; Kenway and Willis 1998).

Contemporary Representations 2: Young Men at School – Anti-hero or Problem?

As educational sociologists have documented, there is a long tradition of relative failure at school by working class children in Britain and the USA, disadvantaged by the middle class assumptions and language of schooling. In these established narratives there is a clear gender-differentiation in the explanations of failure. Young women tended to be represented passively as 'at risk', whereas young men, whether working class or black, have been portrayed as actively resistant, rebellious, even deviant (Griffin 2000). Just as in the urban policy literature and governmental debates, this tradition of concern with rebellious working class boys who reject education is readily identifiable in social policy and education debates. And like the urban literature, these debates too may be traced back in the USA to early twentieth century Chicago, where research on delinquent children by Edith Abbott and Sophonisba Breckenbridge (1912, 1916) initiated a tradition of studies that has continued to the present day. In Britain a similar debate is evident, one that has been especially vibrant since the 1960s. Adolescent boys have played a central role in the sociology of youth and education literature, especially in ethnographic studies of working class boys and their rejection of the middle class values embodied in postwar educational reforms. But here the emphasis is an ambivalent one – these boys are undoubtedly trouble, but their lives and attitudes are also represented as part of that long parade of heroic working class rebels. In Britain a range of case studies, from Hargreaves' (1967) ethnography of a boys' secondary modern school in Lancashire through Willis's (1977) now classic *Learning to Labour*, based on a study of working class boys in Wolverhampton, and Corrigan's (1979) *Schooling the Smash Street Kids* to Sewell's (1997) more recent work with African Caribbean youths, introduced an unforgettable cast of anti-heroes. As Delamont (2000: 99) tartly points out in her recent review of this literature,

> the anti-school, delinquent, rebellious young working class urban males have been lovingly chronicled and even celebrated as heroes, even though they epitomize everything no sociologist would actually want to live next door to in real life and are the embodiment of the opposite of the social mobility grand narrative which produced the sociologists.... However, once middle class, they have not only studied but lionized the very type of boy from whom they had to hide in the playground.

The biases inherent in this lionization have been noticed before by feminist commentators (McRobbie 1980; Walker 1986), whereas the authors themselves of these studies were more likely to emphasize the empathy they established with their subjects – Sewell (1997) for example, argues that he could chill with the boys at 'Township' school in Leeds (the boys' comments on this ability were not recorded). In these studies, then, a somewhat uncritical representation of boys is produced, boys who, as Delamont (2000: 99) noted, 'make life hard for their teachers, reject the opportunity for credentials, and try and impose their definition of masculinity on the other males in their schools'. The working class anti-heroes of these studies, at least during the 1970s, passed quickly though school into industrial employment, their lack of credentials restricting them to the working class but not excluding them from regular work. In more recent decades, however, these low achieving boys have been rerepresented as failures and as social problems, for the wider society as well as the schools that have to endure their disruptive behaviour. In their concern to raise educational standards and to encourage employment participation, the Labour Government has identified working class male school leavers as a particular problem. In an exact parallel to the rise of a yobbish culture on the football terrace and public spaces, the 'laddish' culture of schools was identified in 1998 by Stephen Byers, then junior minister in the Department of Education and Employment, as the main cause of boys' educational underachievement in comparison with their female peers (Abrams 1998). Two years later educationalist Mary James was more specific suggesting that 'part of the blame lies with laddish magazines such as *Loaded* and *FHM* that encourage boys to conform to an anti-work culture' (quoted in J. Clare 2000: 1).

Gender, educational achievement and the attainment gap

> The failure of boys, and particularly white working class boys, is one of the most disturbing problems we face within the whole education system. Research shows that white working class boys are the least likely to participate in full-time education after the age of sixteen, and that white boys are the most likely to be completely unqualified on leaving compulsory education . . . The fact is that our most disadvantaged children, especially boys, remain disadvantaged at the end of their schooling. (Chris Woodhead, then Chief Inspector of Schools, quoted in Adonis and Pollard 1998: 54)

As the debates about lads and laddish culture raged, working class youth has entered the discourse in a somewhat different guise. Equally troubling in this representation, the rumbustious hooligan or yob has reappeared as the 'failing boy' whose lack of achievement, indeed often lack of attendance, at school is beginning to trouble policy-makers. One of the most noticeable features of the recent debates about gender and schooling is its change of focus in the construction of boys as a problem. Rather than the 'lads' of earlier decades, resisting the middle class school curriculum, disruptive young men are now portrayed as failures (Phillips 1993), unable to get to grips with the new demands of an assessment strategy that rewards attendance and course work throughout the year, and which is regarded as more appropriate to the working habits of girls rather than boys (Arnot, David and Weiner 1996; Delamont 2000; Epstein, Ellwood, Hey and Maw 1998). Statistical evidence of their failure seems to be provided in a growing gender gap in examination results. For almost a decade now, young men in Britain are underachieving compared to girls in the examinations taken at the end of the period of compulsory schooling, and so they are leaving school less well equipped to enter a labour market in which credentials are increasingly necessary for employment that offers any form of career progression. Consequently, young men may find it more difficult to make the transition from full-time education into the labour market (or into further training or education) than young women at comparable stages in their careers. Official statistics on academic performance for pupils in England and Wales have shown that during the 1990s, in most subjects in school-leaving examinations taken at ages 15 to 16, girls began performing increasingly well compared to boys (Arnot, David and Weiner 1996, 1999). Nationally, approximately 40 per cent of boys and 50 per cent of girls achieve five or more passes at grade C and above (the recognized benchmark of academic success); girls are also now outperforming boys in science, maths and technology, re-versing the conventional associations between gender and subject choice. These patterns at 16 have an impact on post-compulsory schooling. In the mid-1990s, 87 per cent of young women compared to 67 per cent of young men stayed at school or moved into other forms of full-time education until they were 18 (Stafford, Heaver, Ashworth et al. 1999).

These differentials inevitably carry into higher education and in the last year or so a comparable debate about university access has begun to be apparent. In a controversial study by the National Audit Office (Baty 2002), young white men were identified as the group currently propor-tionately least likely to enter higher education. In a statistical analysis of participation rates among 18- and 19-year-olds in 2000, it was found that only 27 per cent of white men were in higher education, compared with 31 per cent of white women and 59 and 48 per cent respectively for women and men from ethnic minority groups: the latter groups were also more highly represented in universities than in the population in general. Key questions remain to be addressed, however, about the distributions of white and minority students between subject areas and

As the inquest starts on boys' exam results, **Caroline Davies** and **Matt Born** try to find out why females are coming out on top

Girl Power leaves lads lagging behind

Boys lagging in class for years

[23.09.2001]

Billy Elliot has cinema-goers in tears — not least because it highlights what is going wrong for men today

Masculinity in question

[21.10.2000]

A-levels show girls forging ahead amid new fears about under-achieving boys

Schools told to root out 'lad' culture

[18.08.2000]

Black youth culture blamed as pupils fail

[20.08.2000]

Teenagers like those on a lads' night out in a club often seek refuge in antisocial and laddish behaviour to hide their insecurities and fears about the world they inhabit, say experts.

Photograph by Jeff ▮▮▮▮▮

NEW LADS TO NEW SADS

The trouble with boys

Getting them to study is no easy matter

[21.08.2000]

3.2 Boys as failures

between different institutions. As I argue below, white middle class men continue to retain their dominance in many of the elite institutions and high-status subject areas.

The relative success of girls at school in the 1990s, and increasingly in higher education, is not solely a British phenomenon but has been documented in other industrialized societies, including Canada and Australasia (Teese, Davies, Charlton and Polesel 1995). In Australia, for example, this phenomenon has led to what educational researchers Kenway and Willis (1998: 37) have identified as a

> curious reversal of the gender politics of the 1970s. Boys are currently being constructed as the ones with the educational problems, the ones suffering injustice. Regularly calls are made in the press and in government circles for schools to restore the balance, to offer boys equal opportunities for success. Things have come full circle, it seems.

They continue:

> Strutting and fretting at the centre of the gender reform stage in the mid-1990s is the 'under-achieving boy'. Statistics on girls' and boys' academic achievements in their final year of schooling in certain prestigious subjects are being widely aired in the press to show that girls are out-performing boys. This story gained considerable coverage in the press in Australia, Britain, the United States and some parts of Europe in the mid-1990s . . . It has come to dominate government policy on gender reform and also holds considerable sway in the popular consciousness in many Western countries. The boys' story has become gender reform's biggest dilemma. (1998: 47–8)

In Britain the educational broadsheets have also focused on this story of gender reversal. Skelton (1998), for example, noted that the *Times Educational Supplement* had carried an article on boys and schooling in virtually every issue between 1995 and 1998, usually about boys' underachievement or their lack of motivation; and every August, since around the early 1990s, when the national exam results become public, a debate about the gender gap, even though the statistical gap between the overall success rates is still relatively small, is represented by the press in a language of crisis and panic (Mitos and Browne 1998) that is echoed by policy-makers and politicians (see plate 3.2). An interesting conundrum remains about the current construction of these gendered patterns of achievement, albeit not one that is the central concern of this chapter. Why have girls' achievements not been acclaimed as a major success, as an indication that things are evening out, as greater equality for girls rather than as a crisis of masculinity? Indeed, there is anecdotal evidence that this very success by girls has been posited as the reason for boys' relative failure. It is also apparent that the evidence about the 'under-achieving boy' is not as clear-cut as it would seem. What appears to be a question about gender is one about class, or rather about the connections between the two. Distinct patterns of class difference are also evident in educational achievement. The gender gap in achievement levels is widest at the bottom end of the socio-economic order and narrowest at its peak. It is working class boys, not boys in general, who fail to fulfil their potential, gaining few credentials, perhaps after school careers marked by truanting and/or exclusion (four times as many boys as girls are excluded from school during their careers [McConville 1998]). These are the boys who leave school as soon as possible and who may find it difficult to gain access to employment and to hold on to jobs for sustained periods. What the gender gap in attainment really shows is the relative success of middle class, and to some extent working class, girls who have begun to catch up with the levels of achievement that have long been documented among middle class boys but have also begun to challenge the male dominance of certain subjects, especially mathematics and the hard sciences. As Kenway and Willis (1998: 49) suggest:

> It is clear that the core issue is that girls appear to be outperforming boys in those high-status knowledge domains which high-status males like to keep to themselves. . . . [further], as if to bolster the case, statistics on boys' and girls' comparative performance in *other* areas are being widely aired. Whereas once it never mattered much to boys, and to men generally, that girls succeeded at things they despised, suddenly it matters that boys are not as successful as girls in the less prestigious subjects.

They conclude that 'the general process at work here is the mobilization of a "competing victims" discourse and boys are constructed as the new disadvantaged, much worse off than girls – failing at school, failing at life' (1998: 50). In Britain in 2000 the then Secretary of State for Education, David Blunkett, drew on this discourse to suggest that boys needed positive discrimination in schools. He proposed to experiment with single-sex lessons for boys and to find ways to encourage men to become schoolteachers, so providing better male role models for boys (quoted in Woodward 2000: 5) and challenging the 'lad culture' that is assumed to dominate schools where boys are underperforming (J. Clare 2000).

These policy and media debates about boys who fail, leave unaddressed, however, a number of significant questions. The key one among them is not whether girls as a group or boys as a group are more disadvantaged, but *which* girls and which boys in which schools and geographic locations. As Kenway and Willis (1998: 62) note:

> The idea of boys *per se* and girls *per se* makes it very difficult to ask sociological questions such as, 'What is it about particular masculinities and femininities and their relationship to certain aspects of schooling that leads certain boys and certain girls to systematically fail?' or 'what is it that leads schooling to systematically fail certain socio/cultural groups of boys and girls?' Further because the dominant discourse is couched in terms of conventional academic achievement, it makes it difficult to ask questions about other forms of success.

The relative undervaluing of vocational achievements and credentials has long been an issue of concern in Great Britain at a range of different levels in the system (see e.g. Hutton 1996), despite a number of innovations in the national examinations system, introduced in attempts to redress the balance between academic and vocational certificates. Continuing problems here will be examined in chapter 9.

In the UK at present it is working class boys, not boys *per se*, who are experiencing a relative decline in educational achievement, workplace exclusion and who are consequently facing growing polarization and social exclusion (MacDonald 1997). There is also an unexplored assumption that girls and young women's relative success automatically transfers into workplace advantages, an assumption that is challenged by the development of a gender pay gap in the labour market that is evident by the age of 19, although not among very young workers. It is important to remember that for many young women the future is still one of low-paid, non-unionized, part-time work combined with continuing responsibility for domestic labour. It is also important to take a longer look at the success rates of working class boys. Many working class boys have, of course, always 'failed' at school but it did not matter so much when there were plenty of jobs for unskilled and unqualified youths. Susan Griffin (2000: 167) has argued, for example, that the now-popular representations of 'boys who fail' operate as 'a form of collective and selective forgetting', ignoring previous debates about academic underachievement among working class boys in poorly resourced schools, about girls' relative underachievement compared with boys' in maths and science subjects and, particularly, debates about low achievement among African Caribbean boys.

Rather than providing evidence of failure, the figures for educational attainment since 1977 actually show a remarkable improvement, not a decline, in success rates in Great Britain. A far higher proportion of all young people now achieve some degree of success in school-leaving exams and there has been a huge increase in the number of 16-year-olds who now continue into some form of post-compulsory education. Among the cohort of young people who completed their compulsory schooling in the summer of 1999 (a cohort that includes the young men with whom I worked), by autumn 2000, nearly two-thirds were in full-time education, around one in ten were undertaking some form of Government supported training and one in seven were in full-time employment (DfES 2001). The remainder were in part-time jobs (4 per cent), out of work (5 per cent) or doing something else such as looking after family or home. Young women were more likely to be in full-time education (68 per cent compared with 61 per cent) and young men in full-time work or undertaking Government training (30 per cent compared to 20 per cent). The figure for those in full-time education is a remarkable increase compared to a generation earlier when less than 25 per cent of young people stayed at school or went to college.

Class differences, however, remain extremely significant. Sixteen-year-olds whose parents were in manual occupations are much less likely to stay in full-time education (42 per cent of them leave school at 16); this difference is exacerbated as low achievers, persistent truants and those who have been excluded from school during their career are also both more likely to leave and more likely to be out of work by the age of 17. There is also a noticeable ethnic difference in participation patterns. Young white people were more than three times as likely to have started employment than ethnic minority school leavers (15 per cent of whites compared to 4 per cent of those from the main ethnic groups). However, there are also significant differences within the non-white population. Those of Indian and Asian origin have higher rates of educational participation than African Caribbean 16-year-olds, especially among boys. But nevertheless, 84 per cent of black 17-year-olds were still in full-time education in September 2000, compared with only 64 per cent of white youths of the same age. There is, however, a marked gender difference among black school leavers, and in the next section I touch on some of the reasons why African Caribbean men do less well than other minority groups and their black sisters, as well as exploring the connections between ethnicity and class, which produce a particular version of black masculinity that disadvantages boys.

The residual group – those who leave school at 16 with few prospects of secure employment – with undereducated, troublesome young men disproportionately represented among them, has become the focus of Government concern. A range of reports and schemes, for example, have been produced for a particularly problematic group of 16- to 18-year-olds, those dubbed the Status0 group (Williamson 1997) or in more recent Government terminology NEET (not in education, employment and training). According to the Youth Cohort Study (DfES 2001), 6 per cent of all 17-year-olds were in this group in autumn 2000. The aim of these schemes is to provide ways to bridge the gap before these young people become eligible for the New Deal: a workfare programme, which young people, once they reach the age of 18, are obliged to participate in. Under the New Deal, different mixes of further training and work experience are available with the aim of ensuring that participants become more employable.

Contemporary Representations 3: Racist Discourses – Black Masculinity and White Envy

> Black culture has become a class culture . . . as two generations of whites have appropriated it, discovered its seductive forms of meaning for their own. (Gilroy 1990: 273)

There is a further issue about the connections between educational attainment, gender and ethnicity that needs to be unpacked, for, as Woodhead suggested in the quotation at the head of the previous section, it seems that it is *white* working class boys who are the new disadvantaged in Britain. Certainly they are the majority of those who leave school at the age of 16. Elsewhere in the educational literature, however, boys from African Caribbean backgrounds have been identified as particularly at risk of failure. Black children, especially boys, are over-represented in lower-subject sets and sit proportionately more lower-tier exams and have higher rates of both temporary and permanent exclusion from mainstream schooling than boys in general (Berliner 2002; Gillborn 2002). As I argued in the first chapter, the social construction of masculinity intersects with class, 'race' and sexuality in ways that both privilege and exclude African Caribbean men as the Other. As Lynne Segal (1990) and others have documented, in the USA and the UK, racist discourses construct black men both as sexualized and as a threat, in which embodied characteristics such as size and appearance are emphasized rather than the disembodied rational virtues of hegemonic masculinity.

In schools, as a great deal of research has shown, African Caribbean boys are both feared and envied by their peers (Ball, Maguire and Macrae 2000; Frosh, Phoenix and Pattman 2002; Mac an Ghaill 1994; O'Donnell and Sharpe 2000; Sewell 1997). They often position themselves as superior to white, as well as Asian, boys in terms of their sexual attractiveness, style, creativity and 'hardness' (and in the next chapter I show how the white boys to whom I talked understand these discourses). Sewell (1997) suggests that black boys locate themselves in school within what he terms a 'phallocentric framework', in which they both resist racism but also depend on and reinforce white stereotyping of black men. In the USA, Majors and Billson (1992) have identified a parallel version of 'cool' masculinity exhibited by black men, they suggest, as a particular response to their adverse socio-economic circumstances. In Britain, Gillborn (2002) has argued that these stereotypes of a 'hard' masculinity, as well as the behaviour of black school students, result in white teachers tending to regard them as difficult, often labelling them as educational low achievers.

More recently, Sewell has been reported as suggesting that the materialist emphasis in black youth culture on style and appearance is not only a key part of the explanation of the relatively poor success rates of African Caribbean boys, but is also a source of envy and imitation among white working class boys (*Independent*, 18 August 2000). Here is a clear link back to the earlier work on youth culture that emphasized the ways in which style and clothing are appropriated as symbols of resistance in youth culture (Hall and Jefferson 1976), which, as I argue in the succeeding section of this chapter, is also a key factor in the ways in which style and appearance may exclude young men from service-sector employment. And in the inner areas of British cities, as well as in schools, as Back (1996) and Gilroy (1990) have argued, black style is imitated by white urban youths. Young black men, despite being problems at school, are also the 'heroes of a street fashion culture that dominate most of our inner cities' (Sewell 1997: ix), forcing them to negotiate a complex positioning that gives them credibility among their peers but which disenfranchises them among society at large. As I argue later, in the more empirical chapters that follow, this is a more general negotiation that faces many working class young men.

While it must be emphasized that this form of hyper-sexualized masculinity is rejected by many African Caribbean pupils (see e.g. Frosh, Phoenix and Pattman's [2002] recent study in London schools), the ways in which these racist stereotypes interact with the class connotations, constructing working class boys, and in particular black working class youth, as problems have been discussed by Griffin (2000). In an interesting analysis of one of the numerous articles about failing boys carried by the quality press in the mid-1990s, she suggests that the media 'uses signifiers/markers around class (and to a lesser extent "race") which are seldom specified, because in the British context they do not *need* to be made explicit' (Griffin 2000: 177, original emphasis). She illustrated her argument with a piece from the *Independent* in which the journalist, Catherine Bennett, referred to 'feckless, jobless chumps' and boys doing 'much better...as skilled muggers, talented burglars and gifted car thieves' than girls (*Independent*, 5 November 1996). The class connotations are clear, and further, as Hall (1978) argued many years ago, the term 'muggers' is a racialized one. Indeed, in her article Bennett went on to ask 'why should boys be sliding towards primitivism so much faster than girls?' (*Independent*, 5 November 1996), which, as Griffin notes, is 'a discourse which draws on the Great Chain of Being to locate white middle-class "civilization" at the top of the cultural hierarchy' (Griffin 2000: 177), with black working class youths at its base. In Britain as the ethnic minority population remains a small proportion of the population as a whole (less than 3 per cent are of African Caribbean origin), the visibility of black pupils in school and in the labour market is much less than in the USA for example, reinforcing the claim by Chris Woodhead that the problem in Britain, at least in numerical terms, is one essentially about young white men. However, this is not to deny the ways in which race and gender intersect to reinforce the disadvantages of working class black youth, but rather to emphasize the significance of arguments in chapter 1 about the ways in which masculine identities are constructed and are interconnected in Britain.

Images of 'whiteness' and 'blackness' are a key part of the ways in which masculinities are constructed and experienced in Britain in the twenty-first century. If white youths envy and imitate black youths at school, in the labour market it has been argued that envy more typically turns into blame and to racism, especially in declining industrial areas where restructuring has had a particularly severe impact on employment opportunities for young men. In a study in deindustrializing towns in upstate New York, Fine, Weiss, Addelstone and Marusza (1997) found that young white men aged between 18 and 24 tended to blame men of colour for 'stealing' their jobs rather than understanding the impact of economic restructuring. In Britain too there is evidence of growing intolerance, especially in northern textile towns such as Bradford, Burnley and Oldham (where the minority population is predominantly of Asian origins) where the disaffection and disengagement of young white working class men, themselves victims of economic change, is exploited by far right groups such as the British National Party. According to the Commission for Racial Equality (CRE) white working class men aged between 16 and 30 are the group most likely to be involved in racial harassment and violence and, in an effort to increase understanding, the CRE announced at the end of 2001 that it was to make addressing the grievances of these white men a priority in the next year's programme (Ward 2001).

Contemporary Representations 4: Working Class Youth as Redundant Workers

The final element in the crisis of masculinity that I want to explore here is that of young men as unwanted labourers, constructed in the labour market as unsuitable and forced by changes in state policies into longer periods of dependence on the family. As I argued earlier, the shift in advanced industrial societies towards service industries apparently has advantaged young women compared to young men. Many of the conduits which turn boys into men are drying up for the working class. In the workplace, for example, industrial apprenticeships for school leavers are less common, and manual labour for the unskilled is a disappearing phenomenon. In this final section of the chapter, I want to look not only at the structure of the youth labour market but also at the ways in which the construction of masculine identities among young working class men might disbar them from a growing range of employment opportunities. I conclude this section of the argument with a brief assessment of the purchase that ideas about risk and individualization have for studies of young people's transitions to adulthood in the 'new' economy, so connecting the more general arguments in the preceding chapter with the specific consideration of young people here.

The youth labour market has always been subject to deeper cyclical changes than the adult market and so during recessions youth unemployment rates are consistently higher than those for adults (Makeham 1980; Raffe 1985; Raffe and Willms 1989; Roberts 1995), emphasizing their 'redundancy' at particular periods. Young workers are exceptionally vulnerable to economic change for several reasons. When unemployment rises, recruitment falls and so new workers are adversely affected. Secondly, when profit margins are threatened, training schemes for new young workers are often cut. Thirdly, there is greater competition for the available jobs in periods of high unemployment and experienced workers may have the edge, although young workers tend to be cheaper to employ and so may not be completely excluded. One response to the rising rates of youth unemployment in the UK in the recessions of the early 1980s and 1990s was to introduce a range of training schemes for less educationally able young people without plans to stay at school beyond the compulsory leaving age. At the same time, more young people were encouraged to continue their full-time education through the expansion of places on both academic and vocational courses in further and higher education and, as I noted earlier, the fall in the rate of young people entering the labour market directly after finishing their period of compulsory schooling has been noticeable since 1977. When the UK economy expanded from 1982 until the onset of recession in the early 1990s, and again from the mid-1990s to the present day, general levels of unemployment fell, but there was no associated rise in the numbers of 16- and 17-year-olds in full-time jobs. Economic growth failed to recreate youth jobs, largely because, especially in the 1980s boom, the key area of expansion was in business services and in occupations with no tradition of employing this age group. Whereas one in seven men after the Second World War was employed in service-class occupations (higher grade non-manual), by the 1980s the proportion had risen to one in four, and by 2000 to one in three: most of whom had completed some form of further or higher education.

Unskilled young people, especially young men, then, have been the recurrent victims not only of recession but in recent decades also more permanent victims of economic restructuring. As I argued earlier, the transformation of the labour market is not only because of the decline of manufacturing jobs and the corresponding rise of service jobs but also the rise of a more a polarized economy in the 1990s. As well as an expansion in white collar service-class occupations at the top end of the service sector, where the possession of high-level educational credentials is an essential passport to entry, there has been a rapid expansion of low-level 'servicing' jobs in recent years in Britain, as well as in the USA. But at the bottom end of the service sector where educational credentials are less significant, the expansion of job opportunities has largely been in part-time employment, and adult women are often the preferred workers. While young men are the most vulnerable to these changes, as they may find themselves completely excluded from the labour market, young women are also not immune from the impacts. They too are adversely affected by the restructuring of formerly full-time jobs into part-time ones. In addition, the young workers of the 1970s had, by the 1990s, largely been replaced by university and college students (Christie and Munro 2000) and, increasingly, by school pupils (Mizen, Bolton and Pole 1999) undertaking temporary and casual employment, as well as by trainees on workplace-based and state sponsored schemes, so reducing the prospects for young school leavers looking for permanent full-time work. Indeed, in Britain at the end of the 1990s a third of all 17- to 20-year-olds not undertaking education or training experienced a period of unemployment in their initial years in the labour market, and rates of unemployment were noticeably higher among young men than young women. In the UK 24 per cent of young men compared to 9 per cent of young women in this age range had experienced a period of unemployment in the late 1990s (Iacovou and Berthoud 2001). As might be expected, the risk of unemployment was greatest among those with the lowest level of qualifications.

Employment for young people is also often insecure as well as discontinuous. In the UK, and indeed across the whole of Europe, younger workers are more likely than older workers to be on insecure contracts: half of all employees aged 17 to 20 at the end of 1990s were on insecure contracts. It is hard to tell whether this is a feature of the youth labour market *per se* or because, unlike their elders, young people entered the labour market at the time when 'jobs for life' have become less common. In fact, in the UK, perhaps contrary to expectations, the percentage of young people on insecure contracts in 1999 was lower than the European average – 24 per cent of those aged 17–25, compared with 37 per cent in France and 39 per cent in Finland (Iacovou and Berthoud 2001). The net consequence of these features of youth employment is, of course, low wages. In the UK young workers aged between 17 and 20 earn on average about 50 per cent of the wages of older earners, rising to two-thirds among 21- to 25-year-olds. Workers aged 16 and 17 are also excluded from the provisions of the Minimum Wage Act (as well as all apprentices and members of the Armed Forces), leaving them vulnerable to exploitation. But, as I noted earlier, even their older colleagues, aged 18 to 21 are not eligible for adult rates of pay, qualifying only for a young workers rate, of £3.60 per hour in late 2002, compared with the adult rate of £4.20 per hour, and so resulting in young people and young adults under the age of 22 being less able to achieve independent living.

The notion of a lengthy period of dependence is also increasingly evident in the welfare and benefits system in Great Britain as young people have become progressively less eligible for individual support in their own right. The increasing participation in education and training after the age of 16 outlined above clearly increases the period during which young people remain dependent on financial support. As well as full-time education, a wide range of youth training schemes were introduced during the 1980s and 1990s that combined training and employment in a range of different ways. From the early 1980s, for young working class school leavers, the one-step transition from school into employment was replaced by two-step transitions via youth training or post-compulsory education, often employer-based, and in 1986 a range of new vocational qualifications was introduced: National Vocational Qualifications (NVQs), recognizing skills required in particular occupations and industries; and General NVQs (GNVQs), to recognize broader-based pre-career vocational preparation. Level 2 is roughly equivalent to a good set of GCSE passes and level 3 is equivalent to two A levels. In 1994 Modern Apprenticeships were introduced, where young people combine employment and periods of employer-based training leading to level 3 NVQs, in an attempt to strengthen the training route to skills and into the workforce. This programme was updated and expanded in 2001 and, as I shall show later, was important for a small number of the young men whom I interviewed.

At the same time as these employment and training measures were introduced, the then Conservative Government deregulated the labour market and allowed youth rates of pay to float down as a measure to increase rates of employment. It was generally assumed that the problem of unemployment was not related to structural and spatial changes in the labour market, but rather that people priced themselves out of work or were insufficiently work-ready; although evaluations of programmes such as the Youth Training Schemes later showed that these did not compensate for a student's poor educational attainment or lack of employability but instead performed a 'holding' or 'warehousing' function, followed by unemployment (Banks, Bates, Breakwell et al. 1992). To increase the 'competitiveness' of young people a range of other measures were introduced. In 1986, for example, young workers were removed from Wages Council protection. Unemployment income was also reduced to make employment participation more attractive. In the mid-1980s, 21- to 24-year-olds living at home lost their rights to certain unemployment benefits. In 1988 most unemployed 16- and 17-year-olds lost their right to unemployment benefit, and in 1989 legislation protecting young people and women, which restricted hours, conditions of work and occupations within which they could be employed were repealed. The right to financial support among full-time students was also whittled away. In 1987 students in full-time further and higher education were barred from claiming supplementary benefit in short vacations, and later (1990) in all vacations. In 1990 students lost housing benefit, loans were introduced and grants 'frozen'; in 1993 the student maintenance grant was reduced.

The Labour Government first elected in 1997 continued the policies that constructed young people as dependants. In 1998 student maintenance grants were replaced by loans, and means-tested tuition fees, based on an assessment of parental income for all students without dependants, were introduced. The new Government was also keen to expand the range of programmes for the young unemployed, combining coercion though the loss of right to benefit with new forms of training programmes. Thus the Youth Opportunities Programme was introduced in 1997. Young workers had to have been unemployed for six weeks before they became eligible and were expected to seek and remain available for work throughout time on the programme. In 1998 a more comprehensive programme was introduced for all unemployed 18- to 24-year-olds (DfEE 1997a, 1997b). Younger workers under 18 years of age, albeit declining in numbers, were simply ignored in this employment scheme. Known as the New Deal for Young People, it includes job search assistance, counselling, job training and work experience with the aim of improving their employability, with modest incentives to employers in the form of hiring subsidies. Each entrant to the programme passes through the Gateway (a concept that was extended to all welfare recipients from 1999). This involves a period of intensive training and counselling to get people in shape to join the labour force. 'Job ready' applicants are provided with short-term support to 'improve their immediate job prospects' and so helping with a rapid transition into employment (DfEE 1997c: 3), whereas those with more substantial employability barriers remain in the Gateway to receive longer-term assistance. The Government expected about 40 per cent of young people entering the programme to secure unsubsidized employment during the Gateway phase (DfEE 1997b), although the actual results have been lower than this, with considerable variation between local labour markets (Sunley, Martin and Nativel 2001). Those who do not enter the open market continue to work with an adviser to identify which of four programme options suits their need, but are expected to continue searching for work while they are receiving counselling. The four options for participants are (1) an employer-placement option in the private sector (employers receive a small subsidy for each person taken on); (2) a placement in a voluntary-sector organization for up to six months, where participants receive training towards an approved qualification; (3) work with an environmental task force, cleaning up and recycling (participants receive benefits plus a small additional payment), and training for an approved qualification also provided; and (4) encouragement for those lacking basic educational qualifications to return to full-time education.

While these programmes are both relatively flexible and client-based, they also involve compulsory participation. This combination of choice and obligation parallels new Labour's 'rights and responsibilities' rhet-oric discussed earlier, and although the innovatory features of the scheme have been emphasized by Labour policy-makers, there are evi-dent continuities with the earlier Conservative schemes. Indeed, it is clear that policy-makers of whatever ideological hue assume that they have to resocialize and force young people to accept the types of jobs that are available in the contingent labour market, which have excep-tionally low rates of pay and which, other things being equal, they may prefer not to take. It is also clear that despite an age of majority in Britain of 18, most young people are expected to remain dependent on family support for longer and longer periods. This is reflected in the expanding numbers of young people, especially men, who continue to live in their parental home until their mid-twenties. Working class men are the group who leave home latest, perhaps a reflection of their desire to have their mothers look after them until they have wives to take over (Wallace 1987), but also a reflection of the changed material circum-stances that produce greater dependency which is often not freely chosen. The coincidence of labour market changes and the workfare emphasis of welfare state restructuring has created a new generation of working poor. Further, the segmentation of young workers and their construction as 'less eligible claimants' has reinforced their dependency on families that have been adversely affected by economic restructuring. Clearly, there is a widespread belief, held by both main political parties in the UK, that young people are neither independent, nor should be adequately financially rewarded so that they may be. Like women before them, young people's wages are regarded not as a 'breadwinner's' or 'citizen's' wage but rather as a component in a total household wage. This distinction is based on Siltanen's (1986, 1995) comparisons of male and female wages. What she termed 'citizen's wages' are full adult wages that permit the costs of living as an independent household to be met, whereas 'component wages' assume access to the income of other house-hold members. Carol Pateman (1989) has argued for the necessity of a full wage as an essential prerequisite of full participation in citzenship rights and obligations, whatever the legal status of an individual. And reversing her argument but making the same point, Byrne (1997: 31), in an assessment of two decades of welfare and labour market changes up to the late 1990s noted that

> it is an interesting comment on the UK that the triumph of neo-liberalism here has been so pervasive as to permit market restructuring on an essentially domestic basis, in other words low wages and domestic exploit-

ation have been imposed on people with full citizenship rights, not on a separate basis of non-citizen and/or illegal immigrants.

And, as he concluded, young people have been the group most adversely affected by neo-liberal policies. 'The most dispossessed group in the UK are definable not by gender or ethnicity, but *by age*' (Byrne 1997: 32; emphasis added).

But as I have documented here, not all young people are disadvantaged. Indeed, the majority of Britain's youth is now more highly educated and achieves greater examination success than ever before, and, arguably, many of them have more opportunities than in earlier generations. However, the most disadvantaged are excluded from the expanding opportunities of the majority, unable to benefit from the consumption-based lifestyles associated with the 'new' service economy and increasingly trapped on the bottom rungs of all ladders to social mobility. The dispossessed identified by Byrne include, indeed are largely composed of, those working class youths who leave school too early and are constructed both as 'folk devils' or 'yobs' and as cheap labour to be exploited or, worse, as unsuitable labourers and so excluded. I want to turn therefore to a general assessment of the relative disadvantages of these young men as they search for work in the new service economy.

Suitable work? Local networks and embodied masculinity

For the students who decide to leave school as soon as they are able and to search for work, perhaps the most significant factor in their job search is the locality in which they live, as most early leavers look for work close to their homes. Clearly, local labour markets are marked by different histories, traditions and sets of local institutions (Peck 1996; Sayer and Walker 1992) as well as by different combinations of particular types of employment and segmented labour forces. As chapter 2 demonstrated, the industrial and social history of earlier eras has a significant impact on the extent to which the decline of manufacturing employment affects opportunities for male school leavers. The areas, for example, that contain most of the New Deal clients – unemployed 18- to 24-year-olds, many of whom left school at 16 – are spatially concentrated into a few local labour markets. Within these labour markets the clients are further spatially concentrated, many of them living on deprived housing estates (Turok and Webster 1998; Peck 1999). These spatial variations not only affect the types of jobs open to young people but also influence their aspirations. As numerous studies have demonstrated, small-scale, locally based experiences, at school, at home and in the immediate neighbourhood, play a part in the social construction of ideas about self-identity and appropriate labour market behaviour. Local networks and personal contacts are important in getting jobs, especially at the bottom end of the labour market (Glennester 1999; Granovetter 1996; Hanson and Pratt 1995; O'Regan and Quigley 1993; Putnam 1995). Indeed, the key role of local contacts has been recognized for many decades. As Llewelyn Lewis (1924: 55) noted in the 1920s, unskilled parents 'were obliged to inhabit very poor localities and to dwell among people of similar habits', so restricting their access to wider experiences and contacts who might assist in their children's employment.

Ideas about appropriate work for 'people like us' are constructed through childhood socialization. The cultural and social capital that is built up in these years, which is to a large extent still neighbourhood-based for less affluent members of society (Allatt and Yeandle 1986; Bowlby and Lloyd-Evans 2000; Bowlby, Lloyd Evans and Mohammad 1998; Fernandez Kelly 1994; Lee 1995), has a crucial impact on access to and retention of employment, especially low-skilled and unskilled jobs. The concept of social and cultural capital, derived from Bourdieu's (1984) work, includes social knowledge, social skills, and culturally valued qualifications, especially from elite institutions. Social capital includes the set of skills related to and affected by changes in the local labour market. The tradition of male employment in manufacturing, for example, produced local social capital whose value has now declined: there has been a decline in number of industrial apprenticeships and in the role of familial connections in securing them, as well as the loss of valuable social networks constructed through the workplace. Although the distinction between social and cultural capital is blurred, cultural capital is typically defined to include educational qualifications, general cultural attitudes and perhaps reputations: for example, family 'respectability' is a key part of distinguishing the 'deserving' from the 'undeserving poor' in Britain (Skeggs 1997). Cultural capital also includes the reputation of an estate or neighbourhood as 'respectable' or 'rough', as well as the inculcation of 'proper' attitudes, work and authority: each of which influences young working class people's ability to achieve and maintain employment.

The significance of place has been recognized in a long tradition of studies that have linked social disadvantage to location, originating with the now largely discredited notion of a 'culture of poverty', that is purportedly shared by residents in certain urban localities (Lewis 1961, 1966; Valentine 1968). This has been a particularly dominant notion in the USA where there is a far greater degree of residential segregation by class, especially based on ethnicity, than in Great Britain. Thus in a study of the US, urban sociologists Massey and Denton (1993: 9) argued that 'residential segregation is the principal organizational feature of American society that is responsible for the creation of the urban underclass', creating the conditions for the development of a kind of subculture or counterculture in which a job, good education and strong relations between people are no longer part of the prevailing system of norms and values. Schill (1993: 443) has the same view: 'this concentration of poverty generates attitudes, behaviours and values that impede the ability of residents to grasp whatever opportunities exist for social mobility'. In his magnificent study of the impact of job losses in US cities, Wilson (1997) has also documented the corrosive personal and social effects on local communities devastated by unemployment, but from a perspective that recognizes the significance of structural economic change rather than 'blaming the victim'. In Britain, the same connections between class, poverty and location were reflected in rounds of urban policies from the 1960s until the present day, focusing on small urban areas within cities. In these localities, both inner areas and peripheral housing estates, households are faced with the adverse impacts of deindustrialization, inadequate levels of investment in the local infrastructure, low-wage employment, class subordination, social isolation, and low levels of support for families dealing with issues such as problems at school, including truancy and exclusions (Hobcraft 1998). It is in this sort of area that the transition to adult independence is problematic for young men. As Dixon (1997: 92) concluded on the basis of a study carried out in the early 1990s in an urban school serving a predominantly white working class community in a city economically and socially transformed by long-term economic recession and the collapse of heavy manufacturing industry:

> It is this moment and its relationship to global, national and local narratives of masculinity and work that affects the 'making of men' going on in the school... For many school leavers, traditional patterns of gendered labour division have little relation to life experience. Part-time labour, casual work and unofficial self-employment have established a new working pattern. The notions of a 'job for life' around which identities can be constructed and publicly maintained and presented and a 'living wage'/breadwinner's wage which maintained gendered patterns of economic dependence have limited relevance now to urban working class life.

But these notions maintain their ideological significance and power and become objects of fantasy. Young men leaving schools similar to the one

Dixon studied carry with them idealized versions of masculinity, which they play out in the streets and also take with them into the labour market, in consequence often reinforcing the disadvantages they already labour under because of their age, location and lack of credentials.

It is clear that earlier hegemonic versions of working class masculinity are inappropriate in post-Fordism as new types of employment and new forms of labour practices value different attributes. The attitudes and behaviour inculcated in their sons by generations of blue-collar fathers no longer map on to the sorts of behaviour expected in the workplace. At school, however, low-achieving working class boys still tend to be directed into vocational or low-status subjects, 'whose culture continues to reflect the masculine world of manual labour [emphasizing] chauvinism, toughness and machismo' (Mac an Ghaill 1996a: 42). And in their leisure time, many young men seek an affirmation of masculinity 'in personal embodied activities like sports, fighting or sexual prowess' (Canaan 1996: 116; and see Connell 1989 2000). In an absorbing study of working class youth in a low-income part of Manhattan in the early 1990s, Bourgois (1995) has vividly documented the ways in which a locality has an impact on employment prospects for young men. He explored the intersection of local attitudes developed by young men growing up in a previously blue-collar neighbourhood and the shift towards a polarized service-dominated economy in New York City, which placed these men at a particular disadvantage in attempting to find work. He showed how the social networks and social capital possessed by the residents magnified the disadvantages faced by young people, especially young men from the majority ethnic minority group, originally from Puerto Rico. As Bourgois (1995: 14) argued:

> Perhaps if their social network had not been confined to the weakest sector of manufacturing in a period of rapid job loss, their teenage working class dreams might have stabilized them for long enough to enable them to adapt to the restructuring of the local economy. Instead they find themselves propelled headlong into an explosive confrontation between their sense of cultural dignity versus the humiliating interpersonal subordination of service work.

The sort of tough, even violent, machismo, valued on the New York City streets ran profoundly counter to main employment opportunities open to them. For poorly qualified young people leaving school, low-paid, often feminized, office support service work had replaced manufacturing employment, both in the neighbourhood and in the city more generally. If these young men were taken on in the service sector, as photocopiers or messengers, for example, Bourgois found that they quickly lost their position, as their social and cultural capital was inappropriate to the workplace. As Bourgois (1995: 142–3) made clear:

> Their interpersonal social skills are even more inadequate than their limited professional capacities. They do not know how to look at their fellow service workers – let alone their supervisors – without intimidating them. They cannot walk down the hallway to the water fountain without unconsciously swaying their shoulders aggressively as if patrolling their home turf. Gender barriers are an even more culturally charged realm. They are repeatedly reprimanded for offending co-workers with sexually aggressive behaviour.

Conclusions: Youth and the 'Crisis of Masculinity'

The representation of young white working class men as both disruptive hooligans and as school and workplace failures, as this chapter has shown, has widespread currency as well as a long historical trajectory. It is legitimated, and constructed as a regime of truth in Foucauldian terms, through the widespread circulation of academic and policy discourses that portray young men as folk devils. The pejorative discourse of dangerous masculinities is reinforced in a paradoxical coincidence of arguments from commentators at either end of the political spectrum, a coincidence that is particularly troubling by its recent emergence in feminist discourse. From the left, there has been a slippage in analyses of the problem of white working class youth as located in social disadvantage and economic restructuring to blaming the victims, who are constructed as 'a disorganized, racist and sexist detritus' (Haylett 2001: 358). This position is starkly portrayed in, for example, Bea Campbell's (1993) study of what she termed 'Britain's dangerous places' – local authority estates where a range of social problems are attributed to young white men's destructive, violent, and often criminal, masculinity. Thus Campbell concludes that a 'lads' culture of predation ... tyrannized the places of the poor' (1993: 322). This conclusion has long been a key staple of right wing explanations of urban unrest that 'blame the victim' (Valentine 1968) or assert a culture of poverty among the undeserving poor (Lewis 1961, 1966). As Coward (1994) notes:

> these images would not work unless legitimated. Two discourses have provided them with a respectable gloss – underclass theory and a

quasi-feminist critique of masculinity.... [this] critique of masculinity, which was originally intended to undermine traditional claims to male power, has now become a way of attacking the least powerful men in our society. That critiques of gender can be used in this way should warn us that they are not necessarily progressive. Women's protests against male dominance have, at times, intersected with, or even reinforced, middle-class efforts to subdue and 'civilize' the male 'underclass'. And the history of this link between feminism, and efforts to 'reform' lumpen masculinity, serve as a contemporary warning. (quoted in Charlesworth 2000: 156)

This image of destructive, predatory masculinity is currently reinforced by the pervasive terminology of the popular press, constructing trouble-some young men in terms that emphasize not only their antisocial and criminal tendencies but, in the most exaggerated versions, imply that they are less than human: 'beasts' or 'feral children' were common terms in the moral panic about street crime that dominated popular and policy debates about youth reported in both the broadsheets and red tops in Britain in 2002.

At the beginning of the twenty-first century, these debates about working class men are given an extra twist by their association with a pervasive, and innovative, discourse about masculinity: the so-called 'crisis' afflicting urban men in industrial societies. Whereas in earlier debates about youth, working class men were demonized because of their masculinity, or more accurately their social construction as sexually aggressive, in contemporary versions, these men are unsexed, or demas-culinized, because of the threats to their dominance in the education system and their growing redundancy at work. What the consequences of this crisis may be, however, for individual men and for different localities and spaces, is an empirical question. In cities and localities where high youth unemployment or low-paid casualized work are the only options for working class youths, they may cling even more firmly to outdated notions of masculinity that previously dominated the area. Do perceived threats to masculinity result in young British men exagger-ating their 'macho' characteristics and behaviour, as Bourgois found in New York? Are they demanding, even unteachable at school, aggres-sively rejecting middle class norms of achievement for instant gratifica-tion in imitative versions of black streetstyle? Are they resentful or unwanted in the labour market and do those young men who are able only to find low-status service work in British cities blame the 'Other'? Or does their sense of themselves as failures perhaps mean that they turn to other arenas and activities, to sport perhaps, to recreate a sense of acceptable masculine success?

Stephen Frosh (1995), a psychologist with long experience of working with urban school students in Britain, has suggested that the erosion of traditional, work-related spheres of male activity makes not only masculinity *per se* but the individual experiences of each man problematic. Thus he suggests that despite attempts by educationalists and others to construct alternative ways of becoming and being a man, some young men might hold ever more resolutely to the middle class norm of an integrated rational masculinity or to the working class version of an embodied masculinity, perhaps even aggressively rejecting emerging alternatives. Similarly, the sociologist Anthony Giddens (1992) has suggested that clinging to dominant versions of masculinity, based on a supposed superiority to women, is a common reaction among many men – young and old – to the growing uncertainty of late modern society: a reaction that he suggests may be reflected in growing violence against women.

It is, however, important to re-emphasize here that young men's relative failure is neither a cause nor a consequence of young women's relative success, but rather a reflection of fundamental changes in urban and industrial economies. Furthermore, the power of the phrase a 'crisis of masculinity' denies the social and spatial variations in the ways in which economic and social restructuring work out in different places and among different groups in society. The idea of a crisis itself, as well as the implicit gender polarity it embodies, needs deconstructing. What seems to be emerging in Britain, rather than being a crisis *per se*, is an uneven challenge to the automatic associations between masculinity and privilege, which has particular impacts on different groups of men. As well as the young men who inhabit the pages of this book, men from minority groups find themselves disadvantaged in ways that are not new but rather reflect the long history of inequality, as hegemonic masculinity has always been raced as white. As well as young men, other groups are also adversely affected by contemporary socio-economic transformations, including middle-aged middle managers as well as manufacturing workers in general. However, as I have argued before (McDowell 1991, 2001b), a singular emphasis on gender, on the problems associated with the repositioning of the comparative positions of men and women in contemporary Britain, is an insufficient analysis of socio-economic change. To associate the 'problem of men' solely with a new form of gender division successfully hides the class and ethnic bases of the growing inequalities among young people.

In the next chapters the voices of young men in two British cities, reflecting on their hopes and aspirations and their opinions about school, about work and about their own lives compared with those of young women, take centre stage, as I attempt to add empirical detail to the general arguments about young men outlined here and to establish the different ways in which young men in contemporary Britain make sense of themselves as they move from compulsory schooling into more adult independence. While the next chapter focuses on young men's school lives, the main emphasis of these chapters will be on their employment trajectories. Giddens, and the other theorists whose predictions about working lives were examined in chapter 2, have shown how uncertainty and risk have transformed the old certainties of working class employment. While middle class school leavers may face a more varied set of opportunities, albeit associated with greater uncertainty, for low-achieving working class leavers, admittedly a much smaller percentage of the age group than a generation earlier, the prospects of individual autonomy, let alone social mobility, are extremely limited. As MacDonald (1998) has noted in an assessment of the utility of debates about risk and individualization to youth research, although the pathways to independence for privileged school leavers might be compared to a journey undertaken by car, in which multiple locations are accessible, for the less privileged, the journey is better imagined as one undertaken by train, constrained by tracks that lead straight to a life of hardship and inequality.

4

Living on the Edge: Marginal Lives in Cambridge and Sheffield

Place makes the most difference to the least qualified young people.
(Roberts 1995: 45)

The lives of different class groups are situated in different spaces and take
place through different sites. (Charlesworth 2000: 220)

As geographers, sociologists and anthropologists have all demonstrated,
place or locality, the set of socio-spatial relations that constitute the
particular meaning of a place, is a significant part of the social construction of identity and people's sense of belonging, whether to a class, to a
neighbourhood or to a spatially defined interest group. The significance
is both material and representational. As I suggested in the previous
chapter, young people's job prospects depend not only on their class
background, their qualifications, their gender and their personal qualities but also on the place in which they live as they start their working
lives. Clearly, starting to search for employment in a depressed local
labour market restricts the range of possible opportunities, and for
disadvantaged young people geographical differentiation is especially
significant. As the fuller version of Roberts's claim at the head of the
chapter (1995: 45) makes clear:

Place makes the most difference to the least qualified young people. Those
who succeed in secondary school are able to progress into higher education after which they typically seek jobs in the national labour market or,
at any rate, in other areas apart from where they received their school

education. Young people who leave school at age 16 and 17 and enter the labour market are more affected by the local labour market conditions, whatever these may be.

These young people usually live in their parental home; they seldom have access to private transport and so they are often restricted to looking for work within their own locality, whether in the inner areas or the peripheral estates of large cities. And as I have argued, in these areas local social capital and networks of personal contacts in securing work are crucial. Even before the opportunities for labour market entry are a consideration, young people, especially those growing up in working class families, live tightly defined localized lives. While there is an interesting debate about the extent to which young people's attitudes and style in contemporary consumer societies are 'placeless', in the sense of common reliance on a postmodern pastiche of styles (McDowell 1997b; Skelton and Valentine 1998), a considerable number of ethnographic studies, often of young men and typically carried out in inner areas of towns and cities, have documented the spatial limitations of young people's everyday lives, revealing their rootedness in a small number of places. The majority of young people from a range of ethnic and class backgrounds, with the exception of perhaps the most affluent, still lead locally based neighbourhood-based lives, especially when they are still in school (Baumann 1996; Callaghan 1992; O'Byrne 1997; Pearce 1996; Taylor, Evans and Fraser 1996; Watt 1998; Webster 1996; Westwood 1990). Local ties, lack of transport, relatively low incomes, even though many young people are now labour market participants while still at school, and for young people from minority groups, fears of racial harassment, combine to tie them to their neighbourhoods (Back 1996; Bowlby and Lloyd-Evans 2000). In Britain, the extent of neighbourhood differentiation and its close association with access to compulsory schooling, for all but a minority (in 2001 only 7 per cent of children were educated in private schools), means that spatial patterns of class segregation largely confine children to close association and friendship networks with their peers. Class-differentiated patterns of speech, ways of being in the world, including bodily gestures and comportment, as well as differences in social attitudes and aspirations thus take a geographical form in Britain, and to a large extent are mirrored in noticeable differences in school pupils' examination success at the age of 16, varying, as I documented earlier, by region but also within towns and cities. Typically, results are lower in schools located both in the inner areas and in outer estates, where local authority housing provision is common.

To capture some this geographical differentiation, to explore its significance and to assess the impact of place-based identity in the construction
of masculinities in late-modern Britain, the empirical research on which
the rest of this book is based was carried out in different locations. I
wanted to assess the different ways in which economic restructuring was
reshaping the patterns of opportunities for young men coming of age at
the turn of the millennium and struggling to find an acceptable sense of
themselves as masculine as the labour market changed around them. For
this reason, and following the long and honourable example of authors
and commentators including Elizabeth Gaskell and Benjamin Disraeli,
I adopted a North–South comparison. As more recent commentators
have argued, among others geographers (Hudson and Williams 1995;
Martin and Townroe 1992), economists (Erdem and Glyn 2001) and
social policy analysts (Hills, Le Grand and Paichaud 2002), opportunities,
standards of living and lifestyles in Britain continue to reflect a North–
South divide. As I argued in chapter 2, the rapid expansion of high-tech
and high-status jobs at the top end of the service sector has been predominantly a South-East phenomenon, whereas manufacturing decline and
low-status service expansion has affected the old industrial heartlands of
the country. While the annual average pay of full-time workers who had
been in employment for at least a year in April 2001 was £24,067 in
England, as table 4.1 shows, all the English regions with the exception of
Greater London and the South-East fell below this average.

Table 4.1 Average gross annual pay of full-time adult
employees by region, April 2001

Region	Earnings
Greater London	£34,777
South-East	24,944
East Anglia	23,176
West Midlands	21,705
South-West	21,194
North-West	21,164
East Midlands	20,686
Yorkshire and Humberside	20,567
North-East	19,831
English average	24,067
Scotland	21,110
Wales	19,901
GB average	23,607

Source: Labour Force Survey data.

I chose to carry out the empirical part of the study in towns in two different regions: Cambridge in East Anglia and Sheffield in the Yorkshire and Humberside region. I decided to work in East Anglia rather than the South-East as the former region is the most rapidly expanding part of the country at present, where the rise of house prices, with the exception of Greater London, has been highest. For the less affluent in this region, then, dependent on low-income employment, the ability to establish an independent household is particularly difficult.

Two Cities: Manufacturing Employment Versus 'Servicing' Work

The differences between cities are probably more marked and certainly more noticeable to their inhabitants than regional differences. Within England regional loyalties and attachments are rather tenuous, with the possible exception of the 'Geordie' identity in the North-East. But even so, as geographers and sociologists have long argued, geography matters (Massey 1984; Massey and Allen 1984), especially at the local level. The industrial and social history of a place affects identity of its inhabitants, creating a local sense of place, or a local 'structure of feeling' the term used by the critical theorist Raymond Williams, which, as I noted in chapter 2, captures the dense network of locally specific connections that distinguish one locality from another. Cambridge and Sheffield could hardly be more different cities in their image, their employment structure or their local cultural identity. The nature and culture of local industries and working practices, especially the long dominance of a major employer – the steel industry in Sheffield and the university in Cambridge – affects the image and realities of the two cities. In the popular imagination, Sheffield is forever a dirty industrial town, whose decline was documented in the film *The Full Monty*, whereas the popular image of Cambridge is of a medieval university city, remote from the bustle and danger of manufacturing employment (plate 4.1). These differences continue to be reflected in local social practices and urban daily rhythms (Allen 1999), in gender divisions of labour, and political attitudes, despite the transformation of both cities into service-dominated economies (Crang and Martin 1991; Taylor, Evans and Fraser 1996). Traces of practices accumulate over time and seep into local consciousness and the construction of local identities.

In Cambridge, for example, the local working class have long been defined in opposition both to the professional classes employed by the

4.1.1 Cambridge: Medieval shopping streets. Photo by author.

university and more recently the high-tech employees of the new science park firms (Massey 1997) and the students – town versus gown. A culture of service and deference developed, encouraged often by the provision of tied housing by the richest colleges for college 'servants', where generations of the same family worked for a particular college or for the university. Many of these college-based bottom-end 'servicing' positions have long been open to women, as well as to men. The city has had little history of male manufacturing employment with the exception of agricultural-related industries and some light engineering. It is, therefore, a labour market that has always had limited opportunities for stable and well-paid work for poorly educated young men: working in poorly

4.1.2 Cambridge: Kings College. Photo by author.

4.1.3 Sheffield: Victorian municipal city hall and square. Photo by author.

4.1.4   Sheffield: Industrial heritage and 1960s municipal housing. Photo by author.

paid service-sector jobs is a well-established trend. This labour history has led to a resident population that is overwhelmingly white, as well as Cambridge's small-town ambience and conservative traditions and politics, even though the city is now represented by a Labour Member of Parliament.

In Sheffield – historically a working class industrial city rather than a city dominated by a service-based economy – equally strong links developed between a local economy dominated by steel and cutlery and a local employing class – what Taylor, Evans and Fraser (1996: 35) termed 'an enclave of "community" and mutual dependence'. As the economist Alfred Marshall writing in the early twentieth century argued, in its heyday Sheffield was a key example of an 'industrial district' (Marshall 1920: 119) – a tightly geographically defined district with a highly developed level of co-operation and flexibility, and inter-industry linkages between cutlery and steel. In Sheffield, Methodism, rather than the established Church of England as in Cambridge, was the most important religion and a sturdy self-reliance developed among the small craftsmen in the cutlery industry, compared to the deferential social relations of the university town. Sheffield was also a male-dominated city through its industrialization, where fewer women worked than in neighbouring cities such as Leeds where the textile industry relied more heavily, at least initially, on women workers.

The development of the steel industry throughout the nineteenth century led to the rise of a dual economy based on large-scale steel production and the smaller-scale cutlery industry. Steel dominated the landscape of the Don Valley, now the site of a Development Corporation that is attempting to resurrect both the local economy and the industrial landscape. From the mid-nineteenth century until the early 1980s, almost the whole of the East End of Sheffield was dominated by miles of steel plants and forges, as well as small workshops and engineering works, providing physically demanding work for fit men. Interestingly, Sheffield never became a company town dominated by a single employer but it remained a city with over 100 firms of varying sizes until the nationalization of some specialized steel firms in the postwar period. But even then, at least until the strike of 1980, industrial relations were not acrimonious. Instead of capital and labour facing each other as two monolithic and antagonistic blocks, there was localized negotiation within the numerous firms. Unlike Cambridge, Sheffield has long been a Labour-voting stronghold, where five of its six constituencies have regularly returned a Labour candidate by a large majority in the postwar decades. In the 1970s and 1980s, before the national resurrection of Labour as new Labour, local politics in Sheffield were dominated by a particular form of radical municipal socialism, gaining the city a brief but prestigious reputation as the Socialist Republic of South Yorkshire. Somewhat ironically the leader of the local council in these years was David Blunkett, now MP for Sheffield Brightside in the former industrial East End of the city, and conservative Home Secretary in the second Blair Government.

As Taylor, Evans and Fraser (1996) documented, the old industrial heritage of Sheffield is reflected in derelict or empty sites and in a deindustrialized landscape. However, the city still reflects a residual 'northernness'. For example, the heritage of steel lives on in urban imagery (for example in the monument in the foyer of Meadowhall Shopping Centre (see plate 4.2)), in television advertising and street hoardings, and in *The Full Monty*. The economy, however, reflects the impacts of deindustrialization and globalization, as new flexible industries are developed, and service-sector growth accounts for the majority of new jobs. However,

4.2 Sheffield Steelmen: statue in Meadowhall Shopping Centre. Photo by author.

the city still ranks high on the list of Britain's deprived areas. The old heavy male employing industries and their associated camaraderie and political and cultural infrastructure of trade unions, working men's clubs and a particular form of traditional labour politics have been decimated. Women's employment has increased and Sheffield now has a more ethnically diverse population, with significant minority Asian and African Caribbean populations. Male unemployment rates, however, remain high, both among minority men and older white working class men. At the peak of unemployment in 1991, for example, un-employment rates stood at 40 per cent among the Pakistani and Bangla-deshi population compared with 12 per cent among the white residents. At the same date, in Cambridge the average rate of unemployment was less than 3 per cent. At the end of the 1990s, the rate in Cambridge was less than 2 per cent, while in Sheffield it remained at just under 8 per cent.

Despite these differences between the two cities, however, for young men looking for their first job in Sheffield, the opportunities are now more similar to those facing the same cohort in Cambridge than they were in their fathers' generation. For Sheffield youths, who leave school at the first possible moment, the old reasonably well-paid industrial jobs have disappeared, whereas they never existed in Cambridge. Whether these young men have a sense of themselves that is connected to the industrial histories of their specific towns and reflected in different attitudes and labour market aspirations is the subject of the final part of this chapter, where I explore their lives in the last year at school. By establishing a geographical comparison as the basis for this study, I do not intend to imply that there is a straightforward or simple relationship between the construction of local identities, including gender identities and the changing socio-economic context of a city or a neighbourhood, nor that gender identities are fixed, coherent or invariable. Indeed, as I argued in chapter 1, gender identities are continuously in production, mutable and spatially and temporally variable. However, as earlier research on masculinity has indicated, gender practices are inflected in local regimes of work and vice versa and, as Taylor and Jamieson (1997: 153) have suggested in their work on variants of masculinity in Sheffield, 'nostalgic evocations' of earlier industrial practices resonate through masculine imagery and practice. Whether these evocations continue to influence young men in Cambridge and Sheffield and are reflected in their job aspirations and decisions is an issue that informs the comparisons presented later in this and in other chapters. First, however, I want to outline the local areas in which I worked, the research methods adopted and some of the ethical issues raised in working with less-privileged young men.

Two Schools and Two Estates

Although Sheffield and Cambridge are distinguished by their different labour histories, the circumstances of young white men growing up in working class families in the two cities are relatively similar. Taught in the main in schools whose achievement rates are at the low end of the spectrum in their respective cities, white working class youths typically live in local authority accommodation on peripheral estates, with one or both of their parents. Urban theorists and analysts of contemporary cities have argued that whereas such estates were initially constructed for and let to 'respectable' working class families with household heads in manual employment, the recent rounds of economic restructuring have dismantled these older residential working class spaces. Many estates have become unstable, with a mobile population among whom growing numbers of families are in poverty. Campbell (1993), as I noted earlier, has defined such marginalized outer estates as 'dangerous places'.

Whereas the dangerous spaces of the Fordist era typically were defined as the inner city, urban scholars such as Sassen (2001) and Zukin (1995) have suggested that in many cities these latter spaces have now been transformed through residential and commerical gentrification and (re)claimed as both residential and leisure spaces by the 'new' middle class. Thus the inner areas in some of Britain's largest cities, often surrounding a city centre dominated by finance capital, might now be designated postmodern spaces where the growth of cultural industries and new forms of conspicuous consumption have made the streets safe for the aestheticized employment and leisure activities identified by Bauman (1998). In contrast, the spaces of outer estates, in many smaller as well as large British cities, have literally become post-industrial spaces occupied by the new working poor as well as the workless and socially excluded, where employment prospects have declined. These areas are sometimes the sites of localized unrest and racialized conflicts as the 'abject' white working class identified by Haylett (2001) protest at their perceived social exclusion in the 'new' Britain.

Both Sheffield and Cambridge exhibit some aspects of these characteristics of contemporary urbanization. While gentrification is less well developed in Sheffield than in the neighbouring city of Leeds, for example, inner areas are increasingly occupied if not by the new service class then by the growing number of students at the city's two universities. In Sheffield, however, inner city wards are still at present among the most deprived wards in that city (DETR 1998). In Cambridge the particular nature of the city – with its high demand for accessible housing in the inner areas both for gentrification by academic households and for renting by students at the city's two universities, its limited supply of decent-sized Victorian housing and the widespread designation of the inner part of Cambridge as conservation areas – means that low income households have been housed in the main on peripheral estates, in both local authority accommodation to rent and speculatively built housing to purchase for owner-occupation. Thus one of the differences between Cambridge and Sheffield is that in Cambridge 'inner city' poverty is actually located on the outskirts of the city. The area of the greatest concentration of both local authority housing and low incomes is in the north and north-east of the city. In Sheffield similar households, as defined by class and income level, live in inner areas as well as on peripheral estates of local authority housing. However, to achieve some degree of similarity I decided to focus on an outer city estate in each city, identifying areas where the majority of the children between the ages of 11 and 16 living on the estate attended a single school.

Drawing on Paul Willis's (1977) sterling example in his classic study of how young men learned how to labour in manufacturing industries, I decided to trace the transition from school, whether into employment, training or further education, of a sample of young white men who were designated as low achievers or underachievers. I interviewed a small number of school leavers three times in the space of about 18 months, talking to them in detail about their school and their home lives, their sense of themselves in this transitional period, and the mechanisms and institutions they used in their search for a job or a training place. I met them at three key stages: first in the final few weeks as they prepared to leave school, then between four and six months and, finally, twelve months after leaving. A longitudinal study is the best way to capture not only the changing nature of these young men's aspirations as the reality of daily working life or unemployment challenges their earlier assumptions, but it is also the only way to track their complex movements accurately as they become employees at the bottom end of the labour market. Although the national Careers' Guidance Service in the UK (a Government-funded service for school leavers) records the employment position of school leavers, it first does so in the November after the end of the school year in the previous June, by which time new employees may have held more than one job, tried and rejected college, or moved from work into unemployment. Through the co-operation of the head teacher and year 11 class tutor in a school in each city, I made contact with the 24 young men who were involved with this work over the 18-month period (details of the selection methods are included in appendix 1). In Sheffield the school, which I have called Park Edge School, had just over 1,000 pupils on its rolls at the beginning of the academic year 1998/9, whereas the Cambridge school – Fenland Community College – had less half this number. Both schools provide places for 11- to 16-year-olds, and both are regarded as 'underachieving' schools, with problems of low attainment on entry, literacy and numeracy levels, some behaviour difficulties and bullying and, especially at Park Edge, problems of authorized absences as well as truancy and exclusions. During the research period, Fenland Community College also experienced more serious problems, including a knife attack on a teacher and a pupil.

As might be expected because of the way of selecting the schools, their location and intake reflected the characteristics of the locality. In official reports[1] commenting on inspections of these two schools, they were described in the following terms:

Fenland Community College is an 11 to 16 comprehensive serving areas of high social disadvantage. The proportion of children eligible for free school meals[2] is high by national and local standards at around 30 per cent. The standards of attainment on entry are low by national standards and are reported to be amongst the lowest in the country.

Park Edge is situated in one of the most socially and economically deprived areas in the United Kingdom. The local community is characterized by significant unemployment.... 43 per cent of pupils are currently identified as eligible for free school meals, which is well above the national average. There are increasing numbers of ethnic minority students. 22 per cent are from ethnic minority backgrounds and 13 per cent speak English as an additional language. The instability in the local community is reflected in high levels of student mobility.

The main difference between the schools, therefore, apart from size, is the far greater ethnic diversity among the Park Edge pupils. Fenland, like Cambridge, is a dominantly white community. Indeed Ofsted inspectors omitted to record the proportion of minority pupils on its roll during their 1999 inspection, noting only that 'the proportion of students speaking English as an additional language is small by national standards'. School records suggest that less than 6 per cent of the pupils came from ethnic minority backgrounds, some of them, of course, with English as their first language.

Both schools recruit pupils who enter at age 11 with low standards of literacy and numeracy and, although each is successful in raising the self-esteem and confidence of students, their academic attainment by the age of 16, when they finish compulsory education, is low. In 1999, less than 18 per cent of all year 11 pupils at Park Edge School and 29 per cent at Fenland Community College (a remarkable improvement of the previous year's success rate of less than 20 per cent) gained five or more good GCSE passes in 1998 (at grade C and above) – the indicator of 'good' achievement – compared with the national average of 45 per cent. On a national points score constructed on the basis of achievement in school-leaving examinations at the age of 16, both schools fell into category E, on a scale from A to E, where A is well above average and E well below average. The corollary of this categorization is that both schools were at the bottom end of attainment levels in their respective city, where wide disparities are evident. In state schools in Cambridge the variation in 'good' GCSEs ranged from a high of 68 per cent to a low of 18 per cent. In Sheffield the range was greater, from over 90 per cent to 8 per cent as the city maintains a number of schools where pupils are selected on the basis of academic ability. In Cambridge, by contrast, the state schools are all fully comprehensive and select on the basis of local residence rather than ability. In both the schools, in the mid-to late 1990s, year 11 girls had consistently outperformed boys, with a gender gap ranging between 6 and 16 per cent in the proportion of male and female pupils gaining good passes, until at the end of the decade Fenland Community College unexpectedly reversed this trend, which, as I argued in the previous chapter, is also evident at the national level. In 1999 the gender gap at Fenland was 6 per cent in favour of boys, and the school inspection report noted that the boys' performance between the ages of 14 and 16 had begun to improve at a faster rate than for girls. Thus they suggested at Fenland 'special attention should be given to raising the expectations of and standards achieved by girls'.

Overall in the city of Sheffield, only 37 per cent of 15- to 16-year-olds gain five good passes, lower than the national average, whereas Cambridge's average is almost identical to the average. This is reflected in differences in the proportion of pupils who decide to stay on in full-time education from the age of 16. In Sheffield 59 per cent of pupils stay on, compared with 68 per cent nationally and 77 per cent in Cambridge. Figures from Cambridgeshire Careers Guidance Service showed that of those not listed at school or in further education colleges at post-16, 14 per cent entered employment or training and 4 per cent were unemployed. A further 5 per cent had left the area or were destination unknown. In Sheffield, according to the Careers Guidance Service, 10 per cent entered employment, 20 per cent had some form of apprenticeship or careership involving employment combined with training, and 7 per cent were unemployed, while 4 per cent were unaccounted for. In both areas, more girls than boys continued in full-time education at school or in sixth form colleges, paralleling the national trends discussed in the previous chapter.

The estates where the boys in this study lived while they were at school are on the edge of the city and are both distinguished by ranking highly on a series of indicators of deprivation. In absolute terms, a higher proportion of the population of Sheffield than Cambridge lives in poor conditions and has low incomes. However, as the school inspection report noted, the Cambridge estate was the locality in Cambridge that is classified as the most deprived and has a reputation in the city as a dangerous place. In Sheffield, as I note, the poorest wards are still concentrated in the inner areas, but the ward containing Park Edge School was among the most deprived of the outer wards and, like the Cambridge ward, had an extremely small proportion of residents with educational credentials or sufficient social and cultural capital to help their children aspire to opportunities that they themselves had been excluded from. Each estate was troubled by higher than average levels of theft and burglary, by arson, street crimes, and antisocial activities such as car theft and joyriding: all of which made daily life more complicated and less agreeable than in other parts of the respective cities. In both wards housing provision was dominated by the local authority: in Sheffield predominantly 1930s and 1950s houses, and in Cambridge a mixture of houses and flats built since the 1970s (plates 4.3, 4.4). In Cambridge, however, the outer edge of the estate abutted a new development of relatively low-priced new housing for owner-occupation. In each area the estate was served by a local shopping parade that provided a range of basic services. For many of the residents, especially for women and school-aged children, everyday life was a predominantly local affair, carried out within constrained spatial boundaries.

Doing the Research: Prior Assumptions, Positionality and Ethics

The main method that I used was semi-structured interviews based on a life history approach, somewhat similar to the approach adopted by both Connell (1995) and Mac and Ghaill (1996a) in their work with young men. As Connell noted, an interview-based life history approach seems to be the most successful method to use in these types of investigations. Whereas the chronological format of the life history seems straightforward and relatively unthreatening, providing identifiable pegs for the interview, the format of an otherwise relatively unstructured interview allows the ways in which young men construct and talk about their sense of themselves to emerge. I undertook all the interviews myself to ensure continuity and comparability between them. Collecting life histories is a time consuming method, even when the subjects involved are still in their teens but, as Connell (1990b) has argued, it allows the interplay of social structures, collectivities and institutional changes to be assessed at the same time as changes in personal lives, capturing the 'interplay between structural fact and personal experience that is at the centre of contemporary feminist social science' (Connell 1990b: 455), and so enabling connections to be drawn between materialist and post-structuralist analyses of gender identities.

While all interviewing raises difficult questions about positionality and ethics, perhaps interviewing children and young people is the most challenging, as the relations of power and authority so firmly place the interviewer in a dominant position (Fine and Sandstrom 1988; Valentine 1999). In Britain it is also important to be aware of the provisions of the Children's and Young Persons Act and ensure that under-16s are not interviewed without parental consent. Although I contacted the young

4.3 Peripheral housing estates in Sheffield. Photo by author.

4.4 Peripheral housing estates in Cambridge. Photo by author.

men through the auspices of their school, neither the school nor the interviewees knew who was included in the research – at least initially, as inevitably some participants learned the identity of others through friendship networks once they had been contacted. Each time I contacted the young men they knew more about who was involved, leading to mobile phone conversations during interviews when an explanation 'It's that Linda again' (McDowell 2001b) was sufficient explanation of why somebody could not talk just then. I tried to carry out the interviews in neutral spaces. As Allison James and her co-authors (1998) noted, the school is the most usual site for research about young people and significant life course events (see e.g. not only Willis 1977 but also Askew and Ross 1988; Brown and Gilligan 1992; Davies 1982; Delamont 1980; Edley and Wetherell 1996; Hammersley and Woods 1984; Hargreaves 1967; Pollard 1985; Thorne 1993; Whyte 1983). However, working in a school not only naturalizes the model of the developing child but, as James, Jenks and Prout (1998: 176) ask:

> As an age-based institution which is hierarchically organized into age classes and shot through with particular power relations might it not shape the form and style of the research process? ... Would our findings about sexuality, gender, ethnicity, friendship, bullying, play and work, for example, look different if they had been gathered outside the context of the school or other child-specific, age-based institution such as youth clubs or day-care centres?

This comment codified a set of vaguer worries that had persuaded me to interview outside school premises but also clarified an anxiety I felt about Paul Willis's (1977) study. Not only did he interview in schools (as well as undertaking a range of participatory observations, without discussing how his presence as an adult male transformed the social interactions inside and outside the classroom) but he also selected an identifiable group of non-conformist students who had established friendship patterns to observe.

I hoped to be able to include a range of young men with varying social attributes and different ideas about their future, not just the 'disaffected', although as I suspected through initiating a longitudinal strategy, it was the more organized who committed themselves to participate over more than a year. Even so, persuading 24 teenage boys to keep coming to meet me took considerable effort. The growth of mobile phone ownership was key to the success of the study as I was able to track down even the most recalcitrant among the youths and rearrange meetings at short notice. Our meetings took place in a whole range of places, from pubs in the afternoon, cafes, a swimming pool, to public spaces in shopping malls. With their agreement, I recorded our conversations which lasted between 30 minutes and an hour and a half in most cases. This led to some embarrassment and subterfuge to ensure that nobody, especially their peers, saw the encounters. We often kept our back to the crowds or hid the recorder under the table. Inevitably, as I talked to the young men, hoping to be able to access through in-depth interviewing the meanings they attributed to their experiences and social worlds, the interaction between us was coloured by our different positions and perspectives. It is, of course, now widely accepted among human geographers interested in qualitative methods that each story is told to a particular person and that it might have taken a different form if somebody else had been listening. How and what we present of ourselves affects our interviewees' ability and willingness to tell various sorts of stories and, as Miller and Glassner (1997: 101) argue, based on their own work with adolescents, this is particularly important with young people: 'The issue of how interviewees respond to us based on who we are – in their lives, as well as the social categories to which we belong, such as age, gender, class and race – is a practical concern as well as an epistemological or theoretical one.'

If we do not belong to the group we study we may not know enough to ask the right questions. As Miller and Glassner (1997: 102) note, 'the meaning systems of adolescents are different from those of adults, and adult researchers must exercise caution in assuming they have an understanding of adolescent cultures because they've "been there"'. For parents of adolescents this 'being there' might perhaps be partially updated through their involvement in the lives of their own children and their friends, but the warning is still applicable and differences of class, ethnicity, gender and locality remain in place. I was careful, based on experiences with my own son and his friends, to guard against making assumptions about the youths involved in this work. However, Miller and Glassner (1997: 102) also suggested that 'adolescents are in a transitional period of life, becoming increasingly oriented to adult worlds', with more in common with an adult researcher than have younger teenagers and children. As I met and then reinterviewed these young men in Cambridge and in Sheffield over the course of 18 months, it became increasingly evident that they were moving beyond their childhood, and even adolescence, as they began to take on responsibilities for their own lives and workplace decisions. Sometimes, they reversed our position, becoming the interviewer and asking questions about me, both about my social circumstances and my opinions. I tried to answer the questions in the spirit in which they were asked and as honestly as possible. As the feminist scholar Sandra Harding (1987: 9) has insisted, interviewers should appear 'not as an invisible, anonymous voice of authority, but as a real historical individual with concrete specific desires and interests'. When these interests have a significant relationship to the interview process, it seems appropriate to reveal them.

In the early stages it was often difficult to encourage some of the young men to talk freely. Some of them were not verbally adept, perhaps unused to exploring their views and feelings with a stranger, or too often, as they explained, used to being told to 'shut up and be quiet' at school. As Charlesworth (2000: 138) noted in interviewing in Rotherham:

> asking people to 'speak' about their lives immediately institutes a difference. It immediately institutes issues of linguistic competence and introduces the spectres of the state education system and the normally encountered institutions in which its competent products work: the Department of Social Security, the Job Centre and the local council, none of which are well trusted.

A number of the participants wanted to establish that I was not a social worker or a 'lady from the council' before they shared some of the details of their lives with me. As the research moved into its second stage, however, the conversations became longer and freer and I think that most of the young men enjoyed the interaction. A number told me that they looked forward to meeting me again, welcoming the chance to reflect on their futures, as well as to comment on what they had told me on the previous visit. Indeed, a number of them talked to me in ways that seemed particularly frank and honest, although in some cases this was clearly painful to them and they told me things about their personal circumstances or about semi-criminal activities that I was not sure what to do with. I had initially assured them all of confidentiality and I was anxious not to break this. In all the interviews I was careful not to seem judgmental or to condemn or praise responses. I tried to make them comfortable enough to set their own particular views and responses into a wider 'cultural story' about their social world, situating incidents into pre-existing narratives and challenges to these – about changes in family life, or problems at school, for example, but in a number of interviews I was faced by quite complicated ethical decisions. In a small number of cases I suggested other adults or advisory services to which the young men in question might turn to discuss the problems that they had revealed to me. In all cases I have assumed that what each young man told me was valid, in the sense of representative of how they viewed the world and their place in it at that time, unless factual contradictions were evident (and in most cases I managed to sort these out with additional questions). In a somewhat similar study of young men undertaken in three areas of Britain – Newham, Salford and Leicester – Lloyd (1999: 10) noted that he and his interviewers had made the same assumption:

> We have taken young men's accounts and testimonies as valid. Given in particular, the media's view of young men, this is not an assumption that some would share. The combination of being young and male would lead some to be very doubtful about the truthfulness and accuracy of young men's testimonies, and we are also not so naïve as to think all young men are angels.... However, our experience has been that a general positive attitude towards most young men, brings the same out in them. We have approached young men assuming that they will talk openly and straightforwardly with us both about their attitudes and experience, and to a very large extent we think they have.

I was told about drug taking, fighting, semi-criminal activities and family problems, as well as about deeply held beliefs and feelings. These young men sometimes surprised me, sometimes I was shocked by what they told me but I also developed a considerable respect for them, as I hope will become clear in the chapters that follow. Some of them may have looked like ruffians or hooligans, tattooed and pierced, sometimes dressed to outrage conventional views – the sort of boys, as a Cambridge teacher commented early on in the research that 'you'd cross the road to avoid if you met them in a group' – but they all turned up over the year and often displayed courteous attitudes and helpful behaviour. All interview-based research is laborious and often stressful – there were difficult moments: for example, when I was suspected of drug dealing myself or challenged when taking one of these young men into a city centre hotel (see McDowell 2002). Above all, however, this research was enjoyable. As I shall show, there is a great deal to respect in the attitudes and behaviour of young men such as the 24 represented here: respect, that is, as I demonstrated in chapter 3, often denied to working class young men.

Before turning to an exploration of the attitudes and aspirations that these young men shared with me, I want to return to an issue about positionality, the relationship between interviewers and interviewees and the existing research about young men that I briefly raised earlier. It is particularly noticeable that a great deal of the work about male youth cultures has been undertaken by male researchers who often focus on the deviant or the disaffected and their activities on the fringes of legality. As I have noted, for example, Connell (1991, 1995) argued that the impoverished environment and taste for risk of young white working class urban men in Australia and New Zealand produces a form of 'protest masculinity', distinct from and inferior to a hegemonic middle class rational masculinity. This working class protest masculinity seems to me similar to the versions of masculinity described by, *inter alia*, Bourgois (1995) in New York, Willis (1977) in Hammertown, Campbell (1993) in the North-East of England and to the numerous media stereotypes such as 'the lad' of lad culture, men behaving badly, and football hooligans discussed in chapter 3. However, the dominance of this type of tough and cocky working class laddishness may perhaps have as much to do with the preconceptions of the interviewers as with the 'lads' whom they interviewed or at least to the establishment of a form of male camaraderie between them, as feminist critics of studies of youth culture and the sociology of deviance have noted (Delamont 2000; McRobbie 1980; Skeggs 1997; Walker 1986). Male academics often seem seduced by the 'outlaw' subjects whom they study. Clearly, as a middle-aged woman I am differently positioned in relation to my interviewees than these young male researchers and, as I show later, I found a different set of attitudes among the young men who participated than many of these earlier studies of working class masculinity have suggested. While all narratives are not only a product of distinctive interactions, but are also a re-representation of the voices of those involved, a singular story – even the 'truth' – is not to be expected. But what is possible is to counterpose these different stories, and to compare and contrast the content and the conclusions in assessing the ways in which young men in contemporary Britain produce particular versions of masculine identities.

On the Verge of Manhood: Versions of Masculinity at School

A large body of school-based research has documented the significance of masculinity in schools in defining and policing both masculine and feminine identities and acceptable forms of interaction between pupils. Jordan (1995: 79), for example, has suggested that many of the disadvantages suffered by girls and women are 'the result of being caught in the crossfire in a long-standing battle between groups of men over the definition of masculinity'. In recent research with school pupils it has been emphasized, in parallel with the wider debates about the social construction of gendered identities, that there is no single version of masculinity or femininity, but instead the occupation of, and insertion into, cross-cutting discursive gender positions and multiple regimes of power. In work on girls' friendship patterns (Brown and Gilligan 1992; Thorne 1993), for example, common versions of acceptable teenage femininity are encapsulated in the labels 'slags', 'bad girls', 'boffins', and 'good girls', which construct identities and identifications against, instead of in common with, other girls or boys. Students often position themselves in relation to something they are not.

Similar arguments about multiple gender positions are increasingly common in studies of boys at school (Frosh, Phoenix and Pattman 2002). A dominant version of working class or 'protest' masculinity, similar to the earlier version of the 'lad', seems to have a continuing hold, against which most boys define themselves as similar to or different from. This form of laddish masculinity, with its emphasis on macho values such as physical strength, courage and toughness, seems hegemonic among young men. It has been identified in a variety of locations and has been labelled 'retributive' (Chapman and Rutherford 1988) and, confusingly, 'hegemonic' (Carrigan, Connell and Lee 1985) as well as 'protest' (Connell 1995). Edley and Wetherell (1996), for example, in interviews in the early 1990s in a single-sex independent, and so middle class, school in the Midlands, documented the existence of several separate, and sometimes antagonistic, groups of boys in the school. They found, however, that most of their interviewees identified themselves in relationship to a single version of masculinity – either as a member of the 'hard lads' or in opposition to them. The identity of the 'hard lads' was organized in the main around participation in sport and a whole set of loud and boisterous activities such as play fighting, drinking and small-scale vandalism. When interviewed about school life these boys saw it as unremarkable, as a series of 'good laughs' and even when people were upset or hurt it was regarded as 'just a bit of fun'. It seems, therefore, that these young men, although from a privileged educational environment, are rather similar to Willis's lads in a much less privileged school 20 years earlier, where there was a dichotomous division between the 'lads' and what Willis termed the 'ear' oles' – the boys in the same school and from the same background who conformed to the school's middle class educational ethos and were prepared to compete academically.

Boffs, hards, nutters and negotiating 'betweenness' in Cambridge and Sheffield

The schools in Sheffield and Cambridge proved to be no exception to other school-based studies in demonstrating the significance of an aggressive version of laddish masculinity. Almost all the school leavers to whom I talked identified themselves as members of or in opposition to the 'hard lads'. Here the most-commonly used terms in both schools to distinguish between the dominant groups were nutters/hards and boffs/boffins. Unsurprisingly, none of the young men in my study self-identified as boffs, although four of them did mention the importance of getting down to doing some academic work in the final weeks of their school career. Only 3 of the 24 boys included themselves in the lad/nutter/hard category:

> I suppose I am just a nutter really. I do daft things. I scream in lessons and once I cut me hand on a chisel, cos I just felt like it. (John, Cambridge).

The other 21 boys, however, refused this identity, even though sometimes what defined the 'hard' group or the nutters seemed to consist of minor infringements of school rules. Rick, a Park Edge pupil, for example, suggested that 'the people who smoke all hang out together, you know, at break time and that; they stand in a corner smoking or whatever. And they are usually the popular ones. I suppose you could call them nutters if you want a name for them.'

But most of the boys in this study were, they insisted, 'just normal' or 'average', trying to avoid both labels (boffs or nutter/hards), 'I sort of stay between the two of 'em, like' (Simon, Sheffield) and, in their view, this in-between group encompassed the majority of their peers. Rick also told me with an ironic edge, 'Me, I'm a good boy. I always go to lessons you see, but one of the girls said to me this morning, "You're a clever one, but you are not a boff."'

In both schools, there was a euphemistic reference by school inspectors to the 'boisterous environment' or 'overexuberant behaviour' outside the classrooms, as well as some evidence of bad behaviour and bullying. In addition, the problem of disruptive classroom behaviour, especially among boys, was recognized. These behaviours were used by the three self-identified hards/nutters to define themselves. They habitually engaged in what was on their own admittance antisocial behaviour, including various strategies of classroom disruption, as well as playground bullying and shoving, some fighting and breaking school rules about smoking. A similar range of behaviour to distinguish between hards and themselves was mentioned by the 'normal/between' group. But the line between the behaviour of 'hard lads' and the majority of the young men who insisted that they were not part of this group was fuzzy. Most of the 24 young men to whom I talked confessed to a range of disruptive behaviour inside and outside the classroom. However, in several cases they argued that they were wrongly identified as 'hard' or had been unjustifiably labelled as troublemakers at school by virtue of the fact that they were prepared to stand up for themselves against 'hard lads'. For example, Kurt in Cambridge told me, 'There's this kid who's really hard. He started on me once so I sorted him.' I asked, 'So, are you hard do you think?' Kurt replied, 'Nah, I don't think I'm hard. I just think if anyone starts on me I just ignore them. But if anyone pushes me too far I lose it.'

Most of the young men argued that it was important to be able to stand up for themselves and to hit back at bullies. A high level of physical interactions between pupils in both schools was readily visible from pushing and jostling in the corridors to fights in the playground:

> Yeah, fights are common. We go out round the back where the teachers can't see us. (Lee Cambridge)

This physical aggression is a part of the construction of a version of heterosexual working class masculinity that, as Mac an Ghaill (1996b) emphasizes, is based on expelling effeminacy. Bourdieu, too (1991: 96), recognized the links between class and gender in his comment on physically aggressive masculine working class attitudes and behaviour, which

> is undoubtedly just one of the ways of making a virtue out of necessity. The manifestation of an unreasoning commitment to realism and cynicism, the rejection of the feeling and sensitivity identified with feminine sentimentality and effeminacy, the obligation to be tough with oneself and others . . . are a way of resigning oneself to a world with no way out, dominated by poverty and the law of the jungle, discrimination and violence, where morality and sensitivity bring no benefit whatsoever.

This is a comment perhaps more relevant to a wider arena than local schools but it was quite clear that the young men whom I interviewed saw school as a place where toughness was valued. In most cases, however, I would hesitate to argue as Willis (1977) did that any of these 24 young men – either the self-identified hards or those who were aggressive when 'pushed too far' – were 'mad, bad and dangerous to know'.

Among the group as a whole, more of a 'don't much care' attitude summed up their general response to school and its regulatory environment. The dominant feeling was one of 'well, you just have put up with it' (Paul, Sheffield) when I talked to them in the final weeks at school before moving on to what they all hoped would be a more agreeable life in the workplace, in further education or training or in a mixture of the two. Darren's heartfelt 'I just can't wait to leave school. It drives me mad' was echoed by most of his cohort. But inside and outside the classroom, the young men in this study were not in general troublemakers. Only 3 of the 24 had been arrested and cautioned, for example, and although a number of others engaged in a variety of behaviour bordering on the semi-criminal – petty theft, for example, or trivial damage to cars, smoking 'weed' or 'draw' – they had never been caught or punished. Only one student admitted that he had been involved with more serious drugs, and two spoke about heavy drinking that they themselves regarded as a problem. Outside school, almost half of the young men reported that they were as likely to go for a drink with their dads, or fishing with friends, as get involved in antisocial activities such as joyriding. Rather more common, however, were periods of exclusion from school ranging from a day for a minor misdemeanour to almost a term. Five of the 24 young men said that they had been excluded at some stage in their school career. Voluntary exclusion, that is truanting (or 'wagging it' as it is called in Sheffield) was even more common – almost all the young men reported that they had taken time off when they were meant to be in school, although as it was sporadic and for short periods, it was not seen as serious and only three had been in trouble with the school authorities for truanting. Most of them, though, made sure that their parents did not realize they had been absent, often attending school at registration and then leaving and often going as far as intercepting letters from the school to their parents. At Park Edge, poor levels of school attendance were a particular problem that persisted over several years despite the efforts of the school to reduce both authorized (that is with parental permission) and unauthorized absences. An external agency was employed, for example, to check first-day absences each term and there was frequent liaison between the school and the educational welfare service to discuss the family circumstances of the most infrequent attendees.

Sexist attitudes, boys as 'failures' and girls' success

By the end of the twentieth century most state schools in Britain were co-educational. Both Park Edge School and Fenland Community College admitted girls as well as boys, and mixed-sex friendship groups of girls and boys, as well as single-sex groups, were reportedly common in both the schools, although most of the students to whom I talked also spent a large proportion of their time, both on and off the school premises, hanging around in single-sex groups. In earlier postwar decades and in the 1970s, for example when Willis (1977) was exploring how working class boys were educated just enough to fill factory jobs, single-sex schools were more common and, since that time, a vast range of research has been published that attempts to demonstrate the difference that a mixed intake has on areas such as subject-specific achievement rates, attitudes to further study, the development of sexuality, and social relations inside and outside the classroom. As many of these researchers have documented, the school is, however, even when co-educational, an institution embedded within wider societal rules and regulations within which teachers and pupils draw on and reinforce dominant culturally specific heterosexist and patriarchal attitudes (Dixon 1997; Epstein 1993, 1997; Frosh, Phoenix and Pattman 2002; Holloway, Valentine and Bingham 1999; Mac an Ghaill 1994, 1996a; Paechter 1998; Shilling 1991; Skeggs 1992), and, as I suggested above, a dominant version of laddish masculinity influences the social construction of feminine as well as masculine identities. In most schools, in a multitude of ways from humour to violence reflected in staff and pupil attitudes, in the institutional culture of the school, in its regulatory mechanisms and in everyday classroom and playground behaviour, assumptions about masculine dominance and superiority is maintained. Despite most schools having a commitment to equal-opportunity programmes of differing degrees of effectiveness, as I suggested earlier, the current 'problem' of boys' relative lack of success reflects continuing beliefs about masculine achievement, indeed the superiority that is a 'natural' correlate of being a boy.

In both Cambridge and Sheffield the local education authority has a specific commitment to equal opportunities, and in each of the schools anti-sexist (and anti-racist) policies were in place in, for example, the official school rules and in personal, social and health education (PSHE) lessons. The inspection report at Park Edge explicitly mentioned the success of equal opportunity policies at that school, whereas at Fenland a more 'macho' culture in which boys' dominance was reinforced, as well as evidence of positive role models among the male staff, was identified as part of the reason for the faster rate of improvement in boys' performance between the ages of 14 and 16. However, despite these differences, in the course of the interviews, the boys at both schools expressed a complex and nuanced set of reactions to questions about gender relations. While the majority of them consistently denied sexist attitudes and behaviours on their own part, and often had solid friendships with girls, they also held firm to a simplistic narrative of binary difference, usually based on trivial behavioural traits. None of them was reticent in expressing views about the differences between girls and boys and they were astonishingly cavalier in their assumptions of female inferiority. Neither academic nor popular versions of feminism seemed to have made any inroads on these young men's views of gender differences. Thus they variously described girls as 'stupid', 'wussie', 'gigglers' and 'screamers' and as 'sillier than boys' and when they commented on the mixed-sex groups in which they participated, it was noticeable that their considered view of the role of girls tended to be the traditionally feminine one of supporting the dominant males and basking in reflected (male) glory. In a comment on the girls who were 'in with' the 'hards', in Park Edge for example:

> Oh, the girls are just the girlfriends and that. They just stand about wi' em. (Darren)

Comments about girls in the year 11 group in Fenland Community College included the dismissive

> Well, girls have no sense, do they? (Wayne)

Some of Wayne's peers were more tolerant but similarly dismissive about what they regarded as typical female traits:

> They're OK, some of the girls in our class, but never tell 'em anything that's a secret. (Andrew)

And a puzzled, but typical male, response:

> Well, I dunno about girls; they're a mystery to me. (Gareth, Sheffield)

These comments largely support Mac an Ghaill's (1996b) argument that men become men by distinguishing themselves from the 'other' – including girls and women – often through tactics of disparagement and through the abolition of all indicators of effeminacy in their own attitudes. Even so I was surprised by the levels of casual disparagement of girls of whom respondents disapproved. They included dismissal of the significance of a pregnancy, for example, 'Oh, she's just a slag. It don't matter' (Shaun, Sheffield), to a range of unkind comments about various attributes of the personal appearance of the girls whom they knew, although a small number of young men did speak more fondly of some of their female friends.

What was interesting, however, was the fact that almost all these young men were adamant in their rejection of the widespread belief that boys are now educational failures. I approached this issue prepared to hear a litany of complaints about successful, high-achieving girls and boys' relative failure, paralleling the dominant representation of gender differences at school in the popular discourses discussed in chapter 3, although I also expected that the young men would not be aware of the statistical differences in achievement rates between boys and girls in their own schools nor, indeed, in their own class.[3] However, this story of female success was not common currency in either Cambridge or Sheffield, although these young men seemed in the main to be well aware of their own specific educational limitations. For example, several students in both schools commented, usually disparagingly, on their own potential. 'I'm thick, me' and 'I'm not much good at the writing side,' as well as 'I wish I'd worked a bit harder sooner.' What was distinct, impressive and disturbing about the majority of interviewees was their clear-sighted sense of their own structural position as working class students in an institution imbued with middle class values about the importance of education. One of the Sheffield students spoke with resignation and regret, but an astonishingly mature insight, about the way in which he had been labelled as a troublemaker in Park Edge School:

> You know, once you have got a name, they sort of treat you right differently from other people in the class, right. They talk to you like 'It's him again. It's D. again.' I feel like I've got a sign on me head saying I've done summat wrong. (Darren)

Similarly, in Cambridge Kurt noted sadly that 'I get on everyone's nerves, I do,' adding, 'I think they are just waiting for me to leave.'

Both these young men are unaccustomed to speaking about their experiences and seem surprised that anyone might be interested in their views. Like the other boys, both of them were identified by their schools as low achievers and yet their comments exhibit a sensitivity and self-awareness that is remarkable. Both of them exhibit a sense that their position at school is related to the way in which economic position mediates identity. As many studies of the impact of the culture of schools have made clear, from the classic early work of Bernstein (1971; and see also Bernstein 1996 for an assessment of this work) onwards, working class children often feel alienated by the values of the institution, with its 'hidden assumptions of student inferiority' (Wexler 1992: 133) and by their perceived treatment by teachers). Frequently they intuitively understand that they are marked by their class position, accent and attitudes in ways that lead to their being denied the resources of self-respect, value and inclusion and so they develop what Ball, Macrae and Maguire (1999: 33) term an 'estranged or damaged learner identity'. As John, another Fenland pupil, told me 'I'm just naturally thick, me so they don't bother much,' and Kevin at Park Edge echoed his comment: 'I'm no good at book work; I have a bit of trouble with reading and writing and that, so I'm left to meself mainly.' This is not to blame individual teachers at either school, who seemed to me on visits to be doing as good a job as possible in the face of almost overwhelming problems, including lack of resources, continual changes in the curriculum, new modes of evaluation and large classes of demanding students, as well as a high proportion of pupils with 'special educational needs' – the official designation of low achievers. But as Charlesworth (2000: 240–1) in a study of working class life in Rotherham has suggested, because teachers tend to ignore the less able or denigrate their efforts, these students come to 'understand their competence as belonging to the realm of nature [John's claim above that he is "naturally" thick], to the body, the realm of the physical'. Thus, in common with generations of working class boys, the advantages of a labouring body are privileged over those of the mind by some of the 24 when talking about their employment prospects. While economic restructuring has radically altered the labour market options facing 16-year-old working class boys, their school experiences seem to continue to reflect the attitudes and structures that teach these boys to expect a labouring life. This is confirmed by their participation in a range of vocational courses, especially at Park Edge during their final two years, which emphasize traditional masculine manual occupations such as gardening or house painting.

The labelling of these young men as 'low achievers' tends to be accepted by their families, thus confirming and reinforcing the schools' opinion of their abilities. The official reports on both schools mentioned the low participation among parents in school activities and events and in their children's education more generally. Few of the parents of the young men I interviewed attended school open days, nor did they feel able to challenge decisions by the schools, to exclude their sons for example. A number of the participants recounted tales of incidents that they perceived as unfair, including in Craig's case what seemed to be a serious issue of exclusion for most of the term before sitting his school-leaving examinations:

'We just left it, though. Me mam said she didn't want to go up to the school, so that was it. I think it had a bad effect on me, though. I went back to do the exams but it weren't much good.'

The working class family and the school thus together establish the horizon of possibility of working class youths' existence. As most of the young men told me, their parents just wanted them to get a job and to earn some money when they left school, although as I shall show in the next chapter, the actions of some mothers were crucially important in helping their sons to decide to combine work with some form of training. Working class parents, who have the same practical understanding as their children and so who lack both the authority to challenge the ways their sons are constructed at school as 'failures' or 'problems' and the resources to improve their opportunities, thus reinforce what Charlesworth (2000: 241) terms 'the symbolic violation of their children's dignity'. These young men told me that they did not expect to do well in their forthcoming exams. Indeed, two or three of the Park Edge students had decided to leave and look for work without entering, dismissing their relevance for 'people like us'. As Bourdieu has noted (1984: 387) it is often too easy to overlook the fact that educational qualifications are

> not experienced as purely technical and therefore partial and one-sided, but as total hierarchies, grounded in nature so that social value comes to be identified with personal value, scholastic dignities with human dignity... so that privation is perceived as an intrinsic handicap, diminishing a person's identity and human dignity.

Being labelled as a low achiever in adolescence is too often a deciding factor in closing off opportunities for social mobility in the future. As I shall show in the more detailed case studies of young men with different types of labour market attachment in chapters 6 and 7, this resigned acceptance of their own limitations restricted the ambitions and affected the working lives of those young men who joined the ranks of what I define there as 'disaffected and unattached workers'. When I met the 24 young men for the second time, many of them were reluctant to tell me their exam results, pretending to an insouciance that seemed forced.

But this is to get ahead of the story: while these 24 young men were still at school, although many of them seemed to have accepted the general opinion the school held of them, they did not relate their own disadvantage to a rhetoric of gender inequality. Most of them did not seem to be aware that girls in general, as well as those in their year group, at least at Park Edge, if not at Fenland, were likely to continue to outperform boys in GCSE examinations. A small minority, however, did comment on differences in attitude and motivation:

> Well, I think that perhaps girls work harder in school than boys. Boys are more immature and just mess around. (Simon, Sheffield)

But only one of the 24, also a Park Edge pupil was aware that

> It's girls who usually get better grades. (Richard)

Everyone else, including all ten boys at Fenland, thought that boys were just as likely as girls to be successful or not in the forthcoming exams. Nor did most of the respondents seem familiar with the gender trans-formation of labour market opportunities. Not yet faced with the reality of leaving school and the movement into the labour market or into forms of training, these young men felt that their prospects were at least reasonable, if not rosy. In general, they felt that both young men and young women had a good chance of employment in the local labour market, even if they were not among the highest achievers in their age cohort. There was, however, as I explore below, an awareness of gender segregation in employment opportunities. First, though, I want briefly to examine the construction of whiteness among these young men to assess the significance of those ideas about black style and white envy among school pupils in the construction of masculinity that I outlined earlier.

Deconstructing Binaries: Whiteness and 'Otherness'?

As I argued in the first chapter, young men in Britain, are caught within a complex and contradictory set of discourses about 'race' and racism. Notions of a multicultural society that are presented to these pupils in anti-racist educational material are contradicted by widespread popular discourses of national identity that depend on a unitary notion of the superiority of a version of Britishness. At the same time – as earlier work in schools, especially in Greater London (Frosh, Phoenix and Pattman 2002) but also in Leeds (Sewell 1997), has shown – white youths often both envy and fear popular representations of black style and toughness. At both Park Edge and Fenland Community College, white young people were in a large numerical majority, although in Cambridge their dominance was more noticeable. Less than 6 per cent of the pupils of Fenland Community College were from minority groups compared with 22 per cent at Park Edge School, reflecting the distinctive labour histories of each city. Both schools, however, had an anti-racist code of practice and each taught 'citizenship' in PSHE lessons. It seemed too, from the inspectors' reports that both schools had managed to create environments within which diversity, whether based on ethnicity, gender or ability, was valued. At Fenland, policies to integrate minority and disabled students were commended; and at Park Edge, the inspectors noted that 'the school strongly supports the development of the students' multi-cultural awareness. Students representing many ethnic backgrounds live together and relate harmoniously in a supportive environment'. Partly as a reflection of this environment, then, and of the formal teaching that they received, the young men to whom I talked initially were reluctant to voice their opinions about ethnic difference, seeming to be anxious lest I consider them racist. Rick's comment was typical among the Park Edge boys: 'Well, at school there's whites and some Asian and black kids but we just all hang about together. There's no racism in our school here.'

For some, their modes of engagement with whiteness were refracted through complex family and local social relations. Thus the common statement that 'I'm not racist, me' enunciated in both cities was qualified by a number of Sheffield respondents by 'How could I be? Me nan is black or my sister's husband, he's an Indian, I think, or perhaps a Paki.' The casual use of the derogatory term 'Paki' might perhaps be taken as racist or rather, as I think was intended, as an indication that his ethnic origin was, in fact, insignificant. For these boys, then, located within inter-ethnic familial networks, whiteness and otherness are part of an everyday negotiation of identity. However, in the school grounds and classrooms in both Sheffield and Cambridge, social and spatial separation between boys from different backgrounds was common: 'It just happens; it's not that we don't get on but perhaps we do different things.' In the streets outside Park Edge School, however, this spatial separation took a more serious form, often associated with punishment if territorial boundaries were crossed.

> Well, there some parks, like where I wouldn't go. That's where Asian lads hang out and if you go there, even just to walk through, they'll

try and stop you, push you about a bit, and perhaps try and take something, your money maybe or your phone. (Craig, Sheffield)

And:

There's, like, pubs and some of the clubs in town where the coloureds go. Sometimes there might be a bit of trouble, but it's not real serious, usually. (Darren, Sheffield)

This mapping of skin politics on to male territorial rivalries, however, tends to racialize local spaces, as well as reinforce anxieties about the associations between street crime and ethnicity, even though in the local estates where these boys grew up most of the semi-criminal and criminal activities, at least where an offender was apprehended, were perpetrated by white youths. As I shall show in chapter 8, however, a narrative about the inward movement of Others 'bringing down' the neighbourhood is common in both cities.

A discourse of white envy of black masculinity and style commonly found by researchers in multi-ethnic London schools was evident to a limited extent in Sheffield, although completely absent in Cambridge where none of the ten made any comments about ethnic difference and style. In Sheffield two boys, although one made only a brief reference in passing, made a series of comments that suggested they both resented and also envied what they defined as a black way of doing things. This is Pauly, claiming to be speaking for a wider constituency, exploring the reasons why he felt uncomfortable with what he regarded as many black, but also white, boys' mimicry of a black style, which he regards as inauthentic. The combination of his indignation, sense of exclusion, defence of a 'perfectly good Sheffield accent' and his definition of a black Other as 'Them' results in a complex narrative justification of his stance.

Well, I am not a racist myself but I know that a lot of people think the way that I do and that's it really bugs me to see how they talk and how they walk and all their behaviour really. Not particularly coloured people, but as far as I'm concerned if they want to be like that, they go to Jamaica to do it, because that's what they are acting like. It's like a lot of, there's a lot of, I mean I've got friends that walk daft and talk daft and stuff like that and that's how I'd like it to be. I mean they were originally Jamaican but they are not now and they don't have to speak the way they do and they don't have to walk with a limp. It really bugs me to see it.

There's lots of boys like that in school and what bugs me most is to see a white person trying to be like a black person. That really bugs me. There's quite a few of them. Some are old friends what I fell out with for various reasons. They hang round with black people and act like black people. There's like, can you imagine a Jamaican. A lot of the black people in our school do talk that way. They don't need to. They've got a perfectly good Sheffield accent but they talk in a black way. Well, not a black way, but a Jamaican way, if you know what I mean. And one of me old friends he started hanging about with them and he got talking like that and that's the reason why we've stopped being friends really because he got me so mad and then I told him I didn't like it so. . . .

He uses stupid words. It's, like, sort of words, like, I mean you might not have heard them but around Sheffield it's, like, you 'bloodclaut' or you 'raasclaut', something like that. It's daft. If they don't like you they'll call you it. You dirty raasclaut or something. Stupid slang words. It bugs me; I don't like it.

Asian boys seemed not to rouse the same passion in Pauly: 'Well, there's some name-calling: "You stupid Paki" or something like that. But we grow out of it. I mean most people mostly grow up by the time they are 16, 15, 16.' And as one or two of the other boys explained, Asian boys are the quiet ones, who tend to keep to themselves and who also do not socialize outside school, either through sport or in leisure activities involving drinking or clubbing. As a consequence, Asian young men are often regarded as feminized by their peers.

The significance of ethnic difference, then, seems to depend on the context, and on class and social position, and on the distinction between black and Asian identities. While in society as a whole, there are multiple and overlapping ways in which whiteness is differentiated from a generalized otherness, and situations in which the relation is not always one of dominance, in these two schools 'whiteness' is both dominant and largely taken for granted. However, unlike their undifferentiated attitude to gender difference, some of these young men were located in a more ambiguous set of relations and exchanges based on racialized otherness, both through friendship networks (disrupted on the grounds of difference, or rather its mimicry in Richard's case) or through familial connections. It is interesting that a rhetoric of 'natural' gender difference, and its association with relations of superiority and inferiority, was more widely accepted than a similar explanation of racialized difference. As

Shaun in Sheffield noted about ethnicity, 'well, we are all the same really aren't we, just all boys, after all'.

In Cambridge the negotiations of white identity were less problematic than in Sheffield, as the city is overwhelmingly white. Here, outside the specific confines of school and its local environs, social class was the key dimension of a differentiated masculinity in the central spaces of a city where the streets and leisure spaces are noticeably dominated by the middle class, largely white, student population. For the Fenland boys, class difference became a territory of contestation in some of the city's leisure spaces, where students were constructed as 'snobby' but also resented for their privileged access to local facilities, either based on income or student status that denied local youths the same privileges. In Sheffield by contrast, racialized differences are a more visible part of everyday life in the city and at school, and so a terrain for negotiation. Ways of performing a white class-based masculinity in leisure spaces are the topic of the penultimate chapter. In the last part of this chapter, the work experiences during school years, knowledge of local economic prospects and the labour market aspirations of the 24 young men are assessed.

Young men's attitudes to employment prospects and labour market change

It is clear that a particular, laddish, lackadaisical construction of masculine identity among working class school students remains dominant in Park Edge School and Fenland Community College. The 24 boys interviewed continue to hold to a version of masculinity that would have been familiar among their fathers, perhaps especially in Sheffield, when they left school between 20 and 30 years earlier. The key question that remains to be investigated is what these young men think about appropriate or acceptable forms of work that they judge will be congruent with their masculine identities. And how far will their aspirations and labour market expectations while still at school prove realistic once they start to look for work? To what extent are they aware of the shift to a service-based economy in the country as a whole and in their local labour market areas? Do they hope to achieve 'male' jobs in the manufacturing sector or are they prepared to look for work in, for example, the retail sector or in caring occupations traditionally regarded as 'women's work'? And how much difference does place make? Is there a pattern of less traditional expectations in Cambridge, given that many young men's fathers, as I shall illustrate in a moment, work in the service sector, even in 'caring' occupations? To answer these questions, I explored the 24 participants' knowledge of and views about current employment opportunities and prospects for young men compared to what they knew about those open to girls of their own age. I also asked each young man to speculate about his employment prospects now compared with those that faced young men 20 or so years previously, specifically asking about their father's experiences if he was still present in the household. I also explored the extent of working experience so far, including the types of temporary and casual employment they might have been involved in as schoolboys as well as the work placements they had undertaken through the auspices of the respective schools.

Part-time and casual employment was a common experience among the school leavers in both Cambridge and Sheffield. In Cambridge 8 of the 10 young men, and in Sheffield 10 out of 14, had some labour market experience. The range of jobs in each city is shown in table 4.2. The types of jobs undertaken in both cities are mainly in the service sector, with greater variety in Sheffield than in Cambridge. All the respondents had also had a short period of work experience in either year 10 or 11 at school, although some were unable to remember what they had done. However, about half in each city did recall the type of work and it was noticeable that in Cambridge all the placements were in the service sector, whereas the Sheffield school was still able to find some industrial placements, reflecting the differences in each city's labour

Table 4.2 Part-time and casual employment undertaken by final-year school students in Cambridge and Sheffield, 1999

Type of job	Cambridge No. of participants	Sheffield No. of participants
Paper round	3	3
Shopwork/shelf-stacking	3	1
Waiting/clearing tables	–	2
Call centre	–	1
Post Office sorting	1	–
Office cleaning/security	1	1
Packing in a factory	–	1
Painting and decorating		1
Not employed	2	4
Total	10	14

market history. The types of work mentioned in Cambridge included working in a college kitchen, assisting in residential homes for the elderly and working in shops. In Sheffield, placements in residential homes and shops were also mentioned but so too were placements in, for example, a light bulb fitting manufacturers and in a building merchants as well as temporary attachments to painting and decorating firms. Interestingly, despite their lack of experience in industrial work, when asked about their plans for the following year a number of Cambridge pupils, as well as several Sheffield students, hoped to find work or start a vocational course as a mechanic or engineer. However, only the Sheffield students seemed to be aware of the possibilities of the national modern apprenticeship scheme under which young people are able to gain both educational credentials and work experience. Two of the fourteen young men had applications in for an engineering apprenticeship at the time of the first interview. Clearly engineering apprenticeships are less common in Cambridge, but the Careers' Guidance Service had details of similar schemes in, for example, the furniture manufacturing industry and the water industry in and around Cambridge. What was interesting, however, is that Cambridge students were much more likely to be considering vocational (GNVQ) courses at the local further education college than their Sheffield peers.

The types of jobs and course being considered by the year 11 leavers in both cities were varied (see table 4.3) and included in each case transfer

Table 4.3 Post-school aspirations and plans for the year 1999–2000

Cambridge	Sheffield
Some form of mechanic (2 boys)	Car mechanic (2 boys)
Tattooist	Carpenter
Some sort of art course at college	Modern apprenticeship (subject unspecified)
Engineering course at local FE college	Modern apprenticeship in electrical engineering
IT course leading to job as a computer engineer	Painter and decorator
Radio or TV presenter	Art and design course (2 boys)
Bricklayer	Footballer
Not sure (3 boys)	Army
	Retail work, but must be in a sports shop
	Horticulture YTS
	Just a job, building work or something
	Not sure

to a local further education college, industrial and service-sector work. The ambitions of the 14 Sheffield students seemed perhaps more realistic than the Cambridge 10, including as they did a putative radio and TV presenter (John) and Kurt, the young man who longed to be a tattooist. Pauly, the potential footballer in Sheffield, for example, was already on contract as a junior to a national club that had promised him a placement on a Youth Training Scheme (YTS) with them later that year.

It seems clear that most of the young men in both cities, but rather fewer in Cambridge, had relatively clear aims and generally realizable prospects. Three students in Cambridge and two in Sheffield specifically mentioned a college course, while a number of others planned to combine employment and training. These preferences reflect the changed labour market opportunities facing working class men at the end of the century, compared with 20 or so years earlier when an overwhelming majority of men of their age and backgrounds who left school at 16 went straight into full-time employment. Indeed, when I asked these young men what they thought their chances of work were now compared to the experience of men of their father's age, they were quite clear about the differences. Although many of them thought that there were more and a wider range of labour market opportunities for young men now than when their fathers were the same age, there was also general recognition that qualifications are now more important in gaining access to a well-paid job.

> I would have thought that there is a lot more jobs around now what you need to be more qualified for instead of just going to a local shop[4] and getting a job straight away. I may not be right but as far as I'm concerned there's a lot more jobs around at the moment what you have to have certain grades for rather than 30 years, 20 years ago when you go into jobcentre and get a decent job. (Rick, Sheffield)

> There may be more jobs but there's more competition now, cos you need qualifications. (Simon, Sheffield)

But not all of them agreed about the general availability of jobs, especially in Sheffield where the decline of the steel-making industry has had such a devastating impact:

> There were more jobs when my Dad was young cos all the factories were there and there are none now. (Darren, Sheffield)

At the time of the first interview, however, none of the young men's fathers in either city worked in factories, although in Sheffield a number were employed as machine operators in, for example, a scrap waste recovery plant and a bakery, and another father was a forklift driver (see appendix 2). In Cambridge 7 of the fathers/stepfathers who were present in the home were in employment, another was unemployed and one father was looking after the children. In Sheffield there was also one 'house husband' and one unemployed father, and 11 fathers in employment. In Cambridge only one father had a job in the manufacturing sector – all the others were in service employment including cleaning, security, the Post Office and the police. In Sheffield, 5 of the 13 fathers with whom their sons either lived or visited worked in the manufacturing sector. The others had a range of service-sector employment including cleaning and taxi driving. One father in Sheffield was a local government officer but, as in Cambridge, the majority of men were in working class occupations and many of them had had experience of unemployment, layoffs and precarious forms of work.

Of the young men's mothers who were in paid work (all of them in Cambridge, compared with 8 out of 14 in Sheffield, reflecting the differences in traditions of women's work), all had jobs in the service sector and, as is usual with women's employment, they were concentrated into a very narrow range of occupations. In Cambridge all the women worked in some form of care (of old people or children) or in the retail sector, as did six of the eight employed mothers in Sheffield. One women had a professional job – she was a nurse; the other was an aerobics instructor. Five Sheffield mothers, according to their sons, were not working by choice and one was unemployed. It is hardly surprising, therefore, as I explore below, that most of the young men with whom I talked had an explicitly gendered perspective on employment opportunities.

A Gendered Job Market?

Most of the young men assumed that the opportunities facing them were gender-specific. They also held depressingly traditional views about gender-specific skills and abilities:

> I think there is more jobs mainly for boys really. There are mainly motor places and stuff like that and places where you have got to do heavy lifting and they're for boys, aren't they, cos they think

they are stronger and that. [And referring to his own potential move into the building industry] It's work for men really. (Wayne, Cambridge)

Other interviewees noted that
Girls go into childcare, and boys into things like IT. (Damian, Cambridge)
And:

Only boys are interested in mechanics. (John, Cambridge)

The Sheffield students had equally firm views about the sorts of jobs that lay ahead of them and their female peers. For example:

Well, women can't do the jobs that involve lifting and that. (Craig, Sheffield)

Industry and engineering, they don't usually take girls on, do they? Most girls aren't interested in that anyway; they usually go for office work or journalism or something like that. Young men are better off; they get more opportunities. I think it's more boring for a young girl. They always seem to have jobs in offices and things. (Rick, Sheffield)

Whereas someone else noted that

Women are secretaries, or work in old people's homes, or in clothes shops. (Simon, Sheffield)

A small number, however, thought that young women now had

just the same chance as men really, cos I think there's not a lot of sexism in public jobs as there used to be. It's equal, I think. (Richard, Sheffield)

However, the clear majority of the young men interviewed in both cities had definite views about the suitability and appropriateness of different types of work for young men and young women. In the next chapter I explore whether they are successful in meeting their aspirations and what happens if they do not and are forced to take employment that is inappropriately gender-coded. I had also intended to explore attitudes to race and racism in the labour market but found in the first interviews that this was not possible. While the young men were prepared to talk about racist attitudes and behaviour in their school, it became clear that they had little knowledge of the impact of racism and racial discrimination on the patterns of segregation in the labour market. For this reason I postponed the exploration and analysis of their attitudes about racism in the labour market until a later interview.

Despite the transformation in labour market opportunities in the British economy in the last two decades, almost all the young men whom I interviewed hoped to achieve employment in occupations that have always been regarded as male preserves. Where they do differ significantly from Willis's 'lads', however, is in their recognition that further training might be an essential prerequisite of this employment. It is also clear that the respective schools and the careers service in each city encourages students to think about attempting a vocational qualification, and provides advice and assistance to all year 11 pupils. There is little evidence, however, that the young men to whom I talked are looking for work in the retail sector, in leisure or tourism or the hospitality industry, despite the fact that these have been the fastest growing sectors for less well-educated workers in recent years and also areas where these young men themselves had found temporary part-time employment. Even the single respondent who identified shopwork as a possibility insisted it must be in a sports shop, in keeping with his preconceptions of the acceptable masculine identity associated with sport. As they began to think about employment, these young men had a clear sense of the sorts of jobs that they considered appropriate for men. They expressed no fears about finding a job and had relatively little sense of the extent to which economic restructuring had transformed opportunities for men and women. It was perhaps surprising how little they were aware of the changed economic circumstances that awaited them and they had no sense at all that they might not be able to achieve and maintain the traditional pattern of working class family life in which they were the main breadwinners.

These findings differ from Jordan's (1995) conclusions that young men nowadays are less optimistic about their futures than in previous generations. However, I do concur with the claims in recent studies that versions of a laddish or protest heterosexual masculinity performed in the different spaces in schools – from the classroom to the playground – remains crucial, and is perhaps even more significant and disadvantageous in the face of economic restructuring and the growing dominance of service-sector opportunities for unskilled and poorly qualified school leavers, boys and girls alike. As Kehily and Nayak (1997: 84) noted:

> It may be that in today's economic climate young men are no longer able to attain a recognizable masculinity through manual labour, so are seeking to authenticate this identity in postures of heterosexuality. More research is required to determine the exigency of these claims, although we may speculate on the continuing presence and practice of 'lads' in school, despite changes to the manufacturing base. If they are no longer 'learning to labour' then what exactly are they doing?

On the basis of their study in the West Midlands, the authors (1987: 85) tentatively concluded that

> 'lads' are styling their heterosexual role identities in ways that affirm and consolidate their notions of manhood. It may well be that as long-term manual work declines, in a 'feminized' world of flexible workers and new technologies, male pupils are practising other ways of being 'proper' men that aim to accentuate heterosexuality beyond the emasculating existence of unemployment.

The low-achieving boys in year 11 in Cambridge and Sheffield schools in 1999 undoubtedly exhibited confidence about their sense of themselves as masculine, demonstrating neither ambivalence nor anxiety. Their behaviour in school, however, including truancy and exclusion as well as disruptions in the classroom, failing to do homework and, for many, poor exam performances lower down the school means that they were defined as 'low achievers' and expected to fail. Like many working class boys before them 'having a laff' at school seemed a more immediate goal than getting down to some hard work. Their teachers, parents and the young men themselves expected them to leave school at the end of the period of compulsory education and most of them were planning either to seek employment or some combination of work and training. In preparation for this, most of these boys had been involved in some form of work experience while at school as well as, especially in Sheffield, attending vocational training courses in, for example, painting and decorating, and horticulture. What they were not equipped with were the personal and academic skills necessary to attain any sort of job with a reasonable expectation of security, reasonable wages or career progression.

In the polarized new service economy, these young men were about to leave school without any of the skills necessary to gain access to high-tech work. The high-touch, servicing sector seemed to be their main option but even here they had received little guidance about the sort of personal performance and management of emotions that are essential attributes of these jobs. Instead, they were in the main a group of poorly educated, energetic, aggressive and belligerent young men, apparently with little to offer to service-sector employers. But, on the verge of leaving school, these young men themselves were optimistic, experiencing no doubts that they would be able to find work consistent with their view of themselves as men and as workers and, in the longer run, as breadwinners and family providers. However, as the next chapters will show, as they moved into the job market their aspirations to seek and secure employment in male-dominated occupations were challenged by the realities of the dominance of low-status service work for young men unprepared to undertake further education or, in some cases, even to train 'on the job'. In the initial interviews, when the young men were still at school, the extent of the similarities of the lives and views of boys in each city was striking. However, in their transition from school into the labour market, important differences between the two cities started to emerge. These differences are the focus of chapter 5 where life after leaving school is the subject. In chapters 6 and 7, case studies of different pathways to employment are presented.

5

Leaving School: Pathways to Employment and Further Education

Unlike some other cultures, there are no initiation rites which mark the entry into adulthood; in our society the status of adulthood is partly ascribed and partly achieved. (Allatt and Yeandle 1992: 61)

Entry into the paid workforce marks the transition from childhood to adulthood. (Beder 2000: 124)

To become a fully functional adult male, one prerequisite is essential: a job. (US President's Commission Report, *The Challenge of Crime in a Free Society*, 1964)

In this and the following two chapters the decisions made by the 24 young men in the months after they finished school are the focus. Through a series of case studies, as well as an analysis of the choices of the entire group, I want to show the ways in which the relationships between the preferences and decisions of these 16-year-olds, their local contacts through family and friends and the structure of opportunities both in the immediate locality and in each of the two cities resulted in a series of specific pathways. As Hodkinson, Sparkes and Hodkinson (1996: 149) in an earlier study of post-school transitions suggested, 'young people make career decisions within their horizons for action, which incorporate externally located opportunities in the labour market as well as the dispositions of habitus'. As I argued in the preceding chapter, these young men were leaving school labelled as failures, relatively uninformed about the changing circumstances in the labour market and yet confident that they would be able to find employment. Their horizons are relatively limited, both spatially and temporally and as the case studies will show, their decisions are based on immediate considerations of what is available in the short term and in the locality. Their knowledge about alternative options and their confidence to explore them are limited. Almost all of their parents also left school as soon as possible and only three of them live in families with any first-hand experience of further education. Furthermore, as neither of the two schools took students over the age of 16, the choice of continuing education entailed a positive decision to apply to another school or to a sixth form or further education college. But even so, despite these commonalities in their position, a distinctive set of transitions is identifiable as differences in individual dispositions and identities between these young men, in their material circumstances as well as the differences in local circumstances between the two cities, combine to construct a set of differential pathways.

Based on the narrative reconstructions of their decisions, I have distinguished six particular ways in which these young men made the transitions from compulsory schooling over the first 12 months from leaving school. The first three of these patterns – discussed in the following chapter – I have termed the 'committed worker', the 'reluctant learner/committed worker' and the 'accidental worker': in all three cases, however, for the young men launched on these pathways, continuous employment is their aim and their sense of self-identity is as a worker rather than as a student or an identity constructed in the sphere of consumption rather than production. In chapter 7, three alternative paths are explored where employment is either not the main aim or turns out to be unachievable. In some senses the young men who follow this second set of routes may be regarded as failures compared with their peers, whose decisions are analysed in chapter 6. I have labelled the second set of transitions the incidental worker, the excluded worker and the escape route. Whatever their pathways and decisions, however, the destinations of almost all of the 24 young men turned out to be in insecure, precarious and low-wage service-sector jobs. For these young men, leaving school did not presage the start of a promising working life or the route into higher education, like a growing proportion of their peers. Instead, these young men might be defined as the 'careerless' – most of them probably will move from job to job on the bottom rungs of the labour market for the majority of their working lives. Their family backgrounds and the limited educational capital they acquired through their schooling means that they enter the labour market at a considerable disadvantage.

> By the time that young people leave school they have built up stocks of different types and amounts of capital. Some have economic capital – savings and investments usually made on their behalf, or prospects of inheritance from other family members. However, there are equally important social and cultural types of capital. These consist of social relations (contacts and connections with influential people), qualifications, attitudes and values, behaviour and speech patterns. All these assets can influence individuals' prospects when they enter the labour market. But young people usually need to convert their capital, whatever this might be, into specific occupational attainments, in order to obtain the best possible returns during their adult lives. (Roberts 1995: 2–3)

Working class boys from a tough part of town, expecting poor GCSE results, have little to offer other than their youth in exchange for this acquisition of 'specific occupational attainments'. And yet, as I shall show, especially among the boys who showed great energy and determination in acquiring and holding on to jobs, and to a certain degree among that group who combined employment with further education and training, these young men were optimistic about their future employment prospects. Before analysing these pathways, however, I want to lay out the overall pattern of post-school destinations for all the young men and explore the differences that became evident between Cambridge and Sheffield.

Making Choices: The Diversity of Post-school Transitions

As I demonstrated in the previous chapter, when they were at school these young men had clear views of the type of job that they hoped to achieve based on their assumptions about the ways in which gender structures the labour market and on what sorts of jobs are appropriate for young men. Whether they lived in the long-established service-dominated city of Cambridge or the deindustrialized city of Sheffield, these young men hoped to secure 'masculine' jobs, despite the fact that many of them had worked in a range of service-sector jobs while they were still at school. The jobs that students in both cities identified, then, included the car industry, the building trade and, in Sheffield, the steel industry. By the time of the second set of interviews, carried out over the winter months of 1999–2000, all but one of the 24 young men had successfully begun work, started a college course or, in many cases, were combining further study with some form of waged work. For two of them, however, both living in Cambridge, the job they had taken was seen as a means of filling in time rather than the real start of their working life. In tables 5.1 and 5.2,

Table 5.1 Post-school transitions in Cambridge: employment and educational trajectories in a 12-month period after leaving school

Name	GCSE results	July 1999–Dec. 2000	Jan.–June 2000
Andrew	2Bs, 1C, 1D, 2Es	Kitchen porter	Supermarket checkout
Chris	2Ds, 2Es and 1F	Apprentice car mechanic with day release at local college	Same course
Daniel	1C, rest Es and Fs	IT course at FE college Part-time work at retail office suppliers	Same course
Damian	1C, 3Ds	Mechanics NVQ at FE college; part-time work at Post Office parcels	Still at college and the Post Office
Guy	A few Fs	Security work	Assistant in a dry-cleaners
John	All at E or F	Part-time playgroup assistant	Prince's Trust course
Kurt	1E, 4Fs, 1G	Art Foundation, IT and a GCSE in leisure and tourism; part-time in café in local store	Same course and part-time job
Lee	1A*, 4Bs, 1C	Mainly unemployed till Jan.; casual work in restaurant	Modern apprenticeship: web-page design NVQ
Michael	2Ds, 6Es, 2Fs	Started NVQ in health and social care at FE college; evening job, cleaning	Still at college; same evening job
Wayne	1D, 4Es, 2Fs	Modern apprenticeship with block release, construction industry	Same course

Note: only grades at C and above are regarded as 'good' and are the usual standard required by many employers. Five or more 'good' passes is the usual requirement for continuing with further education, whether on a 'vocational' or an 'academic' route.

Table 5.2 Post-school transitions in Sheffield: employment and educational trajectories in a 12-month period after leaving school

Name	GCSE results	July 1999–Dec. 2000	Jan.–June 2000
Craig	2Es	FE College, Art and Design; left after 10 weeks, found work cutting wood to make pallets	March, left work, back to college; left again almost immed.; Athena kitchen units; laid off early June; went to Employment Tribunal; awarded a week's redundancy pay; looking for work
Darren	Left school at Easter, no exams	Aigg Plant, waste extraction from building sites; laid off Dec.; unemployed for two weeks	Trainee laminator from early Jan.
Gareth	1B, 3Cs, 4Ds, Es	Warehouse: packing leaflets for inserts in newspapers (only 25 hrs a week guaranteed)	Still in warehouse; pay rise from £4 to £4.75; same hours
Greg	3Bs, 4Cs, 2Ds	Started college – A and D; left in Oct.; new course (drama – different college); left end of Nov.; unemployed; mid-Dec. started at McDonald's	Still at McDonald's
Kevin.	No exams taken	Suicide July 1999	
Matt	Es and Fs	Sheaf Training placement: groundsman, Sheffield Wednesday, plus day release	Still at Sheffield Wednesday
Paul	8Ds and below	Unemployed until Nov.; then retail assistant; Sports Soccer	Promoted to stock delivery supervisor
Pauly	2Cs, some Ds, Es	YTS as trainee footballer	Moved and lost contact (left Rotherham FC as not good enough)
Richard	2Es and 2Fs	June/July Sports Soccer; Burtons two days; from July, McDonald's	Still at McDonald's; started NVQ based at work

Table 5.2   (*Continued*)

Name	GCSE results	July 1999–Dec. 2000	Jan.–June 2000
Rick	1B, 4Ds, 4Es	Apprenticeship in metal-cutting firm; left in Sept. as too boring and no training; late Sept. to McDonald's	McDonald's till March (applied to army – turned down); started two-year apprenticeship as sawman at a steelworks
Shaun	Entered 2, failed both	Sheaf Training placement in garden centre, day release; resigned in Jan.	From Feb. SYTG[1] placement: forklift driving; day release: NVQ in warehousing
Simon	5Ds and Es	Sheet-metal worker, left in Dec. as no training offered	Unemployed till April; wood-cutting for Athena kitchen units
Steve	5Cs, 4Ds	Apprenticeship with Vauxhall; block release: Vauxhall College in Nottingham; NVQ to level 3	Still in apprenticeship
Vince	none (not entered)	SYTG placement: Netto supermarket; sacked in Oct.	Unemployed, started life skills course in Jan. Left home and no contact from April.

the examination results and the employment position of the young men in each city at the time of the second and third interviews is summarized.

Over the hump or bridging the divide

As I argued in chapter 2, one of the most significant differences in contemporary labour markets is no longer the old distinction between blue and white collar work but rather a broad divide between generic and specialized labour. Generic labour, whether manual or clerical, includes those who more or less have no specialized qualifications, whereas specialized labour consists of the 'credentialled', those with qualifications that make them eligible to enter specific trades: the semi-professions or the professions. The education system is, of course, deeply implicated in the establishment and surveillance of this divide, and post-compulsory qualifications are the key mechanism for getting 'over the hump' (Connell 2000: 133) between the two labour markets. What is unclear in Britain is how effective vocational qualifications are as a mechanism for bridging the divide, given the long dominance of the more highly valued academic A level qualifications, which remain the 'gold-standard' in the 16–19 education system despite persistent attempts by the governments of the day to challenge this dominance and establish the validity of national vocational qualifications (NVQs).

What is immediately apparent from a comparison of the two tables is the difference between the two cities in the young men's propensity to consider gaining higher level credentials. It seems as if most of the Sheffield group have disqualified themselves from the specialized labour market before they even begin their working lives, whereas the Cambridge group might have taken a first step towards it. In Cambridge all but three of the ten young men were combining employment with some form of study or employment-related training at the time of the final interview, whereas in Sheffield only one interviewee – Steve – was in a similar position, in an apprenticeship with Vauxhall that included block release at college. One other man, Rich, was taking a vocational qualification (a GNVQ) while he was employed at McDonald's, and Matthew had a day a week at college as part of his training as a groundsman. As table 5.1 shows, however, all of the Cambridge college attendees, were also employed on a variety of part-time bases, despite being registered as full-time students. As full-time attendance is officially defined as 15 or more hours at college, this leaves plenty of scope for part-time work. Thus they were working variously in the Post Office sorting office, at an office supply retailers, in the restaurant of a local department store and office cleaning in the evenings – in many cases continuing the job, although usually expanding the hours, that they had held when they were still at school.

Research based on large-scale data analysis has shown, unsurprisingly given conventional college entry requirements, that the main predictor of staying on in full-time further education after the age of compulsory attendance is performance in GCSE examinations, especially the achievement of grades between A* and C, although membership of an intact nuclear family and a degree of familial support is also important. Those with D–G grades are more likely to move straight into the labour market (Payne 1995; Robinson 1998; Stafford, Heaver, Ashworth et al. 1999; Steedman and Green 1996). With the exception of Lee, however, the exam results achieved by the school leavers in Cambridge were not noticeably better than those achieved in Sheffield, although nobody in the Cambridge group actually failed to sit any exams at all. But, whatever their examination results, the ten young men in Cambridge were far more likely by September in the year that they left school to be attending a further education college or to be planning to do so than those in Sheffield. As table 5.1 shows, six of the ten young men in Cambridge had started to attend college in late autumn of 1999, and two of the other four had plans to do so in the relatively immediate future. At the third interview, all the respondents who had started a course were still enrolled. In Sheffield, by comparison, despite stated intentions, at the time of the third interview (table 5.2), almost all of the young men were in the labour market. What is also apparent from these tables is the extent to which the Sheffield sample had experienced change over the year. Several of them had had more than one job, sometimes because of redundancy (Craig, Simon and Darren), because they were sacked (Vince) or because boredom, low pay and/or poor conditions had led them to look elsewhere. From what they told me, it seems that the lack of a local tradition of education in Sheffield, combined with a then ready availability of entry-level jobs, led the young men to assume that job mobility was the main route to attaining better conditions. However, the jobs that they started tended to be precarious, often casual and with little security and no job-related benefits. None of the young men in Sheffield, except for Steve at Vauxhalls and eventually Rick in his third job, had an employment contract or entitlement to holiday leave or pay and, in most cases, they worked 'flexible' hours, which were often less than full-time. Indeed, given their age – they were only 17 at the time of the third interview – they had already gained a surprising amount of experience of the worst aspects of 'poor' work.

In Cambridge, by contrast, despite a booming local labour market and a significantly lower level of unemployment than in Sheffield, the young men whom I interviewed were conscious of the significance of 'getting qualified' in a labour market in which any but the most menial of jobs required some post-school educational credentials. It is here that perhaps there is evidence of the significance of the local in definitions of success. It may be that the social and cultural differences between the two cities, the ways in which these interact with wider educational constraints, including local budgets, and with local and national definitions of academic success and academic expectations affect the choices made by school leavers. The history and significance of education in a city such as Cambridge perhaps acts as a positive spur to young men like these ten, but may also encourage local colleges to accept 'low achievers'. The level of participation in post-16 education in the city is far higher than the national average and there is also intense competition between the three main college providers of post-16 education. Whereas most A level students attend one of the two sixth form colleges in the south of the city, the Cambridge Regional College in the north aggressively competes for lower-level students and for students registering for vocational qualifications. While few of the Cambridge leavers had decent grades (only one of those going straight to college had a C grade in English, and one had a C in Maths; the others had D–F grades, rather low for entry to further education), they had all been accepted by this college. Strong recruitment campaigns, combined with reducing the grades for entry, seemed to be successful in raising post-compulsory rates of participation in education in Cambridge, which, as I noted in chapter 4, are 10 per cent higher than the national average and almost 20 per cent higher than in Sheffield.

This marked regional disparity, reflecting the persistent North–South division in educational attainment at all levels, is inevitably evident in the comparison between the Park Edge and Fenland school leavers. However, it was also noticeable that in this city all but four of the parents allowed their sons to continue to live at home rent-free, whereas the young men in Sheffield were far more likely to be paying rent to their parents and, in most cases, at a higher level. It may be that the booming local labour market in Cambridge partly explains this discrepancy, as the mothers of the young men in Cambridge were, without exception, also employed, whereas only half of the Sheffield mothers were, and so average family incomes were somewhat higher, even though most fathers were in low-paid manual work in both cities. Even in Cambridge, however, several young men specifically mentioned either the cost of their course or the fact that parents had to help them out as a reason for thinking twice about attendance.

While educational traditions differed in the cities, there was a clear similarity in the significance of local social capital in gaining access to employment. In both cities local contacts were the most important method of finding work, whether combined with study or not. In both cities, most of the young men had obtained their jobs either through a family member or friend 'speaking for them' or simply by asking around their neighbourhood. In Cambridge, Damian and John worked with one of their parents: 'My dad's at the Post Office too and he got me took on' (Damian) and 'Mum runs this play scheme, so I started by helping her out' (John). Kurt had found his part-time job through a friend of his mother: 'She gave me mum a ring when there was a vacancy is the kitchen. It were only washing up at first but now I'm serving and doing the tables, which is better.' And Michael, through his friend's father: 'His dad's been cleaning there for ages, so he got me and my friend a job.' Guy had relied on his father to offer him work as a security guard when he was still at school, and when, as he often did, he found himself 'between jobs', he was able to fall back on his father, at least until he was declared bankrupt. Lee and Andrew, who both had temporary catering jobs at the time of the second interview, had simply walked around the locality asking in cafés and restaurants, although both hated their work: 'It's really horrible,' said Andrew, who was a kitchen porter, and 'it's mindless as well as hard work' (Lee) and they had both resigned by the third interview, Lee to start an IT apprenticeship and Andrew to take another temporary job, this time in a supermarket.

Personal contacts and local knowledge were also significant in Sheffield. Darren worked with his older brother in the crushing plant, Simon (in his first job) and Gareth worked with friends of their fathers, and Simon (after being made redundant) with his friend Craig, had simply walked round the street nearest to home, and both of them were taken on at Athena. In Sheffield, however, two other methods of finding work were important: training agencies and advertising. Three of the young men (Shaun, Matt and Vince), who were among the lowest achievers, had been found placements with local employers; indeed, Shaun had been placed in two different jobs. Finally, a number of the Sheffield interviewees told me that they kept an eye on the recruitment advertisements in the large shopping centre, Meadow Hall, only a short bus ride from their homes. Over the year, four of the group had found work this way – Greg, Rich and Rick at McDonald's, and Paul at Sports Soccer (a chain store selling relatively low-priced sports clothing and shoes). In all cases, however, local contacts and personal knowledge were the key way of gaining employment, which results in the reproduction of patterns of disadvantage for working class children. The economic and social capital on which middle class school leavers are able to draw to facilitate their transition into higher education and high-status employment is not available to these young men.

Masculinity at Work: Everyday Working Lives and Attitudes

Despite the differences in these post-school transitions, however, especially the greater variation and experience of precarious work among the Sheffield youths, the everyday lives and attitudes of the young men in Cambridge and Sheffield were remarkably similar. It was here that my tentative ideas about how the 'crisis of masculinity' might play out in their lives were found wanting. Almost to a man, they disputed the notion that young men were relatively disadvantaged in the labour market, compared either to their fathers at the same age or to working class young women of their age. Whether combining work with study or not, almost all of the men in both cities found themselves in environments dominated by men. In the main they worked with men, studied with men and had male friends. In this context, expressed anxieties about the status of masculinity were uncommon. It was noticeable too that they all emphasized the working part of their lives in constructing a sense of themselves as masculine. In Cambridge it was employment, rather than college, that loomed large in their lives and the ten talked more openly and at greater length about their current work or their job aspirations than about college life. Clearly, college attendance was seen as a means to an end rather than an end in itself. In addition, all the young men in both cities (with the exception of Vince, who ran away from his foster home, and Kevin) still lived in their parental homes a year after leaving school. To a greater or lesser degree, they maintained the patterns of familial dependence, and masculine friendship groups developed during their school lives.

In the course of the interviews, I explored in detail the ways in which these young men thought about themselves, about masculinity in general and about gender in the workplace as they left school and moved into employment. As tables 5.1 and 5.2 demonstrate, a proportion of them started their working lives in the service sector, especially in the retail and hospitality trades, holding down jobs that were open to both young men and young women, although it is also noticeable that a number of the young men in both cities had started in 'masculine' jobs: in the car industry, in building work and joinery, in the steel industry in Sheffield. As previous studies of the service sector have shown, however, some service-sector occupations permit the holders of jobs to talk about their work in ways that map on to their own sense of themselves as masculine or feminine (Henson and Rogers 2001; Hochschild 1983; Leidner 1993). Men tend to emphasize the heroic struggle necessary to overcome consumer resistance in selling occupations, or the camaraderie of the long hours/hard work culture of the burger bar, whereas women tend to emphasize personal interrelations, empathy and the emotional exchange between sales assistant and customer. In addition, gendered characteristics are often attributed to retail outlets themselves. Working in a sports shop or an electronic goods boutique, for example, is seen as appropriately masculine, compared to, say, employment in a general clothing store. Thus Paul, working in Sports Soccer in Sheffield, said, 'it's all right for a lad'. He told me how his employer insisted that the staff kept in reasonable shape (or at least looked as if they did) and had to wear items from their current stock as a uniform: 'he [the manager] thinks we have to look the part, like, sort of sporty'. As Leslie (2002: 61) has noted, 'fashion retailing demands particular attention to performance and the body that is not manifest to the same degree in other areas of retailing.

Most employees are expected to wear the product they sell on their body'. This type of 'identity work' in which there is a fusion of self-image and employment is often regarded as a typical part of the 'new' economy. While usually precarious and low waged, it may in some cases such as hairdressing or perhaps modelling lead to a glamorous future. In the retail sector such opportunities are much more limited, although Paul told me that there was scope for promotion within Sports Soccer. However, despite this and the perceived congruence of selling sportswear and an acceptable masculine identity, Paul was planning to leave the service economy in search of a more traditional position in the steel industry. He told me that he hoped to move to Tinsley Wire (a branch of the Anglo-Dutch steel corporation Corus), where his father and older brother were already employed, when he was 18. 'It's higher pay' and, in Paul's eyes, 'better work for a man'. He was never to make the move, however, as, it was announced in July 2000 that the plant would be closed within a year.

Working for McDonald's – as three of the Sheffield group did or had done – is more ambivalent in terms of gender and status. Counter staff are generally both sexes, very young and often members of minority groups. Thus in Sheffield the co-workers of the three young men who had been or were working at McDonald's included Somalis and an Italian, as well as Sheffield-born Asian youths. Richard, whose working life and attitudes are explored in more detail in the next chapter, was the longest-term and most committed employee of the three young men who worked there. Although he is positive about the opportunities for advancement offered by McDonald's, working in the fast-food industry is more widely regarded as among the most exploited form of employment in industrial economies (Schlosser 2001). Indeed, the derogatory term 'McJobs' is often used generically to characterize entry-level jobs that are casual, poorly paid, often involving shifts and/or long hours, with few benefits and opportunities for promotion and with high turnover rates. And yet, as Katherine Newman (1999) in her detailed ethnographic study of a fast-food outlet in New York City has powerfully argued, even McJobs provide workers with a range of values and skills. Regular attendance, dealing with customers and with cash, are all valuable labour market attributes that are inculcated by entry-level employment, but which are widely undervalued and underestimated. Many of the worst bottom-end jobs, which poorly educated youth end up in, often require speed, memory, manual dexterity, social skills, co-operation and persistence, cleanliness and reliability in adapting to the workplace regime, and punctuality and adaptability in shift work, with different daily starting hours. As another of the McDonald's employees in Sheffield noted, 'it's not an easy job actually, you are on your feet all day and its very quick and tiring' (Rick).

Both Greg and Richard, who were still working at McDonald's in June 2000, intended at least in the short term to stay, and both of them will feature again in the next chapter. Greg was much less enthusiastic than Richard: 'yeah, I'll stick at it but it's tiring, and there's no prospects'. Richard did see opportunities for promotion and he told me that 'I'll try and make a career of it, you know what I mean', although he paused and then added, 'but I don't know if I am definite'. His determination and hard work, however, had been recognized by McDonald's. At the time of the third interview, his wages had increased and he had become a member of the training squad in his branch, as well as continuing with his NVQ. But Rick, who had done a five-month stint at McDonald's between metalworking jobs, said that although 'it is an easy job to get and decent money', jobs there are 'not permanent; it's just for young ones, like'. For all three of them, however, the work at McDonald's did not challenge their sense of themselves as masculine – the work was fast and tiring but it also provided plenty of opportunities for them to 'have a good laugh' with co-workers, to 'mess around' and 'joke about' to pass the time and relieve the boredom, and it also provided opportunities to make new friends. In this sense, unworried about getting another job and content to have a laugh, perhaps employment for school leavers in the late 1990s was not so different from the experience of Willis's 'lads' 25 years earlier. Certainly, in Sheffield most of the young men to whom I talked saw few problems with employment mobility and were prepared to try a range of types of work without feeling anxious about their prospects.

For the young men employed outside the retail and food sectors, there was no conflict between their work and their gender identity. Most of them were engaged in essentially masculine tasks – heavy digging and lifting, sawing wood and mending engines – regarded as 'men's work' and which, as I noted above, were undertaken predominantly in the company of men. When I enquired about the absence of women among their co-workers, the responses included 'It's not really a woman's job, is it, working in a garden?' a view confirmed when this young man moved jobs later in the year to find that in his new position 'It's all men on the factory floor; women work upstairs in the offices' (Shaun, Sheffield). Other responses included 'no, there's only men here', 'no, there's no women at all; I'm not sure why' and 'it's just not women's work' in the kitchen unit manufacturers, the laminating firm, and the garages in Cambridge and Sheffield. A sense of the masculine camaraderie among workers in these places was reinforced by, for example, common lunch-time activities. Thus, two of the full-time workers in Sheffield reported that 'We just go to the chippy, come back and play cards or play a game of snooker, pool or that' (Greg) and 'You get about an hour break at dinner time. We play darts, cards, all sorts of stuff' (Darren). Even among the young men who went to college on a regular basis, lunchtime activities were usually shared with a group of male friends: 'A bunch of lads plays pool at lunchtime; we've got about six pool tables and loads of arcades and that [at college], or I go for a drive now me mate has passed his test' (Kurt, Cambridge). By the third interview, only one of the students in Cambridge – Michael – had predominantly female colleagues on the childcare course he was taking, and he had adopted the typical male role of the course spokesman: 'I'm the class rep. And I've just become President of the site that I go to. I like to represent people. I like to get done things that need doing.' In the evening, he did an office-cleaning job, cleaning mainly commercial premises in the company of his (male) friend and the friend's father who got the job for both the youths. Thus, even though cleaning is often seen as 'women's work', in this case, where men are cleaning commercial premises, Michael was able to interpret his work as unsuitable for women and so appropriately 'manly': 'The work's too heavy for women. The industrial vacuum cleaners are really heavy and it's also got to be done pretty fast'.

Conclusions

It is clear, therefore, that in the first year after leaving school, most of the young men had established themselves either in employment or a mix-ture of work and study. For them, the notion of a sea change in the labour market, and a concomitant reduction in the opportunities and prospects for young men like them who had left school at 16, had little resonance with their daily lives. Although all of them were poorly paid, earning less than or just about the basic minimum wage (at the time just under £4 an hour for 18- to 21-year-olds; 16- and 17-year-old employees are exempt from the provisions of the Minimum Wage Act, as I noted in chapter 3), and often working less than a full-time week of 38 hours, compared to the year before, they felt relatively affluent and content with their position. Only one of them expressed regret about not having worked harder at school but, even so, he was adamant that he would never go back to studying and taking exams. In Cambridge the young men recognized that compared with their fathers' generation, credentials were now more important. They believed that their decision to combine work with study would mean that they would get good jobs in the future. Like the young men interviewed by Trefor Lloyd (1999), they made a clear distinction between 'career' jobs in an office or a trade, and 'crap' jobs in shops, fast-food outlets, shelf-filling and so on, accepting that college attendance was the prerequisite of gaining a foot on the ladder leading to a career. However, almost of all of them were registered for basic-level qualifications, which may not bring the anticipated employment benefits. As one young man in Sheffield who had given up college said, 'An NVQ's not worth the paper it's written on' (Simon). In comparison to most of the Cambridge ten, the young men in Sheffield were more confident that even low-level entry jobs would eventually lead to something better.

In general the young men to whom I talked were unaware of or untroubled by reports of a growing gender gap or growing opportunities for young women in the labour market. While some of them did consider that young women had a better chance of getting a job than young men had, they clearly did not attribute girls' success to economic restructuring. Instead, it was commonly suggested that 'girls, they just go for the target and they just do it' (Paul Sheffield), while others thought, 'girls have got a better chance', but 'I dunno why' (Kurt, Cambridge).

> Well, a girl can get a job anywhere can't she? They can get dressed up and look older than they are. They can do waitering and that, hairdressing, all sorts of things. (Wayne, Cambridge)

But just as many young men disagreed with this view, even though they had a similar view of the range of options open to women.

> I think men have got more choice. I think women do a lot of hairdressing and receptionist and all that stuff, office work more, they don't have...I mean they could go in the army but many of them don't want that lifestyle, do they? (Rick, Sheffield)

This chapter has presented the overall outlines of the general picture of life for these young men in the first year after leaving school. Despite the greater propensity of Cambridge school leavers to consider forms of further education, it is evident that all the young men, without exception, regarded employment rather than further education as the legitimate route to adulthood. However, a more detailed reading of their interview transcripts revealed important differences in their attitudes and dispositions toward employment and in the degree to which they actively sought work. In the next two chapters, therefore, I explore in greater detail the types of decisions made by particular young men, distinguishing six different routes into and orientations towards the labour market. While some of the young men took steps to find specific types of work, others seemed to 'fall into' jobs, and yet others regarded their work merely as the means to an end: usually to ensure that they earned sufficient money to enjoy an active social life. Another group, mainly the less-able young men among the group, found themselves excluded from mainstream employment; whereas a final group placed their hopes in the traditional escape routes for working class boys – the army and sport – in a search for material success. Through the words of the young men themselves, these differences are explored in succeeding chapters.

6

Actively Seeking Employment: Committed Workers and Reluctant Learners

[The] value [of waged work] is judged by its capacity to generate pleasurable experience. Work devoid of such capacity – that does not offer 'intrinsic satisfaction' – is also work devoid of value. (Bauman 1998: 32)

This chapter tells the stories of those young men whose primary orientation is to the labour market but who are differentiated by their choices and their approach to work. Three groups of young men will be considered here. The first of these groups consists of those school leavers who were fortunate enough to be able to combine participation in traditional masculine forms of employment with job-related training and who expressed a great deal of satisfaction with their choices. While their employment might not have generated pleasure, at least it endowed its participants with the acceptable attributes of masculinity, associated with hard manual labour. The second group was a less privileged group of young men, imbued with traditional working class ideals about the value of hard work but who found themselves buffeted by the uncertainties of labour market change and more likely to be confined to finding work in the service sector. The final group I have designated 'reluctant learners/committed workers', whose orientations to both work and study were instrumental. While the first and third groups include school leavers from both cities, the second group is composed only of Park Edge leavers. As chapter 5 has demonstrated, one of the most obvious differences between the two groups of young men is the greater propensity for

Cambridge school leavers to consider further education, and this is reflected in the differential choices and patterns explored here. The Sheffield leavers were both more likely to go straight into employment and also during their first year in the labour market to move between entry-level jobs. Despite their mobility, however, and the instability and unpredictability of their transition, it was clear that a number of them were committed workers, keen to find a suitable job, prepared to work hard to keep it and if necessary to fight against what they perceived as unfair treatment. The young men in the first two groups – Steve, Richard and Darren from Sheffield, and Damian and Wayne in Cambridge – all took positive steps to find appropriate work, which they hoped would lead to advancement. They are differentiated, however, in that for three of them – Steve, Damian and Wayne – their choices involved the construction of something approaching a career path, usually initiated in the final months at school; whereas the commitment of Richard and Darren, and of several other young men from Sheffield, Simon and Craig among them, was to employment *per se* rather than to a specific job or occupation. The final group of young men to be considered here are that subset of youths in the main from Cambridge, but also including Greg from Sheffield, albeit for a rather short period of time, who somewhat reluctantly decided to attend college, hoping for more medium-term payoffs, but who, in the meantime, continue as committed, albeit part-time, employees in the local labour market.

Committed Workers 1: Masculine Work and Training – Steve, Wayne and Damian

What unites Steve, Wayne and Damian was their expressed determination while they were still at school to find work in an appropriately manly occupation: 'I didn't want a shop or owt like that' (Steve). 'It had to be a real job, like, you know what I mean?' (Wayne) and so they looked opportunities in areas such as motor mechanics and the construction industry. A year after leaving school, all three of the them had found work that they were committed to in traditionally male-dominated sectors and they were also all participating in some form of vocational training to improve their prospects. The routes that led them there, however, were varied and involved different negotiations and sets of contingencies. While Steve in Sheffield and Damian in Cambridge took what seemed to be rational steps to fulfil choices made while they were still at school, for Wayne the route to his current employment was more contingent. While all three boys grew up on local authority estates in working class areas of the respective cities, Steve had a parent in a lower middle class occupation: his father was an unqualified surveyor working for the local authority, whereas Damian and Wayne grew up in working class households. Damian's father had been a lorry driver who had recently moved to work for the Post Office parcels and his mother was a care assistant, while Wayne's father worked as an industrial cleaner and his mother as a hairdresser. For Steve advice from home and from the career's service, while he was still at school, led to a decision to seek a place as a modern apprentice: a scheme then recently introduced by the Government to provide combined work and training for industrial jobs for school leavers. The aim of the scheme is to boost the country's productivity with a more highly skilled workforce. However, the targets set for numbers of modern apprenticeships have proved difficult to meet, despite continuous revamping of the scheme and there has been some criticism of the quality of training provided by some of the employers who are participants in the scheme.

Despite his desire to find work that was congruent with his developing sense of himself as a male worker, Steve applied for three different schemes in different sectors, with Initial Security, Vauxhall and as a trainee with the local council. After an interview with the first two in late spring 1999, he was delighted to accept the offer from Vauxhall to train as a car mechanic: the most traditionally masculine job among the three schemes he had applied for. He started work in June 1999 before receiving his GCSE exam results and although he did not do as well as he had expected (his mother had suddenly and unexpectedly left the family in February that year and Steve was clearly badly affected), his position was confirmed in August. The apprenticeship involved periods of employment interspersed with block release for training. In Sheffield Steve was attached to a workshop, as an apprentice to a qualified mechanic, and four times a year over three years he was to undertake periods of two weeks studying at a Vauxhall-run college in Nottingham in order to gain level 3 qualifications in the NVQ series: the equivalent of two passes at A level. His preference, however, lay in the practical work in the workshop and although he enjoyed the periods of block release socially, he found he was struggling with the course work involved. 'It's hard work, like. The theory side. I prefer it back at the workshop.'

Wayne too, a Fenland student, had embarked on a similar scheme after school: in his case a modern apprenticeship in the building trade in which the training component was organized weekly instead of in a block. In his first year as an apprentice, Wayne spent two days a week at college and three days working for a local building firm. His route to an apprenticeship, however, was more by chance than Steve's. He had intended to go straight out to work on a full-time basis but when he was looking for work in the neighbourhood in Cambridge, during the summer after leaving school, he had happened to call into the Careers Guidance Service, where an advisor suggested that he consider an apprenticeship. His mother encouraged him to take this option: 'I asked me mum and she said, "Yes, that's all right," cos if I go to college me mum still gets benefits or something; child benefits I think? So she wouldn't be out of pocket and she even said she'd help me a bit, if I needed it.'

When I talked to him in late October, Wayne was struggling, although he was determined to keep going. Like Steve, he found it was his college work that was the problem: 'It's the college stuff. I'd rather be at work doing more practical things, you know. At college I don't like the writing side of it.' This confirms the anxiety expressed by the Association of Learning Providers (the umbrella body for private and not-for-profit training organizations) who in 2002 warned against proposals to make vocational qualifications more similar to conventional educational credentials by increasing the college component. As the association noted, the number of apprenticeships had fallen between 1999 and 2000 when Wayne and Steve started, and in 2001/2 action was needed to counter what was identified as 'antipathy and apathy among youngsters'. It was suggested that 'campaigns which appeal to a young person's esteem amongst peers: for example stressing that an apprenticeship means a job and earning money as well as learning new skills' should be introduced (Tester 2002). That an apprenticeship was not only a route to work, but was a form of employment in itself was certainly what appealed to both Steve and Wayne. They were both determined to stick with the scheme despite finding the college attendance difficult and they were both proud to be settled into an occupational path. As Wayne said, 'I'm sorted now. I really am. I mean at school I used to muck about, I fought a lot and I didn't never do no work, but now I am out at work and I know what I am doing is all right.' Even so, there were plenty of opportunities for 'mucking about' in different ways when he was out on the building sites. Wayne reported a series of typically sexist encounters between the 'public', himself and his co-workers, best exemplified by a period working at a girls' school where Wayne told me he successfully arranged a series of assignations with some of the older girls. 'They were great. I even got some presents when we finished the job.'

Like Steve and Wayne, Damian had also decided on a typical masculine occupation during his final year at school. He too wanted to be a car mechanic – 'I've always been into cars and I've always been better with my hands' – but was not aware of the modern apprenticeship schemes. Instead, he signed on at the local further education college to study for a vocational certificate. Although the course was classified as full time, the required attendance was only 15 hours, spread over two and a half days and so Damian was able to work during the rest of the week. Ideally he had hoped to find employment in a garage but during the first 12 months after leaving school he had not been successful: 'most garages want you full time, or not at all'. Instead, he was working at the Post Office, for Parcelforce, a position his father had helped him secure by 'speaking for him' in his own workplace and, as noted in chapter 4, it was a job that Damian had been doing when he was still at school. But Damian kept looking for work as a mechanic and felt confident that he would find something.

All these three young men in this category felt that they were fortunate: they had decided on a type of work that they thought was appropriate and had managed to secure a mixture of training and employment that they assumed would lead to what, in their eyes, would be a good job in the future. The work suited them; it was practical and skill-based and, above all, it was the sort of work that they felt young men of their age and class background should be doing. For them their identity was bound up with 'getting a job, getting on with life, being a good worker you know' (Steve). Their optimism and persistence, while admirable, is, however, unlikely to lead to secure or well-paid employment with an opportunity for social mobility, although they may be lucky in finding relatively permanent work. Vauxhall, for example, has recently cut jobs and apprenticeships and the building trade is notoriously cyclical as well as a demanding job as men get older. As other studies of working class young men have noted, what these young men were engaged in was

> constructing a subjective career strategy, socializing themselves into becoming labourers – one kind of male working class career. In terms of the occupational hierarchy, these lads were ultimately going into dead end jobs, not open ended careers. (Banks, Bates, Breakwell et al. 1992: 88)

For the present, however, these young men were optimistic and enjoying their new opportunities. Their commitment to work and training did not preclude an active social life. Indeed, Steve told me that the best part of his time in Nottingham was the opportunity to go out: 'there's a good group of lads there and we have a great time in the evenings, going to different pubs and that'. When he was in Sheffield he played football on Sundays with a group of friends, had a training session in the week and also went to the gym on Saturday mornings 'for sort of toning, me legs and that, for football'. Damian, who was part of a large working class family – one brother was a plasterer, another had a fish delivery round and his sister had a cleaning job – spent most of his social life with his family: 'I go to the pub with me dad or one of me brothers, and me and me dad go fishing some weekends. Otherwise I just play snooker with a couple of mates and, oh yeah, I do go to nightclubs now and again.'

But both Damian and Steve were less gregarious than Wayne, who had a particularly active social life. It may seem from what he told me that he confirms the Government view of working class young men as 'lads', even 'yobs', and yet, underlying his words, his central commitment to the work ethic is clear. At school Wayne had been identified as a low achiever, a designation whose meaning he was all too aware of. He seemed to have an equally clear-sighted view of his own abilities as the boys whose views were presented in chapter 4: 'I knew I weren't going to get As, Bs, or Cs and anything like that 'cos I know I ain't no good.' In the event, his highest grade was D. Wayne also suggested that he, and a small group of friends who had been similarly labelled, had caught the blame for all sorts of incidents at school: 'Well, if something happens at school, like, like a child got stoned [stones thrown in the playground] or, like, chopped up [pushed in the corridors], like the teacher would say, "Look, it's, it's the boys again; they done it again, 'nt they?"' But, reflecting on his position in year 11 (the final year of compulsory schooling) during the first meeting we had, he said, 'We're more mature now; we just don't bother. We like to help 'em if they're gettin' picked on, you see. Cuz we're top of the school, we can't just walk down the corridor pushin' them over and punchin' them.' Intimidation may have played a part, though, as Wayne added, 'well, I think it's quite cool actually: walkin' down the corridor and they all just move out of the way'.

Wayne's behaviour and attitudes out of school also seemed to confirm the yobbish behaviour of working class youths. He was involved in a range of dubious activities, although he drew a clear line between what he regarded as semi-criminal acts of little significance and 'real trouble':

> Well, we only ever muck about. In car parks [of a shopping centre] at night, like. We used to muck about with the security guard, like walk past him and swear at him or something. We nicked hubcaps off the wheels too. We used to take them away but it's not really worth it now. We used to, like, just take them and smash them up, just for the fun of it.

He paused and, smiling engagingly, said, 'Sound like a right old thug, don't I?' And, like generations of (stereotypically American) teenagers before him, Wayne also told me:

> We hang about the centre of town. Jamie's got a really nice car, and he's done it up real nice and all the birds stare at it, so we go over there and he sits in it revving it up, and then, and then, then a few of his other mates come over and their cars and they, like, race around the market square. I know you are not supposed to do that, but they just do it anyway.

But Wayne never let these activities interfere with his job: 'I'm not as daft now.' He was a determined worker, attending regularly and reliably, despite having to get up extremely early on mornings when he was working away from Cambridge. Although he was a keen Friday and Saturday-night drinker and clubber, he avoided going drinking on Sundays and during the week as he had to get up for work the next morning. He drinks 'every Friday night; its a regular thing' sometimes in pubs and sometimes taking larger from the off-licence to a friend's house. 'I am not really old enough to drink, but I can get served anyway. I drink nine bottles but it's not too bad as it's usually only one night a week.' He told me that he had tried soft drugs but preferred to drink. When he goes clubbing he sometimes gets into fights, often deliberately, on his own admission, unlike Steve who thought 'there are too many young men looking for a fight. I try to keep myself to myself and walk past.' But Wayne insisted that he always tried to stay out of serious trouble. He had never been arrested and described himself as a 'Jack the Lad', out for having fun, meeting girls but not looking for trouble. 'I'm not bad, you know,' he assured me. He thought the media misrepresented young men:

> People think we are all slobs and that. But we are not, all of us, if you know what I mean. The way I have my hair, people who don't know me would think 'oh he's a bad boy, be careful of him, watch him' and everything, but when you get to know me you know I am all right. I like mucking about, making people scared of me. In some aspects I do like it, but then I don't, you know what I mean. I walked in a restaurant and everyone just stared at me and I felt very uncomfortable. But I like to muck about: I'm still young, aren't I? I don't want to be boring. I want to have a laugh.

However, then he added, 'But if I had a chance to do it all again, I would have not mucked about as much at school and get better grades. But I'll never go back now; I can't be bothered with that. I've got a job and everything; I am secure and everything and I ain't got no need. But I wouldn't go back to school: they'd say, "Dunce is back."'

Wayne was one of the most style-conscious of the 24 young men, with a different haircut each time I saw him, dyed, gelled, sometimes in spikes, sometimes with long strands over a short undercut: 'I don't like to wear a hard hat at work cos it mucks me hair up.' He wore chains and rings – 'I take me rings off if I am going to hit someone. I don't want to cut me hands up' – and was unthinkingly sexist. And yet he was charming, courteous and thoughtful and, like many of the young men to whom I talked, as I shall show later, fond of his parents and anxious about the decline of his local neighbourhood.

Committed Workers 2: Getting a Job is what Matters – Richard and Darren

Richard and Darren both grew up on the same Sheffield estate as Steve. Like Steve, Richard had one parent who worked in a semi-professional capacity: his mother was a nurse but his father was unemployed at the time of the interviews.

> Me dad's, like, one of those housekeepers. While she's at work he cleans up and irons and that. He were always in trouble when he were young. Never did owt right. But now he knows. He tells me 'it used to be different in them days; now you want to keep your head to the ground and keep working'. Cos if he could turn time back he would. That's it. He did get a few jobs when he were young. He worked in a steel factory but he's not worked for years.

His father's lack of work seemed to be a key reason why Richard felt so strongly himself about holding down a job, although he felt sorry for his father rather than regarding him as less manly for taking on the traditional female role in the household.

In some ways it is surprising that Richard became a committed worker. His school career had not been a promising one, involving absences, truancy, exclusions and aggression. He had been excluded several times for bad behaviour, including physical violence.

> I have had some fights at school, cos when you get mad you just like flip. I keep … I don't like fighting. I can't stand it, but when it comes to it you got no choice. It's better than just standing there and getting

beaten up. I just, if someone came up to me and just punched me one, I'd say, 'Why did you do that?' But if he kept doing it and doing it, I'd get mad and just knock his head off.

But like Wayne, Richard felt that, unjustifiably, he was labelled as a troublemaker: 'well, it's not always me, I don't always start it but I always get the blame'. He also had a pattern of playing truant: 'Year 7–9 [aged 11–13] I had about 100 per cent attendance; year 10 I went a bit more sloggy,[1] and this year I'm worse, but I'm just trying to put up with it. It's like, I was off and on. I didn't truant. I just stayed at home. I told me mum I were ill but I weren't. And then the attendance officer came and I had to go back.'

Richard's explanation for his behaviour lay in gender differences – in both boys' attitudes and differential treatment of girls by teachers.

Well, boys want attention from girls and that's why they mess about. And so teachers like girls more because they think girls behave more and boys mess about, like; that's because they pay more attention to girls, so boys mess about to get attention.... So then boys start getting a bit stressed and that and getting upset and mess about more and the teachers get mad with them. That's why boys get excluded and then they just don't come anymore.

He rejected single-sex groups as a possible solution – 'well, that just wouldn't feel right, would it?' – although he recognized that 'they [boys] might do better in lessons, though, cos there wouldn't be so much showing off'. Instead, he had a more radical suggestion for helping boys to improve in school: 'I think year 9 you should have a bit of a break and then come back. It [getting fed up and playing truant] happens to everyone cos there's so many years of school. So you start stopping off.' Richard had also been in trouble, locally as well as at school. He had been cautioned by the police for stealing – 'I were nicking stuff and I got done off coppers' – and he had once been arrested for climbing on to the school roof during the summer closure period. As soon as he was 16 – in March of year 11 – Richard started looking for waged work, ready to leave school if he found employment.

I'm hoping for retail and that. I did work experience at the Co-op this year. I've been for quite a lot of interviews so far. Madhouse in Meadowhall, they sell clothes, like designer clothes, but they said, 'We can't take you on cos you've not left school yet.' I showed them me plastic card [a National Insurance card issued to all 16 year olds] but they said, 'We still can't take you on cos we need GCSEs and you haven't done them yet.' He goes, 'Come back after you've done your GCSEs and we'll sort summat out.' They'll keep me on a list while I'm waiting.

He went back to school, but his aim was to find a job as soon as possible after leaving in early June, and to live at home, thus saving money for going out. Although Richard had had some work experience when still at school, it was short-lived and promised little for his future working life as a deferential service-sector worker: 'I did do a Saturday job but it didn't last long. I think I went twice but they treated me like crap: that's why I didn't like it. I were working in this grocery store and he starts swearing at me, so I swore back and just walked off. But he still paid me. I made sure he did. I weren't going to work for nowt.'

In the event Richard did enter the retail sector, initially as a shop assistant in Sports Soccer. He'd started there in May before he officially left school, going in during the final term just to sit his final exams.[2] In eight months between taking this job and the second time I talked to Richard in Sheffield he had changed his job twice. He left Sports Soccer in July for a better-paying but similar job in Burtons, a menswear chain, but found the atmosphere stuffy and left after only two days. His next job, which he had applied for at the same time as Burton's, was in McDonald's. All three of these jobs were in the Meadowhall Shopping Centre, which was a short bus ride or 30-minute walk from Richard's home. He had found them by scanning adverts placed on a board in the centre. Talking about the decision to leave Sports Soccer, Richard said:

> I were getting bored wi' it; it just weren't good and it's better money thear (at McDonald's) and when it's better you just want to move, you know what I mean, go somewhere else where it's better. I've only been thear seven month and I'm training already, which teks up to two year to do, so I am hoping to pick up a floor manager's job in a year or two.

In this second interview Richard was largely positive about his working life at McDonald's. As he told me, the money was good for his age: 'I'm on about £900 a month' but the shift work was a problem sometimes: 'They like me on early, but at 6.00 when I have to get up, I'm really hurting. It's very bad, reet annoying. I work 6.00 while 2.00, but it can be 3.00, even 4.00, when I finish, and sometimes 10.00 to 5.00 or 11.00 to 6.00, 'fore you do a closing. I ain't done one yet cos I am not 18, but you start at 5.00 and do while 3.00, but you get a free taxi home.' However, he enjoyed the company of his workmates, positively describing their division of labour in classic Fordist terms: 'We all work in a circle as a team. So to do like a Big Mac or something, there's one on table dresses t' Big Mac, passes the bun on to grill, and another takes it off so its reet quick, like a formation cos it only takes 30 seconds to get, like, five or six Macs off.' But as Leidner (1993) has argued, fast-food jobs epitomize the assembly-line structure of deskilled service jobs, so highly routinized and scripted that they leave no scope for individual initiative.

Even as Richard told me, 'I'll try and make a career of it,' he also said, 'I'm looking for other good jobs out thear.... I don't want to waste my life staying in one place.' By the time of the third interview, almost six months later, however, the monotony and sheer hard work of McDonald's meant that he had become more dissatisfied even though he had progressed to become a member of the training squad and played a part in training new floor staff. He was registered for a vocational qualification based on workplace experience: 'I'm learning the till cos I'm doing an NVQ there, I'm training already which takes up to two years to do, so I'm hoping to pick up floor manager in a year or two.' He had also become eligible for holiday pay, although he still had no formal contract of employment to his knowledge. But he had begun to find the hours demanding:

> I just work when they ask me. I often do 45 hours a week. And they watch you, there's people watching you work all the time, passing information on to the manager. And they push people around, management does that.... People often don't last long here. They leave after about two months because they can't handle it. It's like slave labour.

Richard himself had arranged an interview in TopMan (a men's clothing retailer) for the following Saturday after I spoke to him for the third and final time. 'Maybe it's better work: it's cleaner and not as hard in a shop.'

Several of the other young man with whom I talked to in Sheffield had also been employed at McDonald's in Meadowhall, but none of them had stuck it as long as Richard, who had worked there almost 12 months by the summer of 2000. They all told me what hard, relentless work it was, demanding stamina as well as having to conform to a welcoming personal performance, scripted by management. 'I hated it,' said a schoolfriend of Richard's. 'I left after two days. It was just too hard.'

To explore Richard's views about the relative life chances of young men and young woman, as well as to examine the relevance of Fine and Weiss's (1998) findings about blaming the Other in a British context, I asked Richard a series of questions about the local labour market, about sexism and racism and about his own life chances compared to those of his father. While he was unhesitatingly sexist, with a clear opinion of the suitability of different jobs for men and for women and of the natural-ness of the gender division of labour, he did not hold racist opinions. Indeed, he was thoughtful in response to several questions about 'race'. First I asked him about his friends at school:

> I don't mix with the Asian boys much. I am not racist or owt, but I just don't mix with them, except a couple. And there's, like, the black kids. I talk to them all the time. But most of me friends are white. It's because where I've grown up, cos round here there were never no Asian kids or black kids. At school, they do stay separate, cos it's like you were growing up with black people, you'd prob-ably be hanging around with black people and if you grow up with whites you hang around with whites, that why. But that's why secondary schools bring all people together, to try and talk, to stop racism, like . . . I think that's good.

By the time he was working at McDonald's, Richard had met a more diverse group of people. 'I've got loads of friends, and we all go out together. They are from all over the place, from Italy to Afghanistan, girls as well as lads. We all muck in together. There's no trouble.'

I asked him to describe himself to me in the final interview: 'I'm talkative, one of the lads. That means you like having a laugh, tekking piss out of each other, laughing at each other.' But he also emphasized that he was hard working and reliable, a view that his work history certainly supports and which parallels Wayne's views in Cambridge. For these young men, life was a careful negotiation between a rumbustious 'laddish' social life and an adherence to the Protestant work ethic. Richard was also thoughtful in his responses to a series of questions about the position of young men. He thought that life was equally stressful for both young men and for young women but that it was up to individuals how they handled it:

> I know the papers are full of problems for boys and I do think about that: everyone thinks about that. I think that, in a way, everyone has got a hard time in life and you just get through it

the best you can without too much stress. Well, everyone has got to go through stress: without stress it wouldn't be a life; but the best way is to leave all that behind and just go for the future. I mean, it's just like being sexist in a way, the paper saying that.

In a moving final comment he said, 'Me dad has had a hard life, a bad life; it were reet bad but I'll do better.[3] I've had a good life, although I have wasted parts of it. I'd like to go back and reconnect but I can't exactly do that, so I'll just leave the past and hope for the best for the future.' This young man was not quite 18 years old at the time he spelt out this view of his prospects but he seemed already to have given up on the option of further education and was resigned to a life dominated by low-wage labour.

For Darren too, holding down a job and bringing in money was seen as the chief route to constructing an independent adult masculine identity. His father was a car mechanic, his mother worked an evening shift cleaning at the local hospital and his older brother worked at an industrial salvage plant. When I first met him he told me that he could not wait to leave school. He was planning to leave before the Easter break, meaning that he would miss the final term and so fail to sit any exams, about which he had few regrets: 'I just want to get a job and get some money in me pocket each week.' Part of the reason for this decision lay in the fact that Darren disliked attending school, not persuaded of the values of education but also resentful of how the predominantly middle class teachers had labelled him as disruptive. He is the boy with the 'label on his head', whose perceptive views about being designated disruptive by his teachers were discussed in chapter 4. He was also a persistent truant: 'I didn't used to go to school a lot, in year and 8 and 9. I used to go and sign in and then go to play football and that in the park, about four of us did it, a lot of the time.' Identified by the school as a low achiever, he was sent on a part-time release scheme to a local college to 'do painting, decorating, construction, woodwork, all that stuff' because, as he told me, 'I'm not very brainy and that and teachers expect you to do more stuff than you can.' Consequently, in years 10 and 11 'I just used to wag it [play truant] most of the time'. And yet when he left school early, he told me that he regretted giving up German. This was the one subject he had enjoyed and felt he might have done reasonably well in it because 'we have individual lessons for it, you know, like for people who didn't used to come to school, you have individual lessons. There's only abht seven in't class. Teacher's all reet': high praise from an undemonstrative Yorkshireman.

When I went to meet Darren the second time, he'd been banned from the local pub for using foul language. He'd been drinking there for more than a year despite being under age and had a tendency to get into trouble when he'd had too much to drink. This was the first time, however, that he'd been banned, leading to a difficult decision about where we might go and talk on a cold November evening. Once we'd resolved this, I asked him whether he thought most young men of his acquaintance would be seen as yobs, as the sorts of men whose behaviour the Blair Government is anxious to change. For Darren, like for many of his peers, drinking was a key part of a regular, and eagerly anticipated, Friday night out with the lads: 'I'll drink five or six pints if I go to a pub; eight or nine if I go clubbing. I go out with £40 on a Friday and a Saturday, mebbe a bit more on Saturdays.' But he was absolutely clear that although he might get drunk, he was never incapable and nor would he go out looking for trouble. 'I know what I am doing. I like enjoying meself on weekend, but I don't drink on the streets; just go out to the pubs and have a laff with some of me mates. I don't cause no trouble or owt.' And later he elaborated: 'I'm just a lad – someone who doesn't cause trouble but who's sociable and likes a laugh.' For more sober citizens, meeting Darren with six or seven of his friends after they'd drunk 9 pints, the distinction between a lad and a yob might seem rather academic. However, most of these young men perhaps appear more intimidating than they are, adopting a certain style to challenge adult authority. When Darren and I entered the bar of a city centre hotel, his cap, earring and tattoo, as well as his size and height, were the cause of a number of anxious looks. And, as Bourgois (1995) has noted, through their appearance, style and clothes, even their very walk, working class youths' intimidating appearance tends to disqualify them from many of the vacancies in the service sector that are advertised locally.

Darren might look intimidating and sometimes get drunk but he was also a hard worker who, like Wayne, didn't drink to anything like the same extent on weekdays as he did at the weekend. His aim, however, was to spend his working life in industrial jobs where clothes and appearance were of little significance. When I talked to him for the third time, he had a job as an assistant to a fibreglass mould-maker and was learning how to laminate. Before that he'd worked on an industrial site on a concrete crushing machine, a job that, like many working class boys, he had found through personal local contacts, in his case his brother. He had started this job after Easter in 1999, leaving school before sitting any exams, but after several months had been made redundant. He had been out of work for a few weeks but he 'didn't bother with the dole or that'. Darren was committed to the values of work, determined to 'make a go of it', describing himself as 'a reliable worker'. He lived at home with his parents, contributing £15 a week for his food. He spoke fondly of his family, especially his father, to whom he was particularly close. It was clear too that Darren had strong views about his local area, where he said he intended to remain. The estate, built between the 1930s and 1950s, where Darren lived with his parents and older brother, was troubled by many mindless acts: vandalism, graffiti, car thefts and joyriding.

> Well, it used to be a quiet place but it in't no more. Like there's all trouble and that. Fighting, smashed windows and cars getting nicked, all that sort of stuff. Police don't do much, just patrol area every so often, that's it. And there's loads of groups of people that hangs about the shops with beers and that. Just daft. Out in cold weather stood on street corners.... They used to be up at youth club. But now they've stopped it so there's nowhere else they can go.

Notice that Darren does not include himself among these young people, being too busy with 'me job and that'. I shall return to views about the locality held by young men in chapter 8.

When he was younger, he told me, he had been hanging around with some of the older boys involved and had been cautioned for petty theft. But 'me dad told me if he sees me with them again I'm grounded': an indication perhaps that curfews for antisocial youngsters – a proposal that is perennially discussed by a Government that claims to be 'tough on crime, tough on the causes of crime' – would find favour in some areas. When I asked him if his parents were strict his answer was revealing: 'No, they are just like normal parents, like. They want – they don't want coppers coming to the house all the time and that, nowt like that.' Some parents in the area found police visits all too common, supporting the argument in chapter 3 that policy-makers assume that 'yobbish' behaviour is an attribute of working class areas.

For both Darren and Richard, their work was the central element of their lives and they described to me in great detail the specifics of their daily tasks – how to lay bricks, how to sort scrap from reusable mater-ials, how long laminating takes on different materials, how to use the till, what to say to conclude a sale, how to respond if customers were rude – as well as other details of their working lives, including the comments and jokes made by their workmates. They recognized their luck in getting work that was regular and, in Darren's case, would lead to a good trade. And although all five young men whose words constitute the majority of this chapter might be classified as poorly educated and socially unskilled, they were not afraid to stand up for themselves and their rights in the workplace. Steve, for example, had been wrongly accused of smoking in the workshop:

> I've had a couple of run-ins. I had one with the boss the other day. I were accused of something that I didn't do and I weren't impressed. We were doing a job, me and the other apprentices – you just have to do odd jobs around – and the boss said he could smell smoke when she went in afterwards and she called us all across and asked who was smoking and none of us was, so we told her that and she doesn't believe us. So they were threatening to put it down on my record, for smoking in a non-smoking area and for lying, so I had a word with college cos they are, like, above and they look after me at work and they have sorted it out.

Richard was involved in a more serious dispute with McDonald's. He had been putting deliveries away and, as he came downstairs, a trapdoor had dislodged and fallen on his head. He had been briefly knocked out and had eye problems, temporarily losing the vision in one eye. He told me that he was planning to take his case for compensation for injuries to an industrial tribunal. One of the other hard workers – Craig – was also involved in a case for unfair dismissal when I saw him for the third time. Unsupported by either a union or co-workers, one of whom was his best friend and former schoolmate Simon, Craig proposed to represent himself: an impressive decision for a 17-year-old.

Committed Workers 3: Reluctant Learners – Daniel, Kurt and Greg

The third set of young men who might be designated as hard workers included Daniel and Kurt in Cambridge, and Greg in Sheffield. These school leavers, like most of their peers, are participants in the labour market, but when they first left school they were also registered for a variety of further education courses on a full-time basis. Where they differ from Steve, Wayne and Damian – the young men in the first group of committed workers – is in the relationship between their employment and their course choice. While Steve, Wayne and Damian may not enjoy their college work nor find it easy, their commitment to it is enhanced by its direct relevance either to the job they are engaged in or to their future job. For Daniel, Kurt and Greg, however, their choice to go to college and the course they opted to study seemed in the main to be a way of postponing the decision of what type of job to look for in the longer term rather than a positive commitment to studying. They wanted to get through their courses to improve their employment prospects, but several of them referred to their dissatisfaction with some aspect of college life, usually the level or content of the course. As well as attending college, all four young men were working on a part-time basis in a range of jobs, in the main for instrumental reasons – they were saving for driving lessons, for example or for a holiday – and they also emphasized the importance of 'keeping your hand in with a job'. For Daniel and Kurt, however, college proved more attractive than it did to Greg, whose attendance was erratic and who had left before the first Christmas after leaving school.

Staying at college in Cambridge

Daniel was the son of a 'respectable' working class family. His father was a police constable and his mother worked as the morning supervisor in a newsagents, and they had recently bought their house from the local authority. Kurt had a more difficult family life – his parents were divorced and he seemed to be shuffled between them and his stepfather, from whom his mother separated during the year over which I talked to her son. During this year, Kurt lived at four different addresses, part of the time with his mother in temporary accommodation organized by the local authority after she left his stepfather, and at other times with either his father or stepfather. Kurt's mother was a cleaner at one of the university colleges, and his stepfather, who retained custody of the younger children, 'just looked after the kids' (of whom there were four, excluding Kurt) according to Kurt, although by the time of the second interview he had a job as a house-to-house collector for an insurance company. Both boys attended Fenland Community College, although Daniel had a better record of attendance than Kurt: 'I don't nick off really. Lots of people do though, you know, if they've got lessons they don't like and they think they'll get away with it. They'll go and hide, in the toilets or in the shops across the way. One of me friends stays off a lot. He once didn't come for six months but the school threatened to sue him so he came back.' Kurt had a more variable school experience: 'Well, I have been in trouble, cos I hit this boy and I got sent home, but he hit me first and then I hit him back and the teacher just saw me. I got a bit annoyed about that. But usually it's just taking and telling jokes in lessons and that. I can't keep quiet. And I do go most of the time.' This is the Kurt who in chapter 4 explained that he 'got on everyone's nerves', because 'well, I might make one person annoyed and the other person laughs and they get told off and then they blame it on me and ohhh, it just goes round in a circle'.

Compared to Kurt, who did indeed talk a great deal and so might well 'get on everyone's nerves', Daniel was a slow, stolid boy, cautious in volunteering an opinion and not willing to expand on his comments. He has been withdrawn from certain subjects, including foreign languages and was being given extra help with homework and exam preparation in the last months at school. He told me he hoped to go to college to do an Information Technology course, hoping eventually to be a computer engineer: 'I've always liked working with my hands, doing stuff and I like computers.' The course he was aiming for required only minimum entry levels, two low-level (grade D) passes would be sufficient, and 'if I don't get that, I can go for another one which I don't need no grade – the foundation, I think it is'. In the meantime Daniel worked on Sundays at an office supply retail outlet. He had been sent there for work experience in year 10 at school and the firm had offered him a casual weekend position, recognizing his reliability. 'I think they knew I'd always turn up, like. It's OK, but a bit boring. I just put things on shelves, take things off the palettes and ring them up and sometimes help with the customers.'

Daniel's GCSE results were not good and he did start the Foundation course but he told me, 'It's too easy. I want to stay and do the higher course next year.' In his first year Daniel attended college on Mondays and Thursdays all day and on Tuesday mornings, and so he had expanded his hours at the office supply shop. His course peers were mainly other young men: 'I suppose it's cos not many women are into computers. They are more into children and stuff.' He enjoyed college life but did not seem prepared to expand on what exactly it was that contributed to his enjoyment other than 'I prefer it to school. The tutors are friendly and stuff; you have jokes with the teachers.' But his working life seemed more comment-worthy:

I've been there two years nearly now. The pay's quite good. It's £4.36 an hour and I only do 15 hours so I don't pay tax. I might be moving to the furniture department soon instead of office supplies, pens and that and there you build all the furniture up and that. And the office manager in that department has been trying to get me there for a bit.

He said I'm the one he would like on his team. I think that's because I work hard. I am there when I am meant to be. We are a good lot, lots of joking around, stuff about when they go out in the evening and that. There's friendly staff, all ages and some foreigners. But the manager is a pain. She treats you like you were five or six. Telling you exactly where things are even when you know.

He hoped to find work with a small local firm that 'tours round, mending computers for different companies and planned to use the local Careers Guidance Service to identify a vacancy.

When I interviewed him the third time he told me, 'Work's the same; college is the same; it's all the same. Perhaps Mum and Dad treat me more like a grown-up. I'm driving now. I nip me mum up town and to Tescos and that.' While he was at school, he had been going out with the same girl for several months and, perhaps reflecting his father's position, he told me, 'I'm law abiding; I drink a bit, but not much, and I don't smoke or do any kind of drugs. When we go out we go to the cinema. I pay but if we go for something to eat afterwards we share the cost. And I try to keep out of trouble.'

He had no views on how the press portrayed young people – 'I don't read the papers, or keep up with the news and that' – but he was prepared to venture an opinion on his own character: 'I think I'm kind, reliable, pretty considerate, and I'm strong. And I'm good at mending electrical things, too – the toaster and the video and that. I don't think I am ambitious, though: I just want to get a full-time job. It's important now, though, to have qualifications and to be reliable.'

If Daniel's life was determined by his desire to be reliable, Kurt's was more erratic. While he was still at school he had little idea about what he wanted to do, nor any knowledge of the local labour market. He told a local career's guidance visitor to Fenland that he wanted to be a tattooist. As he reported, 'When I tell her, she was amazed by that. She said, "That's the first person I speak to what wants to be a tattooist."' I thought it'd be good cos I'm good at drawing. I do cartoons on the pavement outside, with chalk and then rub them off and start again. But people say they are good.' But he continued:

Well, my uncle's got a job and he reckons once I'm 16 I could start there either a night job or an afternoon job while I'm still at school, and when I've left I can go into it full time. I'm not sure what sort of a job it is. He brings home jars of jam and all that. You get quite a lot of money for that, looking after machines and just taking stuff out of them. Me dad did have a job there too, but he never really spoke about what it was. He just wanted the money, apart from that he said it were a rubbish job. But I think I'll do that. My friend who's just left school's got a good job. All I've got to do is get me little card with numbers on it [his National Insurance card].

At this stage Kurt's attitudes seemed to parallel those of Richard in Sheffield, although his home circumstances were more difficult, involving not only mobility but also violence in the home: 'Me mum and me stepdad don't get along that well and he used to hit her. He clouts me too sometimes; he's put me on the floor a few times and all that. My cousins keep on telling me to tell them about it but I can't be bothered to. It really wouldn't make a difference, just cause more aggravation.' Despite this, it was clear that his uncle and cousins were an important support system for Kurt. His uncle gave him extra pocket money for tasks around his house and Kurt often went there after school 'for tea or to do me homework'. And it proved to be the example of one of his cousins that encouraged Kurt to consider further education: 'Me cousin is 21 now and he's got a really good job. I think he works making computers, making the chips. He gets good money at that. But he went to university. I could never do that.'

By the time of the second interview, Kurt's mother and stepfather had separated and, as Kurt explained, 'it's funny, but now I get on better with him. He really helped me when I left school.' Kurt's exam results also proved to be disappointing. Even in art he failed to reach an adequate standard, which was a blow as by then Kurt was planning to attend the local further education college to take an art foundation course. 'But me stepdad was great. He rang up the college and got me in, even though he said he really wanted me to go straight to work. I'm doing art and a GCSE in leisure and tourism and an IT course.'

Like Daniel, Kurt was also employed on a part-time basis and it became clear that for him too employment rather than college attendance was the most significant part of his life: 'Well, I like college but it's not that serious. I'm not sure now that I'm good enough at art, though me cartoons are still good.' Like Daniel, Kurt found college a 'good laugh' but he also told me that some of his teachers were tougher than the ones at school. 'When we get in there, I really have to zip it' – meaning his talkative mouth. And like Daniel, Kurt was also employed as well as attending college. He worked at Debenhams (a local department store), in the kitchens as well as clearing tables in the snack bar, earning almost £300 a month, out of which he contributed towards the running of his mother's household.

I don't pay here [at his stepfather's] cos I am only here a night or two every week, and I help with the kids, but I give me mum a £100 a month. She gives me some of that back cos she don't like taking money off me, but when she's got like no money I always take it out of my bank account and give her some of it. . . . And I was thinking, well, perhaps I should stay at Debenhams, if I get that much already for weekend work, I'd be getting quite a lot for working full time. And it'd be a Monday to Friday job. I'd have the weekends off, or I'd be working like my mum does. She works every other Saturday.

For the Fenland school leavers, further education college was at least an option, even though for these reluctant learners it seemed a less than fulfilling experience and was clearly a step on the path to employment rather than an intellectual experience in its own right. For the few Park Edge boys who were even prepared to consider further education, it proved to be a dead loss. Here Greg's pathway is an exemplar.

Starting college in Sheffield

Greg was the youngest son of a family of three children. His father and one brother worked as machinery operators in a welding company in Barnsley, a town near Sheffield, whereas his older brother and his mother were sales assistants. His mother worked locally in a part-time job; his brother was employed at the Meadowhall Shopping Centre on the north-east periphery of the city and, like his father and brother, worked full-time. Greg too, while still at school, worked in a shop: 'I've got a job Monday to Friday; it's two hours a day, five till seven and sometimes I work over, closing up shop.' Like Richard, he was a forceful employee, not prepared to put up with bad treatment: 'I used to work at another shop, just across the road but they treated me reet bad, so I found another job. It weren't about wages; it's like they were always swearing at me and that, so I got fed up and left.'

Greg was a lively and energetic boy, whose father had been a professional footballer until he reached his mid-thirties, although his career had never been a great success. During the course of the year, it became clear that sporting prowess was a contested issue in the family. Greg felt that his father ignored him, even disparaged his own success in the martial arts field (Greg won an under-18s regional award in 2000) as he pinned all his hopes on Greg's eldest brother who was a talented footballer. He spoke with considerable feeling and sensitivity about the relationship:

My brother plays football a lot and he wants to get, like, professional and that and Dad used to play for Sheffield Wednesday
Reserves and I think it's, like, quite a close bond and that. I like
football but it's like they are both right good players and he wants
him to...cos my dad could have turned for the first team but he
never made it and I think it's like he wants my brother to, and he's,
like, trying to push him all the time and...you know what I mean?
He's different with me. He's always on me back. He shouts at me
all the time and, I dunno, every little thing I do, he's on me back.

Greg was also involved in the dramatics group at school and had
played several major roles in end of year productions but, as he told
me, 'me mum says that she doesn't know who I take after in the family;
they're all different to me'. He hoped to be able to make a career in the
arts world and had decided to move to a local further education college
in September after leaving school, and to register for an academic course
leading to A levels: the requirement for university entry. Despite being
one of the few students at Park Edge gaining five good passes at GCSE
and surprising his teachers who had placed him in the low-ability range,
Greg registered for a less academic course, opting to take an intermediate-
level GNVQ in art and design. Greg found it hard to explain to me why
he had made this decision, muttering something about 'technical drawing: it would have been useful' but it seemed that he quickly realized that
this was the wrong course for him.

I stayed for three of four weeks and then I went to talk to them. I
said, 'This is not what I want.' I said, 'This is,' and they tried to,
like, they said, 'We want you to stay' and that, but I ses, 'Well, I'm
off.'...I found another course: acting this time. It were on erm,
you know, them sheets what you get when you leave school; it were
on one of them booklets. And I read it and I just phoned up. And
they ses, 'Well, we've got no places left.' So I waited about a week
and then they phoned back and said they've got some places. This
time it was an advanced GNVQ.

But, once again Greg quickly became dissatisfied. It was not clear
from what he said to me whether he disliked the course or the college
generally, or whether peer pressure, combined with the lack of strong
guidance from home pushed him into a second change of plan. But the
combination of all these factors led to a decision to leave college
altogether.

I were there about two months but it were mostly theory, not acting, and I wanted to act, you know. And I decided to chuck it. I wanted some money, like. I wanted to work. Me mam and me dad said nothing much. They ses, 'Well, it up to you. We can't make your mind up for you.' I were at home about a month and me mum ses, 'I want you to go and find a job.' So I came down to Meadow'all and looked for a job, but I couldn't find one and so I went to McDonald's and asked for an application form and they give me one. I filled it in and they phoned me back about two weeks later and ses, 'Come down for an interview.' So I went for an interview and they offered me a job there and then.

By this time it was almost Christmas before he started work: 'It were right busy then. It was just before Christmas, Christmas week and that. I were chucked in at the deep end; I were rushed off me feet. When I got home all I wanted to do was go to bed but now I know I have made the right decision.' His decision seemed to be strongly supported by his family, if not through discussion, then in terms of actions, which made Greg's working life less difficult. His father gave him a lift to Meadowhall when Greg worked a daytime shift, whereas his mother eased his everyday life:

She makes me meals when I am in. In the mornings she gets me bag ready with me shirt, hangs me uniform and washes it every night, puts me bag out with money on top and everything. Yeah and when I come downstairs, me breakfast is all ready for me and all that. Me dad doesn't do anything like that, though. He says I've got to . . . he ses me mum is too soft on me. But she does it for him too; she does it for everyone.

Like Richard, Greg worked shifts and initially had no contract nor any rights to, for example, paid holidays. His hours changed almost on a daily basis.

It changes all the time: there's not one set of permanent hours. They put you on a . . . You get a full-time day and then two days off, or sometimes only one, in the week, and you work early morning 9.00 while 5.00, and at night I work 12.00 while half eight or something like that. And work's not guaranteed. You might go, like, four days with no work. It's hard to make arrangements and have a social life.

Six months later, Greg also worked the late shift, starting at 8pm, and although the branch closed at 11pm, he was often not able to leave until after 1am. Although McDonald's pays for a taxi for these late-shift workers, Greg's father insisted on picking him up.

Greg was paid on an hourly basis and, despite not being 18, received the basic minimum wage at the youth rate, £3.60, when he first started: 'They ses 18 and overs only normally get that, but that because there's that much staff working there, they said it is easier just to do a set pay and that, like.' After six months his pay had risen to £3.90p.

Working in McDonald's is exhausting and difficult work, entailing a range of demanding tasks, as well as moral dilemmas. These latter tend to revolve around the often-complex negotiations of different identities, especially when that of worker and friend collide, or when a customer's behaviour challenges masculine attitudes and pride. Greg told me, 'Too many people I know from school come in here. And they expect free drinks, and fries and all that. They come up to me, talking loud. I hate it cos we are watched all the time, you know. I can't give stuff away.' Friends were not the only customers who were difficult to deal with. At peak periods, when queues were long, people became impatient and sometimes aggressive: 'I hate it when customers are rude to you. They sometimes speak to you like dirt, you know; I think they think they are better than us, just because they might have a suit on, but some of them only work in s shop in Meadow'all, just like us.' Like all fast-food workers, Greg, in a brief induction programme, had been taught that deference to the customers was the most highly valued attribute but 'it's hard to keep your temper sometimes. You want to lean across the counter and thump some of 'em, but I'd be sacked if I did, so it's not even worth thinking about.' His comments echo Newman's (1999: 89) conclusions from her study of low-wage fast-food employment in New York:

> Servicing the customer with a smile pleases management because making money depends on keeping the clientele happy, but it can be an exercise in humiliation for teenagers. It is hard for them to refrain from reading this public nastiness as another instance of society's low estimation of their worth. But they soon realize that if they want to hold on to their minimum-wage jobs they have to tolerate comments that would almost certainly provoke a fistfight outside the workplace.

Service work challenges the right to 'stick up for yourself', an attribute that many of the 24 young men had valued during their school years. And yet, for some of them, perhaps Richard among them, years of being told they were no good at school, meant that they accepted the indignities of fast-food employment in exchange for a feeling of pride in working hard: a pride that Greg too exhibited: 'I sort of like being tired at the end of the shift. It means I have worked hard and earned me money.' Both Richard and Greg denied my tentative suggestion that this was demeaning work.

Initially, Greg was not involved in customer service but instead flipped burgers, fried potatoes and assembled orders for the counter staff. These tasks, albeit menial, entailed a high level of manual dexterity and the ability to work accurately at speed and under pressure. As Greg noted earlier, a high level of surveillance ensured they worked hard and, as he also told me, the supervisors are too demanding: 'The managers are a bit like they threaten you all the time. They are only young, about 21 or 22, and it goes to their head, I think; they take it too far in what they say to you. Outside work, it's different. I've got a lot of friends. It's like a big group, like, who respect you. That's missing here.'

Greg was still working at McDonald's a year after leaving school, but was considering leaving. He kept an eye on the vacancy boards at the shopping centre and also read the weekly jobs supplement in the local paper. He had applied for a job as a lifeguard at a sports centre, which was part-time hours initially, but would, he told me, eventually have offered regular hours and a good basic wage – but his application was unsuccessful. He had considered going to work as a welder with his father and brother but his dad had discouraged him: in an unconscious echo of Kurt, Greg reported that 'he told me I'd get on his nerves'. Greg was optimistic, though, that he'd find another job: 'there's plenty of work around here at present, and who knows I may eventually go back to college'.

Whereas Kurt had drifted into college, both Daniel and Greg had made a more positive decision and of the three of them it was Greg who seemed to have the academic credentials and enthusiasm to make a success of his choice. And yet he was the one who chopped and changed courses and who eventually left college for casual employment. Unless he does decide to return to college in the next few years, his prospects of securing permanent employment look slight. However, for Kurt too, engaged on a set of courses barely above GCSE standard, college attendance may not prove a gateway to other than bottom-end employment. Perhaps of these three 'reluctant learners', only Daniel, the reliable plodder, will find some degree of labour market security in the next few years comparable to the more committed threesome – Damian, Steve and Wayne, whose commitment to training was a more significant part of their early post-school transition.

7

Uncertain Transitions: Accidental and Incidental Workers, the Excluded, and Escape Attempts

For millions of people in precarious employment, the old rhetoric of the self-made man and work leading to success has little grounding in the reality of their experience. (Beder 2000: 145)

Just as the reluctant learners seemed to have chosen their college course as much by accident as by choice and their college lives were mainly incidental to their working lives, the incidental and accidental workers dropped into employment as much by chance as through positive actions. Among the accidental workers I have included Shaun, Gareth and Matthew in Sheffield, whereas the exemplar of the incidental workers – young men whose work is secondary to their social lives – is Guy in Cambridge, whose commitment to the work ethic was minimal, reliability uncertain and job mobility over a 12-month period astonishing.

Accidental Workers: Gareth, Shaun and Matthew

Gareth and Shaun came as a pair. They had been inseparable friends throughout secondary school and they turned up together to meet me. Physically they could not be more different. Gareth was a tiny scrap of a boy, thin and wiry, looking years younger than his age and about a foot shorter than his friend. Shaun was large and slow-moving, a ruddy chubby lad who thought hard before he spoke and, indeed, was often content to let Gareth speak for him. I attempted to interview them independently but they were insistent that I see them together, or not at all. Gareth was clearly the brains of the partnership and, although his exam results were not particularly good (as I noted earlier, good results are five passes at C and above) he proudly told me that he had only failed Religious Education and had gained a B and two Cs. He never even contemplated continuing his education, however, as his mother was a single parent and the household needed his wages. In his case, therefore, domestic circumstances dictated his post-school pathway. His mother, he told me, had three jobs, all of them cleaning: both private houses and office premises: 'She's got one in the morning. She wakes up at 5 and she starts at half past 6 and then she finishes that one at 10 and then she goes to another one, 10 while 12, and then she goes to another one in the afternoons, 3 while 6.' And, he commented sadly, 'I wish I could see me mum more, but she is always at work.'

Gareth, who was working in a bulk warehouse, packing leaflets to insert into the local paper, had found the job by chance:

> About a month after I left school, this man that I knew worked for the *Sheffield Star* and he were packing it in cos he found a better job. And I know him and he were asking me if I'd like to do it and that, to just go down and speak to the manager. So I went down and I spoke to him and showed him me reference from work experience and he said that I'd got it thear and then, and I've had it ever since.

Gareth said he enjoyed it and that it was quite good money. He was paid £4 an hour in early 2000 which was more than the then-current minimum wage, to which, as I noted earlier, under-18-year-olds have no entitlement in any case. He worked with two other men: 'there's me, Terry who's gaffer, and there's Phil, so it's all right; we have good laughs and that'. The two older men (Terry was near retirement age and Phil 26) teased Gareth, but he tried not to mind: 'you live with it, don't you? You've got to live with it; just see it as a funny joke and laugh with them'. His work was monotonous and physically demanding.

> What it is, the leaflets come from all companies to our warehouse to store 'em. We've got great piles of leaflets on the floor, one, two, three, four, five, six, and we've got wrappers that says van, for example, van six, drop 15 and we look for square number six and put it on pile 15 and then the *Star* drivers, our drivers, come and pick 'em up and tek 'em to whatever area it is, and we just do the same

every week. It's not hard really. It's just bending down and bending back up that does your back in really, but I've got a back support.

To counteract the monotony he told me that 'I bought a snooker table from somebody and I took it into work and we have a mess about with it at dinnertime and that. It's summat to do, init?'

Shaun's passage into the labour market was equally incidental. He passively accepted a placement offered to him by a vocational training programme in the city. Shaun was one of five brothers; his father worked shifts at a bakery: 'He, like, moves these pallets that's got bread in them and that and keeps an eye on the machines and if owt goes wrong, he has to ring alarms and sign papers and that.' His mother was a housewife – looking after the four younger brothers but she also raised border collies for sale. In his school career, Shaun had constantly been in trouble. As he rather disarmingly told me during our first exchange, 'I have been involved in some things I must admit. I'm not going to hide it. But it were just messing abaht. I'm a kid, aren't I?' The list of 'just messing about' included heaving a brick through a bus window when he was ten, 'nicking stuff', and punching a boy on a bike who'd thrown a brick at him, but in doing so breaking his ribs. I began to feel that Shaun's size and evident strength were a positive disadvantage. His younger brother, he also told me, had got into even more trouble than Shaun. 'He has a problem with fire, you see. You have to watch him. You can't let him out of the house.' His parents were struggling to manage and Shaun told me that they were short of money. 'We haven't been on holiday for years, we haven't had t' money.'

Shaun's brother attended a special school and Shaun himself, an educationally disadvantaged student, who had been entered for only two GCSE exams (maths and English, both of which he failed [see table 5.2], was, by year 11, only partly at school. 'I go to this training scheme where we do painting and decorating and construction, things like that. So I am only fully in school on Wednesday.' When he was there, he told me that he and Gareth used to mess about: 'We act stupid and get done and all that. We try and get the teachers mad so that they throw you out of the classroom. Then we start messing about outside too. I can't wait to leave school.' When he did, he told me, 'I'm going to go on to college and do an interior design course, painting and decorating again,' although he had doubts about whether he would actually succeed in this aim. 'I have to go for an interview but I'm not reet sure about it. I'm a bit scared about doing an interview. And then there's some writing as well as physical work involved.' As for so many of these boys, 'writing' was a problem in applying for jobs.

In the event, Shaun was not accepted at college but immediately he left school, he started a placement with a training provider as a landscape gardener. This is what he had to say about his work in January 2000:

It's hard, really hard work. Carting barrels of mud and stuff up hills and down hills and stuff. And turf and planting plants and cutting mazes and that in the firm's area, a big garden, like. It's half eight while four o'clock, five days a week. The training's for two years. We get paid an allowance, like: £45 a week, which is not much. It's a bit boring too so I'm looking for another job now. I've looked in Meadowhall and had an interview in a leather shop but I've not heard owt.

In fact, Shaun was offered a placement by a different training provider in the South Yorkshire region and by the time I met him again a year after leaving school, he seemed transformed, far more confident and articulate. He was working for two days a week, at a local firm that put together spirit levels and made spanners and other tools, and at the same time attended college for three days a week to study for an NVQ in warehousing. The two days spent in the workplace were long – from 8.00 in the morning until around 9.00 in the evening, Shaun said, although the workers had five or six short breaks, which could be taken in the workplace canteen. Part of his duties at the firm, as well as working at a bench 'where I put the bubble in spirit levels', involved driving a forklift truck to move supplies around. The firm had sent him on a two-month course for driving, somewhere in Liverpool, where he told me 'I stayed in a hotel, the first time all on me own, like' and, as he proudly told me, he was awarded a certificate for completing the course.

The firm where he was employed consisted of two segregated areas – 'it's like a big factory; there's the warehouse and the benches where the men work, about 30 of us, downstairs, and the offices upstairs and that's all women'. When I asked him about his co-workers, he told me that they were all white and said, 'I hadn't noticed before, but you never see no coloured people in the factory, although there are some delivery guys who come to pick t' stuff up.' Shaun was hoping that eventually he would be taken on on a permanent full-time basis, and told me, 'I really like it here,' adding, like generations of working class boys before him, 'we have a good laugh'. While this may have been the limit of Shaun's ambition and abilities, he was, nevertheless, positive about his achievements and committed to his job. His future earning capacity might be low but compared to the awkward, belligerent youth of just a year previously, Shaun was a transformed character, content with his opportunities and determined to make a go of his life: 'I might still mess about a bit and the people I hang about with think I m funny, but I work hard now too. I'm easy going still but I'm reliable too. I arrive on time and I work hard.'

A year earlier, Shaun might have seemed the stereotypical male school failure at the centre of current policy-making. While he is unlikely ever to excel academically, he is holding down a job, enjoying life and contributing financially to his family and, like Wayne, he finds satisfaction in labour market participation.

A failed transition?

Like Shaun, Matthew too was an incidental worker who accepted a placement on a training scheme on leaving school. If Shaun's story is one of relative success, Matthew's by contrast is one of relative failure, marked by lack of ambition and indifference to conventional career aspirations. Matthew came from a large family including four sisters, three of whom were his half-sisters and considerably older than him. During his years of secondary schooling, Matthew lived with his mother and his younger sister. His father had died four years earlier, when Matthew was 11, and the family had been rehoused, which involved a change of school and of circumstances for Matthew. Matthew had previously been living with his father, who had never married his mother and who lived apart from her in the final years before his death. Matthew was a small, thin, laconic young man, answering my questions briefly in short phrases rather than full sentences, often reluctant to expand on a comment. It was clear, however, that the transition in his life after his father's death had been a difficult one and he often referred to his father during the three conversations I had with him. By year 11, Matthew had negotiated an agreement with his mother and they seemed to get on reasonably well, although he told me that she preferred him not to ask his friends to their home. His mum is, he said, 'too cautious about things' and although Matthew would not explain further this might have been a coded explanation of racist attitudes as he later told me that his best friend was black. Although Matthew had lived nearby with his father, he did not really like where he currently lived: 'it's a bit rough round here. Worse than it used to be, loads of graffiti on local walls, and you get gangs hanging around. Sometimes cars go; joyriders around.'

At school he was in the low-ability groups for most subjects. In previous years his attendance record had been poor: 'I didn't go at all in year 7,[1] I don't know why. I just didn't. Thought it were boring. Nobody came round or owt. They didn't bother; perhaps they didn't notice if you hadn't been very much at school.'

When he was there, Matthew was quiet, 'not a troublemaker; just normal' but uninterested in academic work: 'I just want to leave and get a job.' In the final year he attended a local college one day a week on a landscape course, which would lead into a post-school placement about which he was cynically clear sighted: 'I've got a training thing next year, horticulture it's called but it's just gardening, making garden paths and that and planting; it's a placement. It might be all right. I were interested in working in a shop at first but I did that for work experience, in a supermarket, and I thought it were a bit boring.'

He left school in June and by early July he had started his training course. In November after some initial training he was allocated to the Sheffield Wednesday ground where he worked as one of five grounds-men. The trainee position was for two years and he was paid a basic allowance of £45 a week, out of which he initially gave £15 to his mother as a contribution to his board and lodging but was paying more than double this amount six months later, leaving him with only a few pounds for pocket money. On Thursdays Matthew attended college and was working towards a foundation level NVQ in horticulture in a class of 17 young men and three young women about his age. He told me, as did almost all the participants, that he preferred work to college: 'I'm treated like a worker there, one of the proper staff, not a trainee.' He was still there in May 2000 and hoped eventually that the football club would make his position permanent. If not, he felt that he would be able to find work as a groundsman somewhere else, perhaps a cricket ground or a golf course. Overall, he told me, 'Life's all right, maybe a bit boring. But I like work; everyone gets on wi' everyone else.'

Among all 24 of the participants in this study, Matthew seemed perhaps the most fatalistic of them all. He expressed no ambitions, other than to stay where he was, in the same job, in the same area and at least at present living with his mother and his sister. I felt sure that if Wednesday were to take him on as a groundsman after his period of training, he would still be there if I went back to talk to him after five, even ten years, barring untoward events. Unlike Shaun, who seemed to have gained in confidence and energy after six months in the labour market, Matthew remained the same laconic individual that I had first met a year earlier, trapped between the train tracks leading to low-waged dead-end work, to pick up the train metaphor explored earlier. But for both Shaun and Matthew, a locally organized training scheme for less able young people, which they accessed through the Careers Guidance Service, proved an important link into work. The jobs, however, in which school leavers are placed tend to be casual and unskilled, with little prospects for promotion. In the final chapter I address a range of proposals to develop greater links between entry-level jobs and longer-term employment prospects. In the rest of this chapter, however, the voices of several boys, whose transitions to work proved problematic for a range of reasons, are dominant.

The Incidental Worker

Guy's first year after finishing compulsory schooling in Cambridge was spent in the labour market. He had left school with extremely low grades in the small number of subjects for which he had been entered. Indeed, he was not prepared to reveal his results to me, saying only of his final year at school that 'it was a slow year'. Like Richard too, Guy changed his job more than once in the first few weeks after leaving school. The number and range of vacancies at the bottom end of the service sector in both cities made this possible. However, unlike Richard's job path, mobility was a noticeable feature of the whole of Guy's first year in the labour market. If Richard might be characterized as a determined worker – he was, in his own words as well as in the opinion of one of his peers, a committed and hard worker – Guy's attachment to the labour market is an extreme version of a 'flexible' or casualized worker. While employment was clearly a central part of his life after leaving school, it was also an incidental part. He appeared to have no plans and few preferences and was prepared to turn his hand to almost anything. Even before leaving full-time schooling, Guy had been employed for several years in different jobs: 'I did some work for my dad when I was at school because he owns a security firm. . . . I've been doing odd shifts for him since I was about 14.' As he continued:

> I had loads of odd jobs too right through school. I worked for about two years doing cleaning in the evenings. That was with a cleaning company. Couple of hours a night at the Science Park. It was advertised in the jobfinder bit of the local paper. A few of my friends worked with me there too. There was women there, young men, middle-aged people. We were paid in cash, about £50 a week. It was just, do the job, here's your cash and that's it. We didn't have a contract or anything.

While uncertain whether working *per se* had affected his schooling, Guy did recognize that he had not worked as hard as he might have done at school:

> I took the wrong route in school. I went out too much, every night. I was never really one for studying, revising or whatever and that obviously affected my grades and there wasn't anything I could do. I didn't do the work. I didn't turn up for lessons. I didn't even have enough to go back and do retakes. Well, not to anywhere decent. I did go back to the local further education college for a couple of weeks but it didn't work out and they asked me to leave.

I asked Guy whether he thought boys have a tougher time than girls do at school. Here his opinion was different from Richard's, although Guy also identified gender differences as significant.

> No, definitely not. But it was the people I went with. I don't want to sound big-headed but there was, like, the in-crowd, erm, depending on who you were, well, for me. My crowd there was people in the year above and the year above that, all different ages. It was mostly all the lads and that. School was just a doddle; it was, for me, just a big laugh. The teachers probably just gave up on me. Falling into that type of crowd it just went downhill from there. And the teachers just expected it from me, I should think. When you get to the fourth year you do mature a lot but then it was too late. They just leave it up to you.

Here again, many of the young men with whom I talked corroborated earlier findings that working class boys prefer to 'have a laugh' at school, perhaps drifting into the 'in-crowd' rather than positively rejecting the academic values of the school. And in Fenland Community College, as Guy noted, it was boys rather than girls who seemed unable to combine academic work with having a good time: 'The girls seemed to put their heads down and get on with it after that and the lads didn't. I don't know why. It baffles me. Perhaps because we like to be loud and impress girls. I don't know how it is but the girls seem to have a laugh too but do their work at the same time.'

He told me that 'once I realized I wasn't going to carry on my education. I just went straight out to work really.' But he also suggested that his decisions had been partly affected by his personal circumstances at the time: a pattern that was to recur in the next few months:

It was a bit of a funny time for me. I had been going out with a girl for two and a half years and we split up, so my head was...I didn't know what I wanted to do so I went to agencies trying to get some work there but there was nothing I really wanted to do there. I went to Blue Arrow [a commercial employment agency], and the Career Advisors and there was nothing really, you know, nothing that appealed to me. At the Careers they had loads of little cards. There was chefing and there was always manual labour and that sort of thing; none of it appealed to me. I had done work experience as a chef in a restaurant when I was at school. I only turned up for half of it. I really didn't...I hated it to be honest. It is hard work in the kitchens; it really is hard work. It's non-stop you are always getting...it wasn't a job I wanted. I didn't know what I wanted then and I don't now to be honest. I'm just taking life as it comes.

So, despite a more formal job search than Richard, Guy

got a job by chance. I was in the Häagen-Dazs café one night and I got chatting with the manager. She was quite an attractive woman and I said, 'Sort us out a job then.' I was just messing about. A bit of chit-chat and she said, 'Yeah, come in for an interview.' And the next Friday night, about 11 o'clock, we were all out on the town and I saw her in the window. I knocked on the window and she invited me in; we had a little chat and she gave me a job. It started off as a general handyman in Häagen-Dazs, but it ended up as a waiter, dishwasher and a food preparer as well. So I did all of it. I had such a good time on the job. The people there were nice and I really got friendly with them and whatever.... There were about five waiters, a dishwasher and perhaps three others. They were all young, mainly students having a break. I did shifts, 2.30 till 12.00 at night. Often six days, as they were busy.

Like many employees in fast-food outlets, Guys terms and conditions were based on informal agreement:

I didn't have a contract there either. It all went a bit pear-shaped as well. The manager, she got herself in a bit of trouble and got caught dipping in the till and she tried to get me involved. I was having none of it. I am not going to start doing stuff like that at all. I didn't get paid one week and she said, 'I'll sort it out,' and I never got it, so I quit. It was a shame cos I really did enjoy that job. I was there for a couple of months. Not very long. It was September or October time I was working there.

After leaving Häagen-Dazs, it was his relationship with a girl that again influenced Guy's employment decisions.

I met another girl. I wasn't doing much then at all, just bumming around. I occasionally worked with my dad but nothing really set, nothing reliable because my dad's work is contract work, so not too stable. . . . I did some temping work. I went back to Blue Arrow. It wasn't much – a few weeks. I did temping at Debenhams for a day, bagging up shopping as people paid for it, and then I went on to more manual work. I went packing up cosmetics somewhere out in the sticks, God know where it were. A warehouse. A lot of people there. They arranged transport. Picked us up in town. There was about 4 in a group, so about 12.00 at any one time. All packing. . . . That was absolutely horrible. It was cold, you're working with people you don't know and thinking, 'God, do I really want to be doing this?' They gave us a job with thousands of little lipsticks and we had to sort them out. It took ages and ages. We were sitting on the cardboard boxes or standing up – that wasn't a problem – but there were no facilities you could use. You had to bring your own food and drink. You could eat it sitting on a box or in someone's car. It was 8.00 till 6.00, with a little break for lunch. But everyone wanted to eat quickly and get back to work.

I didn't do that long, a few weeks. I really didn't like that at all but they [the employment agency] didn't have anything better for me to do. They did get me another job. It was a cleaning job at a factory, very different to what I normally do. I did that for a couple of weeks too. The job there was probably the easiest cleaning job I have ever had in my life. It'd take me about an hour and then I'd just sit around. . . . I was on my own doing that. It took the pressure off me quite a bit. I did it quite relaxed. When you first start a job you are quite enthusiastic, but after a period of time you start thinking, 'Oh my God. What I am doing in this?' It seems to get harder and harder the more you do it. I definitely wouldn't go back to cleaning again, definitely not. It's boring, you know; it's not a nice job anyway. And sometimes it can be quite hard work, it can, really. Especially in hot weather, it really does get to you. And the pay isn't great, about £4.60 an hour. It was more than the basic wage, though. It felt reasonable to me at the time.

The final time I spoke to Guy he told me he had had several more temporary jobs at the end of the winter including working for a private security firm for which he had lied about his age. Under his girlfriend's influence, he had finally taken a more permanent job as a trainee manager in a dry-cleaners:

> My girlfriend was a full-time hairdresser and she ... got annoyed that I was not working much and she was all the time, so I looked for a job. I started in a dry-cleaners before Christmas. That job was in the paper. I went along and had an interview and that went quite well. They asked me if I'd had any experience dry-cleaning. I told them a little white lie and told them that I did. ... I told them I had some GCSEs too. I said that it was a job with opportunities and I could see myself going somewhere. But I didn't mean it, to be honest. I just wanted a job and I wanted some money. I was fed up.

Whether Guy simply has bad luck or whether it is his evident lack of commitment, this job too did not last:

> They never gave me a contract and everything started getting a bit pear-shaped after a few months. ... I thought this wasn't right for me. I want another job. The manager and me, he was a bit funny with me and we were having a few fights. I used to turn up late, only about five minutes and that but he got funny. And for my cheeki-ness. Apparently I got a bit too comfortable with the friendly relationships everyone had and everyone was getting a bit cheeky with the manager. But I thought this was enough. I started getting bored with it too, to be honest with you. And I wanted more money as well. I was on £4.80 an hour. I got paid monthly about £400 or £500 a month. And it wasn't covering all my expenses. I didn't pay any rent at home, though. I was getting really fed up. I looked around and thought why am I here.

After four months, which was the longest period he had held a steady job, he walked out, as he found the work boring. He also explained that 'my home life at that time was really tense. I was getting into a lot of trouble and my dad was shouting at me. We spent long periods when we wouldn't talk at all.' He was close to his siblings, however, but they no longer lived at home and so he spoke to them every day by phone. Both of them had 'good' jobs in the service sector: in a computer firm and an office manager for a law firm respectively and, although Guy wished he could emulate them, he was clear about his own lack of commitment:

'The trouble with me is that I think about things but I never actually do anything, which is a shame.'

So, like Richard, Guy was devastatingly clear sighted about his own attributes and equally unwilling to attribute his current lack of opportunities and commitment to work to anything but his personal choices. In this sense, then, Guy more closely conforms to the 'feckless lad' stereotype, the school 'failure' that was not prepared to make an effort. And yet, as the extracts reveal, Guy is a thoughtful, articulate young man, clearly able to express coherent opinions verbally. His options, however, in the polarized labour market in Cambridge look grim without a decision to try to gain some educational credentials: a decision that at the time Guy was adamant he would not make.

The Excluded – John and Vince

While it was clear that Guy would be able to talk his way into almost any entry-level job – his problem was holding on to employment – there was another group among the 24 school leavers who found it difficult to find work of any sort, whether a job with decent conditions and some security or even the type of low-wage and insecure work in shops and fast-food outlets that many of the young men had to be satisfied with. This group of young men, including Vince in Sheffield and John and Andrew in Cambridge, were among the most disadvantaged in the group, with low levels of social and cultural capital, either through their familial background, their educational achievements or their personal characteristics. As other studies of adolescents have documented, school failure and problems entering the labour market are particularly marked among children from difficult home circumstances or those with a range of educational and personal disadvantages. As official assessments of social exclusion among young people have demonstrated (Training and Enterprise Council 1998), a number of complex and interrelated factors are associated with social and economic exclusion: interrupted schooling, lack of family support, few formal qualifications and reduced self-confidence, as well as poverty through unemployment and low pay. Many of these factors, especially early family disruption, have strong associations with several of the outcomes in adulthood (Hobcraft 1998: 2), as the case studies demonstrate.

Vince had a difficult home life. Initially, he was living with a foster mother whom he disliked. During the year she had begun to live with a man who abused both her and Vince, which, as I shall show below, affected his commitment to employment, and by the end of the year after leaving school he had run away, leaving no forwarding address. Andrew's birth father was in prison and he lived with his mother and stepfather. Andrew was also an unprepossessing boy at 16, with weight and personal hygiene problems, which disadvantaged him in entry to many of the body-conscious service-sector jobs on offer. He was, however, able to find a part-time job as a kitchen porter and later on as a supermarket checkout operator (see table 5.2). Here, then, I focus on the attempts made by John and by Vince to begin their lives as workers in Cambridge and Sheffield, showing how chance and circumstance affected their differential success.

The value of charitable provision

John was perhaps the most complex of the 24 young men with whom I talked, and his initial behaviour seemed to me to exhibit signs of severe disturbance. John lived with his parents in a local authority house. His dad worked on a casual basis, according to John, 'doing odd jobs at the Science Park'. His mother worked mornings at a pre-school playgroup and was also a childminder for two days a week, taking a three-year old child into her home. At Fenland Community College, John was a self-identified member of the 'nutter' clique. He told me that 'I go around with the nutters and we do weird stuff, act real mad. I think the rest of them think we are a bit weird. Everyone just calls me thick cos I go around doing all sorts of weird stuff, and they've got nicknames for me – psycho and things like that.' He told me that he was also regarded as weird by his parents and on probing explained that he often became hysterical, overreacting to comments or events that he found amusing. His parents dealt with this by sending him upstairs until he calmed down and, as far as I was able to ascertain, John had never received any sort of assistance such as counselling while he was a school student, although he did receive extra help to address his dyslexia.

John was both nervous and aggressive during our conversations, picking his fingers and walking round, although he was articulate and spent a long time talking with me. His strongest views seemed to revolve around physical disgust. He told me he refused to consider part-time work while still at school because 'I can't be bothered: it's too boring and you get idiots everywhere; they're disgusting.' He did not drink, smoke or take any form of illegal drugs: 'No, not at all, no way: it's disgusting; there's quicker ways to kill yourself, i'n' it?' He also found his father repulsive: 'My dad is a right state; he just lets himself go: he's got all tatty clothes cos he works doing pots [washing up] and stuff, and planting things, so he's got tatty clothes and looks dirty. He's a right scary thing. Me friends say me dad's a bit unusual. Me parents do me head in, they're just so annoying.' This was to change, however, as John, after several vain attempts to find work and a period of unemployment, became a participant in the Prince's Trust schemes for disadvantaged youth. The Prince's Trust, established two decades ago under the auspices of the Prince of Wales, is a charitable organization whose aims include the reduction of urban deprivation and rural poverty. It provides training for socially excluded youths, in an attempt both to reduce levels of involvement in crime and to enhance the skills and opportunities of disadvantaged young people.

During the initial few months after leaving school, John found it difficult to settle and could not decide what to do: 'I'd hoped to get on some sort of youth training scheme but that didn't work out. I didn't want to get a job so I just went along with me mum to the playgroup; it's like a community hall thing so they can't leave all the toys lying about, yeah, so you've got to pack all these toys in a sort of cupboard and I get paid £10 for that.' He continued, showing that it's possible to find satisfaction in even the most menial of tasks: 'And it's quite tricky cos if you don't get them all in in a certain way, they don't all fit in.'

At Christmas, John said he had 'no clue' what he wanted to do in the medium term and although he was clearly short of money, he told me he did not spend much as his social life mainly revolved around playing computer games at home or in his friends' houses, riding his bike and 'just hanging about'. However, six months later, his life had changed considerably. He was more enthusiastic and seemed to have an idea of what sort of job he might eventually be able to find. He attributed these changes to his successful participation in a 12-week Prince's Trust course from mid-February: 'I think it was just a stroke of luck that they [the Careers Guidance Service] happened to mention it to me. In May 2000 he was just about to start the course again, 'as I have nothing else to do yet'. Before February, John told me:

> I'd been to the Careers a few times, a couple of times with me mum and then on me own, and they told me about a couple of things but nothing was really working out that well. I had to go to the jobcentre too to sign on cos of not being able to get on a course, but I signed on a couple of times before they told me about the Prince's Trust. I got £61.60 a week, I think.

He then started the Trust programme. The courses involve a mixture of personal and social skills' development, some community service and physical activities. Almost without drawing breath, John told me what was involved:

> It was difficult at first as I didn't know no one there. I kept quiet in a corner. There were about 30 of us at first, in two teams, but by the end there were only 12 of us left. We do all sorts of things. We went away on a Wing Fellowship for a week looking after elderly and disabled people for a week. They can be quite hard. And it was shifts – two, either 7.45 in the morning till the evening, or one with a break and then on again in the evening until 12.00 at night. We went to Derbyshire too, and did rock climbing, orienteering, kayaking and stuff like that. I liked that. At the start of the second time, we did it all again but me and this other bloke had to stay out of bits of it as we had done it before. You have to follow clues and bring stuff back.
>
> I got a general health and safety certificate, and a Wing certificate for looking after the old people. You don't get paid. I got Job Seeker's Allowance and most people get benefits. But you also get people who are working but they come to improve their social skills and that, their talking and that; then they go back to work. You have to do a presentation and keep a folder. We did a play for our final presentation. But most of us were 17 and 18. It's more blokes than girls, not sure why.
>
> It's great. It's fun and useful. You don't actually do that much writing and that. It's mainly have a laugh and you don't actually realize you are learning stuff until you know... plus you get to meet new people. It's much better than school. You are relaxed around everyone, and, the team leaders, last time, they were really nice. I hope it will help me get a job.

I asked him what he might consider:

> I would really like a job with art, but anything outside really, like gardening. As long as I am not stuck behind a desk. I couldn't be doing with that. I am now on this Gateways scheme with the Careers and they will find me a place with training and that, after my second Prince's Trust course. I have got to go back to the Careers, and have appointments and that and then they fix you up.

Like Shaun and Matthew, then in Sheffield, it seemed that basic- level employment in a typical masculine occupation – gardening – would provide an initial entry into the labour market for John that might enable him to live a reasonably independent life dominated by labour market participation.

A transition derailed?

For Vince in Sheffield, this option of independence seemed a more distant prospect at the end of the first year after leaving school. His experiences show how family problems can derail the transition to labour market participation for vulnerable young people. Vince's birth parents had split up when he was four and since then he had lived with foster parents. His foster-father was self-employed: 'He gets body parts for Metros [a make of car] and goes round and puts leaflets through people's doors and mends their cars.'

Vince was a tall, thin, nervous youth and he told me that he often did not attend school: 'I got fed up at school. I got very thin and didn't eat and I got tired. I stayed at home; mostly Mum didn't mind, but some days she did. Me dad didn't mind cos he didn't go to school much either.' And in a sad addendum, Vince added, 'He classes himself as thick,' revealing the internalization of middle class judgements of working class boys who failed to achieve at school. Vince told me that he had never seen a doctor or health visitor, nor had his foster-parents visited the school to discuss Vince's problem. 'It don't matter,' he said. 'I'm thick too. I just want to leave school.'

As his school attendance was so sporadic, Vince's own opinion of his abilities was confirmed. He had not been entered for any GCSE exams in the summer of 1999 and, like Darren and Shaun, he had been placed in a vocational stream involving practical courses in painting and gardening at a local college on a day-release basis during the final year. Yet again, he echoed the typical praise of working class boys for educational experiences they enjoy: 'It were fine; we were a good group and we had a laugh.' He told me that the students who were expected to do well, 'the clever ones, they keep themselves to themselves, they do. I don't know most of them. They're stuck up and not friendly.' As well as the vocational placement, Vince had worked at an old people's residential home as work experience in year 11: 'It was all right. In fact, I liked it a lot and they offered me a job in the end but I just didn't think I'd fancy it full-time.' Once again the Careers Guidance Service proved invaluable and found Vince a position through a training provider, the South Yorkshire Training Group, to combine working in a supermarket with a foundation level GNVQ on a day-release basis. But as it turned out, this position was unsuccessful.

Perhaps reflecting his home circumstances, Vince was one of the very few boys who had considered living independently once he left school. He had a friend who hoped to take over the tenancy of a council flat from his mother's partner and had suggested that Vince might move in too. Vince also knew a group of boys who had been kicked out of school and their own homes and were 'dossing here and there, sleeping on floors and that' and with whom, he told me, 'I smoke a bit of draw [cannabis], and sometimes there's heavier drugs too'. While several of the 24 young men admitted they smoked, only Lee in Cambridge, apart from Vince, was prepared to talk about taking class A drugs, including cocaine. At the time of the second interview, Vince told me he was having serious difficulties at home, and was contemplating moving out. He had a 'new' dad:

> He and me mum have got together recently, since I left school, and he didn't like me a lot. He were too strict. I couldn't go out with all me friends and just do stuff. And he'd come home drunk and start hitting me mum and stuff, and that I weren't putting up with and we got in a fight and police and stuff got involved. . . .
>
> My mum, she never talked when he were around; she just kept quiet and he sort of were dominating the house and he just thought he were a big man. And I got this job, at the supermarket, and I went thear, and the day I went thear, the day I went thear, that morning, he'd not been in all night and he came home drunk and he started in on me mum. So that got me mad and when I came home, she told me cos he'd gone out to work or summat. So I locked all t' doors, shut curtains and just told her to sit down and I did a cup of tea. And then he came home and just started banging on t' door, trying to get in and stuff. I were reet angry. I felt like killing him. Me mum she were just crying. She were thinking about phoning t' police but I did it instead and they came and had a word with him. And after that he were a bit quieter and just went off. The police talked to my mum about it and asked me questions and then they put it all in a file and said if there were any more problems to ring this number. After that he was a bit all right. And then one night me mum asked him if I could go out till half past nine, cos I were going to me friend's house, and he wouldn't let me. He was in a right funny mood so I just walked out and went to his house and he came after me, flung me in the back of the car and I just weren't allowed out. The next morning

I went to work and this kid he were just dissing[2] me mum to the fullest and that got me even more mad and I got into a fight wi' him and I got sacked.

Thus Vince's first job after school came to an end. So too did his mother's short-lived relationship: 'She kicked him out about a month ago, sometime before Christmas.' But his problematic few months seemed to have scuppered Vince's chances of employment. He had nothing to offer potential employees, no qualifications, a record of physical violence and he had been sacked from his first real job. He had also been involved with a number of street robberies, instigated by a friend: 'We just walk up to these groups of kids and take their phones off 'em. Usually they don't do nothing,' and so far he had not been caught.

When I saw him in January 2000, he had been unemployed for nearly three months and, like many young people with too little to do (Allatt and Yeandle 1992), he passed much of the day sleeping: 'I'll stay in bed as long as I can, till afternoon, and then get up and have something to eat; and then I'll stay upstairs on t' computer, just playing games on me own.' Vince was boy who, when I asked him to describe what sort of a young man he was, said, 'A boring one. I just sit in t' house.' But he did tell me that he was planning to try to get a job:

> I don't mind what. I'm not right picky. I just want to get some money in, like, for us [him and his mother] and then I can leave that and go off for a job what I want. . . . I'm thinking of going down to Meadow'all and having a look round. Me next door neighbour works for Woolworths and she finds out about all the jobs and stuff and she just tells me.

He confessed to being 'a bit fed up' but refused to consider trying to pass some exams: 'it probably would be a good idea, yeah, but I didn't like school or that college where I went during school. The staff were all right. It were the other kids, they give you dirty looks and just start with all me mates. I haven't been in a fight there, but all me mates have. I'm never going back.'

Sadly, Vince never did manage to find work and he began to spend more and more time in 'bad company'. According to his foster mother he just packed up and left home at Easter, not telling her where he was going, and by July she had heard nothing from him. One of the other boys said he had seen Vince, begging in the city centre one day, but that he had not spoken to him. All my attempts to trace him failed.

Escape Attempts

Apart from Vince, then, and Kevin[3] the stories so far have been ones of relative success, albeit to different degrees. Even the most disadvantaged boys, from difficult home circumstances or with very low levels of achievement, managed to find employment, and others started and persisted with college courses, which they combined with labour market participation. All that remains in this chapter is to explore the typical escape routes for working class boys: through the exploitation of bodily attributes and, often, brute force. As feminist anthropologist Sherry Ortner (1974: 73) argued almost three decades ago, 'nature is devalued compared to culture and so the categories of people who are perceived as being more rooted in, or having more direct affinity with nature' are themselves devalued and regarded as inferior by the dominant order. The growing number of studies of masculinity have drawn on her argument by emphasizing the significance of embodiment, a key element in the social construction of subordinate masculinity, through which working class men become confined in or identified through their body. Traditional forms of manual labour, of course, relied on male strength. As Charlesworth (2000: 259) has argued:

> Working class men's comportment seems to emblematize a form of rugged masculinity that shuns physical pain and sentimentality and which values the hardness and strength of the body. In their conditions they have to be able to turn their hand to as many manual jobs as they can in order to survive in a labour market in which they are just 'hands' and infinitely replaceable.

In fact, as I argued in chapter 2, the value of 'rugged masculinity' is now largely being replaced in the labour market by forms of embodiment that emphasize docility and deference, and so challenge typically masculine forms of embodiment. However, masculine hardness and strength are still highly valued attributes on the sports field, in the boxing ring and in the army: all of which, for generations, have provided escape routes from monotonous low-paid work for working class boys.

Football as a career

As I have already shown, Greg's father hoped to relive his glory days through one of his son's footballing prowess. Among the 24 participants in this study, only one – Pauly in Sheffield – had the real prospect of escape through sport. A good-looking, robust, physically mature and boastful boy, in the first conversation, Pauly assured me that he was a successful womanizer as well as frequent habitué of over-18 clubs. His main topic of conversation and his evident passion, though, was football. He was, in his own words, 'sports mad' and played as a schoolboy for Yorkshire in the English Schoolboys Championship. On the verge of leaving school he signed a two-year contract with a local club as a youth apprentice.

> I first started playing when I were 9 and reached the highest standard for boys by 12 when I played for Yorkshire. I played for the school all the easy through the years and then, when I were 14, I started playing for Barnsley juniors. It were the PE teacher at school who got me playing at a high standard cuz he was a scout for Barnsley Football Club. He sent me for a trial down at Barnsley and I got in and I played for Barnsley for two years. But I didn't get on with the management down there so I left and went to Rotherham.

When I first met Pauly, however, he was injured: 'I've got shin sprains and I've been out for three months. When I felt a pain in my shin I told the manager and he said, "Right, you're not playing again for three months cos I don't want you injured for life." I'm starting training again next week.' The club were, apparently, prepared to take a risk with Pauly: 'I'm dead lucky to get it [the apprenticeship]. There was 15 of us in for it and me resting me shin, but they've dropped some, cos there are only 6 placements and I'm one of them, so there's only 5 others got in.'

Sadly, however, the club's vote of confidence was misplaced. Pauly was injured again just six weeks after starting to play again and, in the brutal world of professional sport, he was out with no compensation and no future in football. After this humiliating start to his adult life, he refused to speak to me again.

'The army wouldn't have me'

The final story, also one of failure, at least in the short term, is about the army as a route to advancement. Rick was among the most conventional looking of the Sheffield group of boys – short hair, no jewellery and a generally neat appearance and his local speech mannerisms were less pronounced than was typical locally, even though his family had lived in the area for years. His father had, for example, also been a pupil at Park

Edge School. His dad worked as a porter in the main city hospital and his mother had just started as a personal shopper in a department store. He was the youngest of three children and, like Rick, his two older sisters had also left school at 16. In the final year at school Rick told me he hoped to be successful in an application for a modern apprenticeship, preferably to an engineering company:

> I just like practical stuff. I can't sit down at t' desk and right all the time. I like to do something with me hands. . . . I went to Jewsons for work experience: it's like a builders' merchants. That were good there. I got on well there. I just can't wait to leave school. It drives me mad. Teachers boss you about too much. You can put up with it for so long but then, once you've grown out of it, that's it.

Unfortunately Rick's impatience with school and sitting at a desk was reflected in disappointing GCSE results and his route to an apprenticeship seemed to be closed: 'My results weren't that great, to be honest. I weren't right happy with them; I got an E in Maths and that were a surprise, but I did get a B in Technology – that were all right.' But his other grades were mainly Ds and Es and he asked me, rather plaintively, 'So they weren't really bad but, they weren't really *really* bad, were they? Just not too bad.'

After some searching through the local papers and a visit to the Careers' Guidance Service, however, Rick did secure a traineeship with a company that did machining but

> it was a very, very boring job, nothing like I thought it would be like. Basically I was a bit of a skivvy, so I did it for two months, and then I left cos I was supposed to be learning something and I wasn't. It was a waste of time, so I left there. Then I needed a job, you know, for the money, like, so I was prepared to do anything. So I started at McDonald's. It's a very easy job to get, you see, and easy money, and I am still there now. But what I really want to do is to join the army.

Apparently this had been Rick's long-term ambition: he had mentioned to me when I first met him. He'd always enjoyed sports and keeping fit and also knew he would be able to pick up a trade as a soldier:

> So I applied as soon as I was 17, but they turned me down. Apparently, I have got something on me medical record, so I have got to wait until I am 18 and I can go in then. I think it's my asthma. You have got to have no problems with your asthma for four years. So I'll

just have to wait and take whatever job comes along till then. I'm leaving McDonald's for another job as soon as I can, though.

So Rick too was a 'flexible' worker, moving between entry-level jobs in the service sector, after an initial sortie into what remains of the metal industries in Sheffield. As he astutely noted, 'There's no career at a place like McDonald's. It's not a permanent job. It's just for young ones, like. It's just for money really. They have a lot leaving and they have a lot coming on, so it's just one of them jobs.' Unfortunately, 'just one of them jobs, just for money' seemed to be the lot of the majority of the 24 school leavers, as well as for their peers who, as school failures, continue to leave school at the age of 16.

In the final chapter, the current suggestions by policy-makers to affect this choice and to improve the opportunities for young entry-level workers will be addressed. First, however, I want to return to the debates about 'yobs', 'lads' and forms of youthful 'protest masculinity' in spaces of leisure, pubs and the streets in the main, as well as attitudes about sex and sexuality and family life in the locality in order to assess the links between work and home, employment and everyday life, among young men. It is clear from their own words, recorded at length in this and the preceding chapter, as well as from chapters 4 and 5, that most of the men whom I interviewed are reliable rather than reluctant workers, imbued with the values of the Protestant ethic, and determined to make the best of what limited opportunities are open to them. Unlike the older and more settled workers who Sennett talked to in Boston and elsewhere, these young men are not 'corroded' by dissatisfaction but are instead remarkably resilient and cheerful in the face of the monotonous tasks, the often-demeaning drudgery that confronts them everyday at work and the extremely low levels of pay that are their weekly reward. They seem relatively unaware of their lack of privilege and of the lifetime earnings gap that will open up between them and their better-educated peers over their lifetimes. But at present no amount of exhortation from teachers or from Ministers of Education will persuade them of the value of postponing labour market entry for more than a year or two at most. And for most of these young men, their familial expectations merely confirm their choice. What has radically changed, however, since these men's fathers were young is the availability of secure lifetime employment for working class men which enabled them to establish an independent household and support a family. Low-level service employment is no basis for a similar pattern in the future, even though as I show in the next chapter this is what most of these young men expect from their futures.

8

Performing Identity: Protest and Domestic Masculinities

Like gender, sexuality is not given, it is learnt, imposed, acquired, worked at, experimented with, negotiated and, often with difficulty, experienced. (Morgan 2002: 164)

In the previous chapters – in which 24 young men talked about their work lives – I have shown that contrary to popular representations of low-achieving working class youths as idle and unreliable, most of the young men to whom I talked were making serious efforts either to enter the labour market or to combine waged work with further education. In conversation, they emphasized the importance of employment and of earning a living to their sense of themselves as self-reliant and as 'proper' men. Most of them insisted on their trustworthiness and reliability as employees. Indeed, it was the word 'reliable' that was reached for again and again by these young men when I asked them for a handful of words that they thought best described them.

In this penultimate chapter, the key focus is non-work life and social relations with friends and family. I want to turn from the workplace to the other spaces and places that are important in young men's lives, to look at the ways in which they construct and perform versions of masculinity in their out-of-work lives – in leisure activities, in friendships and relationships and in the locality. It is here that the 'laddish' behaviour that dominates the popular press might perhaps be most evident. As Majors

(1990) argued in his analysis of the social construction of masculinity among minority men in the USA as a 'cool pose', all men are expected to conform to hegemonic definitions of masculinity which require them to be successful breadwinners. Too often excluded by socio-economic circumstances from access to the necessary financial resources to fulfil these expectations, black men instead have to look to other arenas, especially in leisure activities, to demonstrate their manliness and masculine style. Similar arguments characterize studies of masculinity among socially excluded and less affluent white men in which aggressive displays of macho behaviour and challenges to authority have been identified. But even here, in their out-of-work activities, most of the young men in this study challenged stereotypical representation of 'protest' masculinity. They were on the whole, if not models of virtue, relatively responsible and surprisingly mature, with strong opinions about acceptable forms of behaviour in both their social and sexual activities.

As I shall show, these young men live spatially circumscribed lives in both Cambridge and in Sheffield. In the main, they seldom venture far beyond a few miles from their homes. For these men popular notions of an increasingly mobile society in which citizens are able to participate in an informational economy, largely untrammelled by the constraints of distance, have little purchase on their diurnal activities. If the wealthy and the work-rich, the specialist 'self-programmable' workers at the top end of the service sector, are constrained by time-shortages, living and working in what Castells (2000) termed 'the space of flows', then these young men, the 'generic labourers' of the service economy, are constrained by location and live in a 'space of places'. Despite the increasing significance of economic globalization, it is important to remember that a large proportion of the global proletariat consists of locally based workers, not only in the Third World but also in the advanced industrial societies. As Faux and Mishel (2001: 95) have argued, in economies and societies in which income inequalities are increasing:

> People at the top end of the income distribution in all countries not only have deeper financial reserves; their income is also more likely to be generated from capital that is more mobile and therefore more able to avoid being trapped in a depressed country. People at the bottom, however, whose income is generated by their labour are tied much more tightly to their immediate economic surroundings.

For unskilled and underqualified young men whose labour market assets are minimal and whose social and educational capital almost worthless in the service-based economy, 'spatial entrapment' (Hanson and Pratt 1995) is extremely significant. These men may often have time on their hands, but their incomes are inadequate and their resources too few to allow them to escape the limited set of opportunities within their localities. Because of their low wages, the 24 men in this study had relatively small disposable incomes and consequently their opportunities for 'hell-raising' were limited. All but one of the young men in Sheffield, for example, contributed between £10 and £25 a week to their parental household, although this was less usual in Cambridge (only four of the ten did so), and so their spare cash for enjoying themselves was limited. Thus, unlike affluent workers or better-educated and more fortunate young people, free to explore an ever-increasing set of educational and leisure opportunities, these young men are trapped in 'place'. As I shall demonstrate in this chapter through a focus on a range of spaces within the locality – the street, the neighbourhood and the home – both current and potential – not only are these young men's lives locally based but so too are their aspirations. They also exhibit a form of territorial loyalty that to a large extent is based on the expulsion of perceived threats to the locality from a range of 'Others'.

It is, however, also important to emphasize that even the least-mobile young people participate in forms of youth culture that transgress the boundaries of locality. Youth cultures – style, music, clothes, clubbing – have long transcended geographical divisions and may cross-cut structural differences within and between places. At any particular time, the consumption of the same 'labels', the same iconic goods, the same music, links young people together across class and spatial boundaries, despite their differential access because of inequalities in financial resources. But, as Bauman (1998) suggests, the young poor may be failed or flawed consumers of contemporary consumption-based cultures rather than full participants. It may be that the increase in income inequality that has been evident in Great Britain since the late 1970s has recut patterns of youth culture, so that class and locality based distinctions are regaining their significance. Whereas analysts of youth culture focusing on the 1960s and 1970s were able to document moves towards an increasingly international youth culture with growing uniformity among young people (Brake 1987), the evidence at present is contradictory (Amit-Talai and Wulff 1995; Sibley 1995). The rapid expansion of university education into a mass system at the end of the twentieth century, as well as increasing difficulties in entering the housing market as an independent young worker, may, for example, have led to a greater uniformity in lifestyle among late teens and twenties. However, these same trends also create greater problems in accessing this common lifestyle for the socially excluded with few educational credentials (MacDonald 1997). For poor working class youth trapped on the outer estates of British cities, new global networks, such as cheap travel and the Internet, that diminish the friction of distance, may only reinforce their spatial immobility if they are out of reach because access is too expensive. Only 6 of the 24, for example, had a holiday in the summer after leaving school. As I explore below, their out-of-work lives, like their work and college lives, are also predominantly local.

Masculine Street Performance: The Lads' Night out

As is common among many of Britain's youth, Friday night out, and often Saturday too (Chatterton and Hollands 2002; Hollands 1995; Miles 2000), was a ritual in Cambridge and Sheffield. Although many of the men to whom I talked went out during the evening on a regular basis, on weekday evenings the main aim seemed to be to find something to do that did not involve spending money. Thus many of them visited friends' houses to watch TV or play computer games, or alternatively they just hung about on street corners or by local shops: the 'hanging about and doing nowt' as Darren put it, that in policy-makers' minds is often associated with petty crime and vandalism. But the weekend was different. Friday and Saturday, and less commonly Sunday, were big nights out, involving drinking in pubs or clubs (Gofton 1990), cruising round town if one of the group had a car, meeting girls and perhaps concluding the evening with a curry or a takeaway.

Just over half of the young men in this study went to pubs and clubs at the weekend, and drank something in the order of 6–8 pints of, usually, lager each evening:

> I go drinking, play snooker with me friends. (Rick, Sheffield)

> If we've got the money, we'd go and play pool and have a few pints. (Kurt, Cambridge)

These young men emphasized, however, that they seldom got unpleasantly drunk and that they made a decision to try to stay out of trouble:

I like enjoying meself on weekends, but I don't drink on the streets; just go to the pubs and have a laugh with some of me mates. I don't cause no trouble or owt. (Darren, Sheffield)

His views were confirmed by both Simon and Paul. Simon, interestingly, did refer to himself in terms of the common media image of young working class men, but he also contested its associations:

I'm a bit of a lad, one of the lads, up for a joke, messing about, going out in a group but we don't cause trouble, fight or that. (Simon, Sheffield)

Whereas Paul insisted on his own distance from popular images and indeed from what he regarded as typical behaviour by his own age group:

I don't like people me own age. It's just that they . . . most people my age want to hang out on street corners and drink on the streets and that, I mean I think you should sit in a pub and have a few pints with your mates rather than sit on t' street with a bottle, smashing windows and things which is what a lot of people do round my area. It's like a normal 16-year-old thing to do that but I'm not into that. I'd rather go and sit in a pub. (Paul, Sheffield)

And in Cambridge too, all 10 men with the single exception of Wayne, whose working life was discussed in chapter 6, agreed with the Sheffield respondents, stressing that, although they liked a drink, they tried to avoid getting involved in physical violence. They explained that drinking was often a problem for men of their age as they 'couldn't hold it, like'. Too much to drink, they suggested, made them feel out of control or, worse, invincible, leading to taking silly risks, ending up out of control if they were not careful, and getting involved in fights when they really did not want to. The men to whom I talked told me how drink makes them feel invincible, able to take (stupid) risks and behave outrageously, sometimes against their better judgement. It often seemed, when they were out, as if they were trying to develop a compromise version of an acceptable masculinity that included drinking but not so heavily that they were in danger of losing control. As Canaan (1996: 120) has noted in a study of young men's behaviour in public spaces, 'masculinity [is], then, fundamentally contradictory'. Young men have to live up to their reputations for 'hardness' while ensuring that they do not overstep their own boundaries or fears of losing control.

Not all young men to whom I talked, however, negotiated a compromise between the contradictory versions of masculinity, whether a compromise based on a rational decision or on the fear of loss of control. Wayne, for example, candidly admitted that he deliberately looked for trouble, and enjoyed fighting: 'I go up there [a club in Cambridge] to fight, to start one. It's my new thing now. You just walk up there and look for someone to start a fight with. . . . I only do it when I have a bad day though.' He also openly admitted his homophobic behaviour: 'I go when all the queers are there, and shout at them. Some of them ignore but others don't and take a swing at you.'

As Mac an Ghaill (1996b) emphasized, one of the key ways of constructing heterosexual masculinity is through differentiation from women and gay men. In leisure spaces this is often achieved though jokes and taunts, calling out in the streets, yelling abuse, sexist and homophobic jokes and comments to more serious forms of harassment and violence of the type that Wayne admitted too. In these ways young men assert their public identities as red-blooded heterosexual males. While homophobic behaviour seemed uncommon among the other 23 men, at least in their own reports, sexist attitudes and behaviour were not and, through casual talk, jokes and various forms of 'messing about' on the streets and in clubs, for example, the young men in Cambridge and Sheffield made it plain to me that not only were they heterosexual, although not all of them were sexually active – 'worse luck' as Gareth candidly admitted – but that typically they regarded also themselves as superior or dominant in their relationships with girls, as well as too young to be in a serious relationship. Thus Simon, speaking about his girlfriend, confided that he felt anxious about commitment: 'It's getting to worry me now; I've been going out with her too long.'

It was also clear that there was a clearly established gender division of leisure time. The ritual of the night out with their mates was clearly separated from seeing girlfriends:

On Friday I go out with 'our lass', and on Saturday it's wi' me mates. (Rick Sheffield)

And:

Well, I see 'the Mrs' on the weekend, but only on a Friday or a Saturday, not both. (Andrew, Cambridge)

While the pub and the club dominated these men's use of commercial leisure spaces, not all of them drank, either to excess or indeed even at all when they were there. In addition, a number of them were also active in other arenas, including sport. Several of them played sport on a casual basis, as well as, of course, the putative professional footballer, Pauly, and, as I noted earlier, Greg was a keen participant in martial arts. In Cambridge, two of the participants belonged to the Boys' Brigade and one of them played in the band. Rick in Sheffield, perhaps the hardest working of all the young men, had put together a rock band that had made a demo tape. But for most of them, local pubs and hanging round local shopping precincts, parks and other open spaces was the key element in their leisure-time activities. And part of their desire not to cause trouble, whether in pubs or in other spaces, was based on what they saw as a series of perceived threats to their neighbourhoods. Before exploring these threats, however, I want first to look in more detail at attitudes to heterosexuality among the group.

Sexual and Domestic Attitudes

The media image of working class men as a threat to middle class norms and values is, as I argued earlier, in part constructed through the opposition of their embodied 'animality' to middle class cerebral rationality. As a consequence, working class boys have long been portrayed as sexually predatory and sexually active from a young age. In 2000, the year after the 24 boys in this study had left school, a moral crisis about teenage pregnancy became evident. National statistics revealed an unacceptably high rate of under-age pregnancies, especially in deindustrializing towns and cities in northern Britain, compared with European Union averages, and the popular press focused on case studies of apparently feckless, sexually active boys, who from the age of 12 onwards boasted about their virility. However, as a number of contemporary studies of adolescent sexuality (Ford 1991; Johnson, Wadsworth, Wellings and Field 1994; West, Wight and Macintyre 1993) have shown, there is a wide range of both attitudes and behaviour among school students and school leavers. Thus, as studies of heterosexual relationships have demonstrated, there are 'several coexisting and potentially contradictory discourses concerning sexuality [which] make available different positions and powers for men and women' (Hollway 1984: 230). Although such discourses organize meanings and actions, they are not necessarily distinctive in behaviours, as the boundaries between them may blur. There remain gaps in the knowledge of how the discourses about sexuality commonly found among young people actually map on to sexual behaviour. Further, the sexual behaviour of young working class men has received relatively little attention (Wight 1994, 1996).

Wight's (1996) own study of young working class men, however, provides an instructive example and useful comparison. Working with young predominantly white working class Glaswegian men aged between 19 and 24, living on a peripheral estate, Wight argued that four discourses are common among working class youth, noting that 'even within a sample that is fairly homogeneous in terms of age, locality, parents' social class, housing and sexual orientation' (1996: 146) diverse concepts of masculine sexuality are common. He termed the four discourse categories the *uninterested*, the *predatory*, the *permissive* and the *have/hold or romantic*, describing them as follows.

Uninterested discourse

This discourse is an extreme expression of homosociality in that contact with the opposite sex is claimed to be of no concern at all (Wight 1996: 152). Wight suggests that it is commonly found among school students up to about the age of 14, illustrated by descriptions of girls by adolescent boys as, for example, 'pains in the neck'. He also suggests that it a discourse that is particularly evident among working class boys, perhaps emerging from 'the rigid gender boundaries that are central to traditional working class culture' (1996: 153).

The ways in which boys at Park Edge and Fenland described girls in their class as 'stupid', 'wussy' or 'gigglers', noted in chapter 4, are good examples of this discourse in classroom-based encounters and exchanges.

Predatory discourse

This discourse 'involves the stereotype of masculine sexuality, in which men gain esteem from their male peers by having as many sexual partners as possible. . . . Within this discourse, heterosexual intercourse is fundamental in asserting one's masculinity, and physical sexual pleasure is also of less importance than the opinions of one's male peers' (Wight 1996: 154). Wight argues that the enormous pressure teenage boys experience to lose their virginity is one aspect of this discourse.

Daniel, then a pupil at Fenland Community College, confirmed this view: 'they all get egged on to do it [have sex], especially boys, at school and that. There's some people who are always talking about that, joking and so on.'

Wight noted that within the predatory discourse, relationships are represented as short term and uncommitted, intimacy and trust are unimportant and among young men there is an overwhelming emphasis on penetrative sex. Women are regarded as sexually passive, although, interestingly, Wight's respondents recognized that these views were influenced by popular attitudes held by and about young working class men and that they were 'sort of stereotyped' (1996: 156). Holland, Ramazanoglu and Sharpe (1993) in their study of sexuality suggested that this predatory discourse was the dominant or hegemonic sexual discourse among young men, whereas the evidence from Wight's study and from my own at least partly challenges this assertion.

Permissive discourse

Although this discourse has many similarities with the former one, Wight notes two significant differences: 'First, in the permissive discourse sexual encounters are valued for their own sake, not primarily in order to confirm one's masculinity with one's male peers, and second, ideally women should play the same role as men, initiating encounters for their own sexual gratification' (1996: 157). However, these assumptions, but especially the latter, tend to be unrealistic, especially in the light of the crucial importance of a young woman's sexual reputation in working class cultures (see e.g. Holland, Ramazanoglu and Sharpe 1993; Skeggs 1997).

This discourse, however, makes a significant appearance in contemporary theorizations of late modernity. Paralleling versions of individualization in the labour market, outlined in chapter 2, the social theorist Anthony Giddens (1992), for example, has suggested that late-modern or 'risk' societies are also distinguished by new forms of sexual relationships, in which mutual sexual satisfaction is at the core with little or no long-term commitment once mutual satisfaction wanes. He terms this new form of permissive sexuality 'plastic sexuality' and links its emergence to the democratization of personal life, which is a consequence, he believes of the changing status of women in the twentieth century. While empirical verification of Giddens's claims is limited, his view is at odds with contemporary research among working class youth.

Have/hold or romantic discourse

The fourth discourse 'refers to the set of ideas and practices associated with monogamy, partnership and family life, though this does not necessarily involve companionate relationships' (Wight 1996: 159). While many previous researchers have argued that this is an explicitly feminine discourse, as young women look for commitment and security, Wight insists that 'men can also occupy a position as a subject within this discourse' (1996: 161).

As I shall demonstrate, this discourse was an important part both of the social construction of sexuality but also of gender identity among the boys from Fenland Community College and from Park Edge School. It also became clear that it is possible to have a contradictory location within more than one discourse, which partially depends on a common distinction between respectable femininity ('good girls') and disreputable femininity ('slags').

Wight found through group discussions with younger boys (14–16) that the traditional moral distinction between 'slags' (or, more commonly in his interviews, 'cows') and 'nice girls' was widely subscribed to by boys of that age (Wight 1994). Other research has found that adolescent girls, as well as boys, reproduce these categories (Wilkinson and Kitzinger 1995). In discussion with the boys from Cambridge and Sheffield in the context of a general discussion about teenage sexuality that I initiated using newspaper headlines, almost all 24 reproduced this rhetorical distinction. Their judgemental views tend to echo those of the tabloid press. I have already quoted Shaun whose reaction to the pregnancy of a girl in his class was 'it don't matter. She's just a slag.' His friend Gareth added, 'No, I don't feel sorry for them [pregnant teenagers]. They did it, after all, didn't they?'

Others echoed these opinions but qualified their statements with an assertion that the blame lay in the main with parents rather than with girls themselves. It was noticeable, however, that these young men generally absolved themselves from any responsibility. Here is Greg's comment on under-age pregnancy: 'It's pretty stupid really. It just shows they have nothing better to do, doesn't it. It's mainly the parents' fault cos they brought them up that way.' And Richard's: 'God, I think it comes from the parents to be honest, cos if you have got rough parents they set a bad example.' And Simon added: 'It makes me sick, girls at that age. They have still got their lives to live and you can't live a life with a kid at that age.'

Interestingly, however, all three of these young men told me that 'I'd support her 100 per cent if I got a girl pregnant,' whether the decision was to have the baby or a termination. Another young man told me, 'well, I mean, if I had a child now, I would be able to support it, and her, now I'm in work'. Clearly, their view of their own conduct was different from their more generally dismissive responses.

As Wight (1996) suggests, the distinction between slags and good girls, often made by boys who are still at school and many of them not sexually active, is a key link between the disinterested discourse and the predatory and have/hold discourses. The construction of a moral dichotomy separating girls who 'deserve all they get' is used to justify predatory masculinity, and uncommitted sex with no strings.

Here is Wayne whose views reflect this distinction and justification:

> Well, girls just ask for it, you know. They are tarty. They get all dressed up and I mean they are asking for it when they go down town all tarted up, don't you think? Tiny little T shirts, split skirts, great big heels. They are asking for trouble when they go out looking like that. But that's what boys go for isn't it? I mean, I know what young girls are like when they go out. They get drunk and go with boys and everything.

His response to my query whether boys should be more sensible was a devastating 'No, I think they should just go for it, me personally.'

Richard, who, like Wayne, was somewhat of 'a lad', noting without boasting that he had been having sex since he was 13, also had a predatory attitude to casual sexual encounters, warning that 'Well, you have got to be careful; you don't just...don't be stupid. Cos you can go to prison for that if you are 16 and the girl is under that. If she presses charges you have lost it cos she can press charges and claim money and that. Cos you know what girls are like [adding in a semi-serious tone] they'd do owt for money.'

Despite Richard's admission of under-age sex, both British and American surveys have found a relatively low frequency of intercourse among teenagers (Johnson, Wadsworth, Wellings and Field 1994; West, Wight and Macintyre 1993): a finding that is too often ignored by moralists and the media. Unsurprisingly, there was considerable variation in sexual experience among the 24 young men who were aged 16 and 17 when I talked to them. In Wight's survey, the age of first sexual intercourse varied from 12 to 19, and the median and modal age was 16. Some men in this study had had no sexual partners, most of them had one or a small number of 'one-night stands', often when either they or their partner, or usually both of them, were less than sober, whereas only three of them, including Simon, whom as I noted above was worried by commitment, and Pauly in Sheffield, and Guy in Cambridge had been or were involved in relatively long-term relationships (longer than 6 months). But several of them had had shorter-term relationships – sometimes of just a few days or weeks – and they described how they enjoyed dressing up to go out, planning to go for a meal after a cinema visit for example. Even Richard commented, with some respect, about a current girlfriend, 'our lass, she sorts me out, she does. She's got a good job as a secretary at a solicitors too.'

What was interesting was that the majority of these young men had a strong investment in the 'have and hold' discourse in the medium term. In answer to a question about how they envisaged their lives in five years time, all but two them specifically mentioned being in a long-term domestic relationship with a woman:

> I think I'll be married, like: a house, a wife and a car: that's how I hope it'll be anyways. (Steve, Sheffield)

'When I'm 20, perhaps 22,' Vince told me during our second conversation, 'I hope I'll have a good job, a nice house, in a nice area and a family.' Sadly, this seemed less likely as by the time of my third visit to Sheffield, as I noted in chapter 7, Vince had disappeared. Without exception, all the young men hoped to become a father, albeit not for a few years, and some of them spoke tenderly of their views about fatherhood. For example:

> Well, I think about taking a little nipper to school and seeing him do what you did an' that. (Craig, Sheffield)

It seemed clear, therefore, that although many of these men had an investment in both the predatory discourse of male sexuality, encouraged by talk at school or in the workplace to exaggerate their sexual prowess, they also believed in a discourse of romantic love and commitment. Whereas this have/hold orientation to sexuality and sexual relationships has often been associated with femininity, it is also a reflection of traditional or 'respectable' working class values that valorize family life. For young working class men on the verge of adulthood, embracing masculinity through labour market participation, the combination of different versions or discourses of sexuality requires a complex series of negotiations. These men must find a way to combine the predatory discourse – which brings both the respect, even the envy of their peers –

with the romantic discourse that will provide the basis for establishing a solid and eventually enduring relationship with a young woman. As I showed in the previous section, one way to do this is to ensure that the protagonists of each discourse remain separate in time and space, keeping 'our lass' or 'the Mrs' away from 'the lads'.

Wight (1996) suggested that these two discourses are commonly embraced by different types of young men. In his study, the early school leavers, the nutters in this study, or a group termed the 'neds' in Scotland in the early 1990s, were the group that was most likely to embrace a macho or protest version of predatory masculine sexuality. The 'boffins' or the 'bright guys', by contrast, tended to enunciate 'ideals of companionate relationships and were more likely to describe some of their relationships in terms of mutual commitment' (1996: 150–1). Wight notes that this latter group conform to Morgan's (1992) definition of Protestant masculinity – sensible and responsible, committed to themselves and future career. I want to suggest, however, that it is perhaps only the means of achieving these ideals that differentiate the former group from the latter. The young men whom I interviewed also enunciated a version of the Protestant work ethic and domestic commitment, despite the lower likelihood of being able comfortably to achieve it. Even Wayne, the most 'laddish' of the lads, told me 'I prefer nice girls, one's you can talk to, have a proper conversation with'.

Despite dire warnings from some of the more populist versions of the crisis of masculinity that men are in danger of being rendered redundant as sexual partners and as fathers (A. Clare 2000) or that 'feckless lads' refuse their responsibilities (Campbell 1993) these young men had clear belief in their future role as a committed family member. Indeed, numerous studies have shown that both men and women continue to define themselves as members of a family (Finch and Mason 1993; Morgan 1996; Morgan 2002; Silva and Smart 1999): a self-definition that may be particularly significant among less privileged men. Thus Fine and Weiss (1998: 47) have suggested that 'white working class men express strong sentiment about the family and specifically about male roles and responsibilities within the family': sentiments which might be enhanced by economic disadvantage and men's sense of loss as their ability to fulfil the role of the main breadwinner is reduced by economic restructuring and challenged by women's growing labour market participation. These 'strong sentiments', however, may be as likely to result in conflict between men and women within the family as the strengthening of reciprocal bonds of mutual obligation and respect and a diverse range of practices. As Morgan (2002: 153) has argued, 'Changing patterns of women's and men's employment, post-industrialization, women's in-creased education opportunities, urbanization, class, cultural capital and globalization are all factors that need to be recognized as influencing how men and women will respond to childcare and family responsi-bilities.'

It is also important to emphasize that discourse and practices are related in a complex way. Discourses do not necessarily provide a clear guide to actions, particularly in an arena as complex as sexuality and sexual/familial relationships, and especially when, as is the case here, these discourses are filtered through the research process. Further, as Wight also concluded, and I endorse his finding, sex as an erotic activity was a rather minor part of many young men's lives. The predatory discourse is only one part of the establishment of a particular version of working-class protest masculinity. Making trouble at school, drinking, fighting and having a laugh at work, as well as sexual activity, are ways in which young men establish themselves as men and construct their masculine identity within and across a range of spaces. At the same time, versions of domestic respectability, family values and the Protestant work ethic, which are key parts of respectable working class culture, are strong coun-ters to this 'macho' or protest masculinity. Becoming an adult man, espe-cially for working class boys, involves negotiation of this dichotomy and the construction of a compromise in which particular aspects of masculine identity are most evident in different arenas and locations.

Life at home

Further evidence of the significance of domestic respectability, often constructed through the lens of loss or threat, is to be found in the young men's relationships with their parents and in their attitudes to their neighbourhood. While their transition from school pupils to more independent adolescents was sometimes marked by a struggle at home – over clothes, music, and especially evening curfews – most of them reported that their parents were lenient and tolerant about their behav-iour and prepared to accept the growing independence of their sons. In return many of their sons held to versions of their families as 'decent', unlike the rough parents who, as the preceding section documented, might be blamed for their daughters' lack of sexual probity. A good proportion of these 24 young men had a continuing and close relation-ship with their fathers and would, for example, go for a pint with them now and then (although two of them noted that, in their opinion, their fathers drank too much), and several went fishing with their fathers on a regular basis. However, many of them also expressed a determination to become a different sort of man to their father:

He's boring, just boring. (John, Cambridge)

And:

Like my dad? No, I hope not. He's full of Yorkshire crap, he is. (Rick, Sheffield)

This dismissive tolerance, however, was missing from the responses of three young men for whom the relationship with their father or stepfather was much more problematic. For them a range of abusive behaviour had to be endured, both personally and towards their mothers and, as I have already noted, in one case the problem triggered leaving home and in another the youth and his mother were rehoused by the local authority. But in the main, these young men had reasonable relationships with their fathers and a small number among them clearly admired their fathers. This is Darren in Sheffield explaining why he did: 'Yeah, I do admire me dad. He does a lot of things for other people, like. See, he's a mechanic and if people round here want to buy a car, he'll, like, go and have a look for 'em before they buy it, and he doesn't charge them or owt, he just does it for a favour.'

Their relationships with their mothers were different and, in the main, seemed to revolve around domestic support – usually, although not always, of the son by the mother – rather than shared leisure activities. Remember Greg's mother in Sheffield who washed his McDonald's uniform every evening and made his breakfast. Many young men made similar comments about valuing home comforts:

I like it at home. I get my meals and everything done for me. (Wayne, Cambridge)

The relationship was sometimes, but less often, reciprocal:

I do some chores for me mum cos she has three jobs. I put the washing in and I do the ironing. (Gareth, Sheffield)

As other studies have shown, living at home in a reasonably supportive household is a key factor in young men's successful transition to adult status (Stafford, Heaver, Ashworth et al. 1999). These men, in the main, valued their familial life and had no plans to leave home, although it is also clear they had insufficient income to be able to achieve independence. While a small proportion of them had thought about leaving home to live with friends, most of them intended to stay at home as long as their parents allowed them to, suggesting that it would not be until they married that they would look for alternative accommodation. In many cases, they had older siblings who also lived in the parental home. The typical pattern among middle class young people of a period of independent living, often associated with participation in higher education, between leaving their parental home and re-establishing a version of the nuclear family, is a great deal less common among working class young people (Jones 1995; Kiernan 1985, 1995). And, as recent national statistics have revealed, the age of leaving home has become particularly extended among young men in Britain and in other west European countries.

Life in the Neighbourhood: Local Reputations and Perceived threats from 'Others'

In chapter 2 I drew on the work of Fine, Weiss, Addelstone and Marusza (1997) in deindustrialized towns in New York State to suggest that poorly educated and socially disadvantaged young men might blame the 'Other' for their relative lack of success in the labour market. In Sheffield and Cambridge, however, perhaps because of the relative youth of these early labour market entrants or because of the high levels of vacancies in the job markets, albeit in entry-level positions in the service sector in the main, sexist and racist attitudes and behaviour seemed to be uncommon. When I turned to a discussion of their local neighbourhood, however, parallels with Fine and Weiss's (1998: 41) work in Buffalo began to emerge. As they noted:

> The sense of assault [felt by working class men disadvantaged by economic restructuring] runs far deeper than in the economic realm alone. It invades the perceptions of many white men in their talk about neighbourhoods, of physical living spaces. They express a sense of no longer belonging, or that their neighbourhood is 'deteriorating', further evidence that it no longer belongs to them in either physical or psychological terms.

Like these young American working class urban residents, most of the young men in the two British cities agreed that their local area had 'gone down' because of the troublesome behaviour of a range of incomers:

It used to be a quiet area but it in't no more. Like there's all trouble and that. Fighting, smashed windows, cars getting nicked, all that sort of stuff. (Darren, Sheffield)

Rick held similar views, explaining at greater length what the 'trouble' involved, and like the US young men, attributing the deterioration to incoming 'others'. In Buffalo, the encroaching instability was often attributed to an influx of blacks or Hispanics, whereas in Sheffield it was less respectable members of the working class:

Well, I still like it round here but it's not that nice now. It's a bit rough. It used to be all right but it's a bit rough now. There's a lot of new people moving in, from down Manorhouse.[1] They are being re-housed here and they bring trouble. Some of them are druggies and they hang around the shops and stuff. There's weed, but now quite a lot of smack going about. We don't use it or hang about with people like that but if . . . er . . . I could pick people out who do it. And there's other stuff. Bikes get pinched and washing off lines, and cars get nicked, screeching round corners and stuff. That's usually young lads, about 17 and 18, you know. I've lived here a long time and I know what most people do and what most people don't do. (Rick, Sheffield)

In Cambridge a similar set of sentiments emerged in conversation. Many of the 10 young men echoed John's comment that

It's rough round here now. (John, Cambridge)

Wayne, in a long and more personal reflection, implicitly drew on the classic distinction between rough and respectable working class families, as he explored the problems of being part of a house-proud family in a 'rough' neighbourhood:

I mean we are the only one down our street that washes our car, cut the grass, washes windows and everything, cuz my dad's a cleaner you know and he does a perfect job when he cleans the windows, and in our house he hoovers the floor and what have you. Yeah, me mum and dad clean everywhere and make it look nice and I mean, then they are embarrassed cuz, I mean, cuz they don't have gardens that they don't cut the grass or let the dog poo everywhere. And so people go, 'Look, there's Wayne, all poshy and that lot.' There are a couple of boys down our street that go like that, but Dad says to me if they start anything, just, just knock 'em out; really duff 'em up.

Me mum wants to move. Me mum says to me, 'Just win the lottery, Wayne, and we'll move.' But, I mean, I'm happy where I'm living at the moment; it's a nice little place and really it's all right round here.

Interestingly, almost all the young men in both Cambridge and in Sheffield expressed a desire to stay in the locality, in the same neighbourhood, not just in the same city, in which they had grown up, as they became adults. Not only are their lives predominantly local, as I argued earlier, but so too are their aspirations. Despite their common representation of their neighbourhoods as 'under siege' from a variety of threats, others, like Wayne, expressed a sense of local pride. As Darren said, 'despite everything, it's a good place to come from, round here. People help one another and they aren't stuck up or owt'.

Conclusions

In their non-work lives, then, the attitudes, values and behaviour of these young men reinforce the view of them as perhaps surprisingly mature, responsible youth who are doing their best to get by and to avoid trouble. I found it hard to remember at times that they were only 16 and 17 years old when I talked to them, as they seemed so set on a path of what might be defined as respectable 'domestic conformity'. Although 'having a laugh' featured in all their lives, these men also planned to hold down a job and to provide for a family in the future. As this and earlier chapters have shown, they were certainly sexist in their attitudes, and adhered to entrenched and traditional views about masculinity and its correlates. While most of them enjoyed a drink and going out with the 'lads', they also hoped to establish a serious relationship with a young woman whom they could respect and to (re-)establish the type of nuclear working class family based on conventional gender divisions of labour that was still predominant in both the Cambridge and Sheffield neighbourhoods. They held strong views about their own attitudes and behaviour and those of other young people in contemporary Britain, arguing that the media exaggerated both the problems of being young, noting that 'they do go over the top a bit' (Shaun, Sheffield) and 'there's never anything good about young men, is there, in the papers or on the box?' (Damian, Cambridge). And despite the recognition that young men like them faced considerable pressures in 'getting settled', they agreed with Simon that 'it's easy now to be a man'. They were also surprisingly independent in their attitudes. In response to questions about role models, for example, the common response was an expression of a clear desire to be an individual, to be themselves or to be unique. Thus most of them rejected the idea of young men in the media as figures to emulate. In both cities, David Beckham, in particular, was singled out for disparagement rather than envy as a possible role model: 'Nah, not Beckham: he's got an attitude, he has' (Darren, Cambridge). And, more decisively: 'Beckham, he's a poof, he is'[2] (Paul, Sheffield).

Instead, most of them were in agreement with Gareth's claim that 'I just want to be like meself really' (Gareth, Sheffield). Lee, among the most articulate of the young men, explained the same desire at greater length:

> I don't admire anyone or aim to be like them. Everyone has their own goals and own personal ways of achieving them. I am not going to admire anyone cos they have done this or that, because I know I can do it if I want to. (Lee, Cambridge)

The anxieties about the establishment of an acceptable masculine identity among white working class youths, outclassed at school and outcompeted in the labour market by their female peers, which dominate academic and policy debates, had little resonance in the everyday lives and attitudes of these young men. On the whole, they were confident that they would be able to find work and re-establish the type of working class household that most of them had grown up in. However, most of these young men were also clear sighted about their limited opportunities and horizons. Remember Vince, who was devastatingly honest about himself when in response to my question about what sort of young man he was, he replied, 'A boring one. I just sit in t' house,' adding he'd prefer to be someone 'with loads of good friends that don't do owt, like wrong and do drugs and that. But', he concluded resignedly, 'everyone does round our area.'

In the final chapter I want to explore some ways in which a wider set of opportunities might be made available to young men such as these at the beginning stages of the transition to adulthood in a 'new' economy that restricts their opportunities to the least well-paid parts of the service sector in the main. Here I move into the arena of what is often termed, somewhat pejoratively, 'applied' social science but, like many self-identified critical human geographers, I should like to believe that one of the purposes of social inquiry is to inform critical public policy-making. Whether to work with Government agencies, with local community groups or in some other way remains the choice of individual researchers. Clearly, writing a book such as this one may be a somewhat indirect route to key economic and social decision-makers, and other forms of publication and ways of disseminating the research must also be sought. I hope, however, also to influence the theoreticians and, of course, the co-researchers, scholars and students interested in the implications of economic change for the lives of some of the least powerful members of the population of British cities who, as I spelt out in chapter 3 in particular, currently receive a very bad press. But I also want to make a theoretical intervention, by returning to those influential theories of identity and employment in post-industrial 'risk' societies addressed at the end of chapter 2 and bring them into sharper focus by counterposing their general claims to the nature and texture of the everyday lives, beliefs and attitudes of the 24 young white working class men who have dominated the intervening pages. I want to redress some of the imbalances in their representation by the media and policy-makers as loutish, unreliable 'lads' and by theorists of work as losers, uncommitted to the work ethic, whose only value to a capitalist economy is as consumers – and even here unvalued, as their purchasing power is insignificant in a society disfigured by enormous differentials of income and wealth.

9

Conclusions: What Is to Be Done about Boys?

Is an economy in which the benefits of growth are distributed in an increasingly lop-sided manner achieving its social purpose? (Faux and Mishel 2001: 94)

Technological change and globalization demand that young people of today must develop knowledge, skills and flexibility for their world of the future. (Tony Blair, British Prime Minister in a speech at Centrepoint, London, 19 December 1999)

While there were profound political and individual transformations taking place in women's lives throughout the twentieth century, they were not noticed by most men. Men were too engrossed in performing the masculine discourses handed down to them by their fathers and others. (Whitehead 2002: 6)

Despite enormous changes in the labour market and, to some extent, in gender relations (Bottero 2000), it seems as if young unemployed men hold to a series of moral beliefs and values that have less and less relationship to contemporary social and economic structures. Although they are largely unaware of this problem, young working class men, such as the 24 whose voices have filled the previous pages, are, in most senses, excluded both from the new economy and from the new moral order that underpins it. This new economy is constructed on the basis of the rejection of an older set of structures and ideas about time, work and masculine responsibilities. Instead, the economic and social order increasingly is based on instant gratification, on the consumption of goods and services that are out of reach of the majority of the working class, on aesthetic criteria as the basis of individual worth and on the construction of an individual portfolio of experiences that both facilitates and demands occupational and residential mobility. For the educated, middle class with potentially high-earning capacities – Castells' (2000) self-programmable labour – the arguments about the growing individualization of advanced industrial societies in which personal biographies are increasingly a matter for reflexive choice (Beck and Beck-Gernsheim, 1995, 1996; Giddens 1991, 1992), which were outlined in chapter 2, may have some resonance, although the vagaries of the Stock Market often remind many high-status, high-earning employees that they too are dependent upon the whims of a capitalist economy. But for 'generic labourers' with few skills and little social capital, especially the type of social capital that is valued in a service-dominated economy, notions of increased agency in the constitution and reconstitution of their lives and the growing ability to construct an employment career that is based on reflexive choice have never had much resonance. Older patterns in which class position and geographical location broadly determine the shape of their future lives for working class young people still have a persistent hold. Like their grandfathers and fathers before them, many working class young men are faced with the prospect of lives lived in the locality, in which low-level work dominates. What has altered, however, in recent decades, is the structure of the labour market, the range of employment options and so the relationships between waged labour and gender, thus affecting the relative expectations and life chances of young working class men and women. Increasingly, working class young men are excluded from the forms of manual labour that brought their fathers a degree of social respect as well as some economic security. The lives of young working class men and young middle class men are becoming more and more sharply divided in their transition to adulthood (Jones 2002).

Class and Gender Matters

I began this study, and indeed completed it, convinced of the theoretical strengths of an approach that integrated the analysis of material inequalities with a discursive approach to the construction of identity. As I hope I have shown here, gender, class and ethnicity are mutually constituted to construct identities that are fluid and variable, in part depending on the location of gendered performances as well as the negotiation of the multiple scripts that construct and constrain the performance of acceptable and respected masculinities. Idealized versions of masculinity, media representations of working class youth, stereotypical ideas about black virility and style, expectations of particular types of performances in different types of workplace all affect the ways in which young white working class men in Britain today present themselves as masculine as they negotiate the complex transition from school student to adult. However, especially for the least advantaged members of society, the material structures of inequality continue to constrain opportunities severely. In Britain global and national economic changes interact with regional and local circumstances to construct a set of labour market opportunities that condemn growing numbers of urban residents to lives of working poverty. As social scientists have argued, the income gap between the rich and the poor widened in Britain in the last quarter of the twentieth century. In an earlier rediscovery of poverty in the late 1960s and 1970s, analytic attention was focused in the main on those outside the labour market. Poverty, welfare dependence and joblessness, especially in inner city areas among minority communities was analysed in a necessary counter to arguments about prosperity and the leisure society. At the beginning of the twentieth-first century, however, a new form of poverty is becoming endemic: poverty among the working poor who are committed to mainstream values about the dignity of work but who are forced to accept undignified conditions. As hooks (2000: 7) has recently argued, in these new times, above all, 'class matters' and she insists that 'race and gender [must not be] used as screens to deflect attention away from the harsh realities class politics exposes. . . . we should all be paying attention to class, using race and gender to understand and explain its new dimensions'. Her plea echoes recent work by geographers (Harvey 2002; Sayer 2001; Smith 2000) as well as feminist theorists (Fraser 1997; Phillips 1999; Segal 1999) to retheorize the connections between class, identity and cultural politics.

As I have shown here, white working class families living in 'respectable' circumstances on outer local authority estates, in different parts of the country, are faced with the prospect that their sons will no longer have better lives than their own. For these young men, the opportunities for experimentation with identity that are often a correlate of late adolescence for middle class youth are virtually absent. As Pauly noted, 'life's tough for people like us, but you've just got to make the best of it and get on with it, like'. Making the best of it for white working class young men involves a complex negotiation between more reckless and hedonistic versions of laddish or protest masculinity and a more dour, serious version of a class-based respectability.

Hybrid masculinities: protest masculinity and domestic respectability

As I have shown in the empirically based chapters at the heart of this book, young working class men in Britain today are portrayed by a hostile press and by a more sympathetic academic literature either as teenage tearaways, challenging authority and middle-class norms through a range of antisocial, if not, criminal behaviour, or as educational failures. Whereas the former 'yobbish' image has a resonance with most of the young men represented here, as the previous chapter made clear, many young men are careful to steer a path between the protest masculinity identified by Connell and many others and a quite different version of masculinity that I have termed 'domestic respectability'. This latter version of masculinity is reflected not only in attitudes towards their familial and sexual lives but also in responsible attitudes in the labour market.

In her influential work on the relationships between class and gender, based on interviews with working class women, Skeggs (1997) has argued that 'respectability' is one of the most ubiquitous signifiers of class. Drawing on Bordieu's significant and long-standing documentation of the ways in which class differences are mapped on to the body as well as reflected in every aspect of everyday life (Bourdieu 1984; Bourdieu and Wacquant 1992), Skeggs (1997: 2) noted that in Britain, the notion of respectability

> informs how we speak, who we speak to, how we classify others...and how we know who we are (or are not). Respectability is usually the concern of those who are not seen to have it [and] would not be of concern if the working classes (Black and white) had not been consistently classified as dangerous, polluting, threatening, revolutionary, pathological and without respect.

Thus, whereas the working class in general, in opposition to the middle class, may be defined as dangerous, there is also a key internal differentiation that is used to distinguish 'respectable' from 'rough' working class lives and values and that as Skeggs showed affected the construction of working class notions of acceptable femininity.

This respectable/disreputable binary is also frequently mapped on to gender differences *per se*. In the enormous literature about working class youth, as I noted earlier, young men are usually studied in exceptional circumstances, often involving social conflict and violence: studies of the inner city gang, for example, have a long tradition in urban sociology (Alexander 2000; Campbell 1984; Schneider 1999; Thrasher 1927). In this work, masculinity is typically associated with physicality, machismo and territorial behaviour and the focus is commonly on stylized behaviour, codes of honour, and sometimes initiation rites. Girls, if they appear at all, are involved usually in subordinate positions and/or represented as sexual objects. If young women are the focus of the study in their own right, as McRobbie (1991) has shown, they are often documented in domestic circumstances: inside rather than outside on the city streets.

In an interesting study that attempts to challenge the association of inner city masculinity with macho behaviour and the lack of respect from wider society, especially among black residents, Duneier (1992) has argued that middle-aged and elderly black men often live lives based on a code of self-respect and mutual respect that rejects the values of younger ghetto residents. Based on an ethnographic study of the customers at a cafeteria on Chicago's Southside, Duneier develops a version of black masculinity that emphasizes respectability. Challenging the binary construction of black masculinity in the USA that contrasts the ghetto underclass with a striving black middle class, he argues that there is a little studied or understood in-between category of decent working men. He shows how the men are resolute, sincere and sensitive in their respect for each other and the way they treat, for example, an elderly and intolerant white customer. They have a respect for age and for the values of civility but also a strong sense of their own respectability. These are men, Duneier argues, who are at 'ease with their own selves' (1992: 45). 'Quiet satisfaction, pride, inner strength, and a genuine expressiveness without effusiveness here coalesce in a type of masculinity that is certainly more widespread in reality than in current accounts of the black male in the mass media and in sociology' (1992: 45–6). Duneier's argument about the variety of masculinities among black men, however, remains an exception. The binary distinctions between 'rough' and 'respectable', masculinity and femininity continue to influence the social construction of difference. However, his distinction between a version of respectability endorsed by older men in opposition to the 'respect' desired by younger Southside residents, based on their reputations as 'hard' or stylish men, has a parallel in work on 'race' and gender in less industrialized societies.

In an interesting coincidence of Skeggs's notion of respectability and the widespread gendered distinction between public and private spaces, work in the Caribbean, for example, has identified a gendered binary discourse on the basis of 'reputation' and 'respectability' (Wilson 1969).

Masculinity and reputation and femininity and respectability, it is argued, are coincident and also take a spatially specific form. Thus:

> Caribbean masculinity is said to draw its forms of expression (verbal wit and displays of male prowess and virility) and primary loci of activity (public spaces such as rum shops and street corners) from African roots and Afro-Caribbean femininity is depicted as mirroring the conventions of European womanhood. If reputation is best demonstrated through informal, face to face, non-institutional exchanges, respectability is best embodied in interior domains and associated values of the church and home – Christian morality, propriety and decorum. (Freeman 2000: 109)

Although this schema has been subject to criticism (see e.g. Besson 1993; Miller 1994 and Sutton 1974) and is clearly more flexible than a straightforward mapping on to masculinity and femininity, as Freeman's (2000) own empirical study of women data-entry workers in Barbados has shown, it is also a persistent and fluid dialectic that parallels debates about white working class gender identities.

What I want to argue here, however, is that working class young men embody both attributes – reputation *and* respectability – in their negotiation of a complex hybrid masculinity in post-millennium industrial societies. Unlike the older black men whom Duneier studied, young white men in contemporary Britain struggle with and negotiate a complex, contradictory construction of masculinity. Their expressed desire to achieve domestic conformity reflects, I suggest, a version of the working class respectability identified by Skeggs that is reinterpreted to become relevant to their age and class. Thus young working class men, as a group, have to negotiate a particular version of the respectable/not-respectable binary. The hegemonic version of 'hard laddishness' may bring benefits among peers, but it tends to exclude young men from wider societal respect. Similarly, while domestic conformity may be generally respected within working class communities; it may be despised in particular circumstances by groups of 'lads'. The attitudes and behaviour of the young men interviewed here, however, demonstrate the possibility of negotiating a careful path through this contradictory position associated with being a young working class man. They seem able to negotiate the construction of masculine identities in such a way that they attain credit and reputation in the eyes of their peers and in the eyes of wider working class community.

In this negotiation, however, working class youths are hindered by the type of popular representations of working class masculinity that continue to dominate the media and so preclude them from the respect of society as a whole. Unfortunately, in the workplace too, despite the sterling efforts made by many young workers to conform to the requirements of the Protestant ethic, the respect of the wider society is often withheld from young men, especially those who find their first jobs in entry-level jobs in the service sector. Despite this lack of respect, I believe that the notion of a crisis of masculinity among young men is exaggerated. As I have shown here, a singular view of a laddish working class masculinity is stereotypical. The attitudes and behaviour of adolescent white youths are more varied and complex; their ways of doing masculinity vary across time and locations. Even so, however, the impression from this study remains one of continued dominance of a version of a traditional, sexist masculinity, in both the laddish behaviours exhibited in leisure arenas and in the domestic attitudes that affect workplace participation and attitudes towards young women and family life. New forms of masculinity more in tune with the dominant attributes of a service-based economy and with young women's changing social position and a more general recognition of the arguments of feminism have yet to find any expression among the young men here. However, as I argued earlier, economic restructuring and growing income inequalities are as likely to reinforce, as to challenge, long-standing masculine attitudes and traditional gendered relationships in working class communities.

Class and gender continue to interact in ways that reinforce established notions that men's place is in the public arena – in the workplace – and that their main responsibility is as a breadwinner. As both Beck and Gorz emphasized in their assessments of the implications of the current trends in the labour market, and as feminist critics (Fraser 1997) have long argued, new forms of gender relations and less constrained ways of being men and women are partially dependent on new ways of valuing different forms of work, including caring labour in the home and voluntary participation in the community. This re-evaluation, however, will depend on initiatives such as the entitlement as a right to a basic citizen's wage, detached from labour market participation. Such a policy currently runs directly counter to current Government programmes that emphasize the duty of all citizens, regardless of their domestic and caring responsibilities, to enter the labour market. It is hard to foresee such a radical change of direction, despite recent Government initiatives to facilitate a more acceptable worklife balance for parents. A more difficult issue to address is the current restructuring of the labour market that is producing a polarized set of opportunities and a polarized workforce where those with few skills and educational qualifications are trapped in 'poor' jobs.

The Working Poor/Poor Work

Accepting low-wage work or, rather, having no other alternative, like most of the young men here, brings with it not only financial hardship (which might be partly alleviated by minimum wage initiatives) and little prospect of occupational mobility, but also social costs, especially for the young men who moved into 'non-traditional' work in the service sector. Although the gainfully employed are more highly respected than the unemployed, low-wage workers in bottom-end, entry-level jobs, especially in the service sector, typically are stigmatized or denigrated. As I noted earlier, the common designation of low-wage service occupations as 'McJobs' sums up their social evaluation as work without redeeming value. As Bauman (1998) has suggested, the replacement of locally based manual employment for working class men, which brought with it some dignity and social respect by casualized service employment that is often highly routinized and entirely lacking in discretion, is one of the key features of late-modern societies. Newman (1999) has suggested that this type of work is without symbolic capital. For teenagers working in McDonald's and other fast-food and retail-sector jobs, employment is often a humiliating experience. Servicing customers means accepting that they are always right, and responding with a smile to customer behaviour that reflects society's low evaluation of the social worth of service-sector work as well as acceptance of poor conditions, unreliable hours and low wages. As Newman noted (1999: 93):

> Thousands upon thousands of [people] line up for jobs that will subject them, at least potentially, to a kind of character assassination. They do so not because they start the job-seeking process with a different set of values, one that can withstand society's contempt for fast-food workers. They take these jobs because there is nothing better in the offing.

However, as I also argued, participation in the labour market, to which all the young men were committed, brings with it a set of attitudes and the development of skills that might be built on to enable these teenagers to move into more highly valued and better paid work. In the final part of this concluding chapter, I outline a number of ways that might facilitate occupational mobility for labour market entrants who are currently at risk of entrapment in poverty-level, minimum-wage jobs.

A small number of the young men here managed to access employment in sectors that bring with it the reinforcement of typical masculine attributes as well as the greater degree of respect associated with male manual work. However, employment in trades in the construction industry relies on bodily strength and the maximum earning capacity for the men employed in these trades often declines with age. These types of jobs are also vulnerable to national economic cycles of growth and depression, whereas work in the car industry, the destination of a small number of the group, is at the mercy of global trends and shifts in the location of production. In Cambridge it was noticeable that more young men than in Sheffield were prepared to defer full labour market participation for further education, although in all cases they combined it with waged work. Whether the acquisition of the sort of low-level vocational qualifications for which they were entered will, in fact, improve their job prospects, remains an open question but the omens are not promising. National surveys show that low-level vocational certificates are seldom the routes to well-paid work. Nevertheless, the Government is committed to expanding this sort of provision through the aegis of the Learning and Skills Council. In the next section I look more directly at possible policy innovations that might improve the life chances and employment prospects of working class school leavers.

Policy Considerations

A study combining economic restructuring with an analysis of the social construction of masculinity raises a number of implications for a wide range of policy areas, including education, the labour market and social services. Many of the these issues and a range of policy recommendations are currently being considered not only by the respective Government departments but also by social policy research institutes such as the Joseph Rowntree Foundation (see e.g. Bentley and Oakley 1999; Johnston, MacDonald, Mason, Ridley and Webster 2000; Lloyd 1999; Stafford, Heaver, Ashworth et al. 1999). One of the key planks of the second Labour Government is an initiative to link services to ensure that a growing number of young people remain in education at the end of their compulsory schooling as well as to encourage more people to consider lifelong learning and participation in work-based skills training.

Educational policies

The main issue being addressed by policy assessors and advisors is how to achieve a successful balance between policies to raise the academic ambitions and achievements of the less intellectually able pupils and those to provide a vocationally relevant curriculum, workplace experience and appropriate careers advice for this group. The young men in Cambridge and in Sheffield seemed to value the efforts made by their school to provide vocational training and placements. However, they were generally dissatisfied with the type of work experience that they had been involved with at school, arguing, even in Sheffield where the schemes were more developed, that it was a waste of time and just a means of taking them out of school for a few hours a week rather than a step towards gaining vocationally relevant skills. The academic orientation of GCSE courses also came in for criticism. They told me that many of their school courses were too difficult, boring or irrelevant, and it may be that some of then had been entered for too many GCSE examinations in which they had little hope of success. When it came to thinking about a prospective job, the respective Careers Guidance Service in each city had been used by most young men and they told me that they had found it to be a useful source of assistance, providing notification of appropriate vacancies and help with applications. In both cities several of the young men had made repeated visits to the Service and praised the assistance that they received.

Despite their dislike of school and their anxiety to leave as soon as possible, many of these young men recognized the growing importance of credentials for future success. Consideration might perhaps be given to new ways of inculcating greater respect for academic achievement that specifically address disaffected young men in schools, perhaps through placements with local employers who might be encouraged to work with schools to demonstrate the links between school achievement and future employment. In the UK a number of innovative schemes focused on, for example, 'macho' and disaffected boys in general as well as on African Caribbean boys who often have particular problems in school, might bear wider introduction, although there are clear implications for staffing levels and financial support (Salisbury and Jackson 1996). However, relatively inexpensive, in terms of finance if not time, schemes are showing some degree of success. In Bristol, for example, in two schools in the city's Education Action Zone, a one-to-one mentoring scheme has been set up in which older pupils mentor younger, disaffected pupils. It is clear, however, that in the new knowledge economy, a range of scholastic skills, including maths and English, are essential entry requirements for the types of jobs that bring any prospect of reasonable wages and that wherever possible students should be encouraged to gain, at the very least, CGSE passes in these subjects.

The British Government's current response to the need to develop the skills and abilities of less advantaged young people is the new Connexions Service and Strategy (DfEE 2000) which aims to co-ordinate the fragmented provision of youth services across a range of areas. The new service is available to all 13- to 16-year-olds still in school and will benefit future 'low achievers'. In its key provisions, Connexions mirrors the assumptions and provisions of the New Deal for 18- to 25-year-olds, based predominantly on a personal advisor for individuals to provide support and guidance and access to skills training. This reliance on personal interaction and mentoring has echoes both of social control and an idealized version of the family in references to 'an elder brother figure' for disaffected youth. A number of financial inducements to remain in education are, however, also proposed, including a 'smart card' with discounts for travel and leisure as well as the introduction of Educational Maintenance Allowances (Piatt 2001) for teenagers from low-income families. This latter allowance was introduced on a pilot basis in 2001 and seems to be effective in raising staying-on levels. It will be introduced nationally from 2004. While these provisions will be valuable (and might usefully be extended to 16- and 17-year-olds in entry-level jobs to facilitate their movement between employment and education), it is also important to recognize that additional forms of intervention may be necessary to improve the links between educational and labour market institutions and to alter the terms and conditions of low-income employment. As some of the initial results from the evaluations of the New Deal for Young People are beginning to make clear, there is a considerable degree of churning in entry-level jobs as turnover rates are high. Further, aspirations for reasonable work and some further training are often not met among both the New Deal participants and those who start a modern apprenticeship (see e.g. Adult Learning Inspectorate 2002). In assessments of the New Deal for Young People, for example, Van Reenen (2001) has argued that too many of the work-based schemes are what he termed 'skivvy schemes'. Sunley, Martin and Nativel (2001) are also pessimistic about the prospects for decent employment for new deal participants in areas where levels of labour demand are low and where there are problems of entrenched high rates of unemployment and joblessness.

Perhaps local connections between particular schools and relatively local employers might be forged. In some cities in the United States, for example, local employers, including hotel and restaurant chains and large retailers, have developed educational programmes in conjunction with schools in deprived areas with high rates of post-school unemployment, guaranteeing jobs to school leavers subject to certain levels of attainment and a satisfactory personal report. A National Youth Apprenticeship Program was, for example, developed by a consortium of employers – McDonald's, the Hyatt hotels and Walgreen's drug stores – and piloted in four Chicago school in the mid-1990s. These and similar schemes have had some success in lowering truancy levels and raising achievements among the pupils involved, although they risk creating a social division within the participating schools between pupils accepted on to the schemes and those who are not. In Britain the example and practice of schemes such as the former Youth Training Schemes and current modern apprenticeships in which links are developed respectively between training agencies and employment placements, and between employers and local further education colleges for pupils aged 16 and over, might perhaps be extended to a younger age group. To some extent the work experience programme for all year 10 or 11 pupils already partly fulfils such a role, as a number of the young men in my study told me that they had been offered work after their placement. That none of them accepted it, however, is an indictment of the types of placements available.

The nature of provision in work-based schemes for school leavers is also often inadequate. In a damning critique of national provision, the Adult Learning Inspector in his annual report (ALI 2002) noted that radical changes are needed as too many providers fail to deal adequately with the type of young people who are being recruited, both into modern apprenticeships (such as Steve and Wayne had begun) and into workplace-based NVQ schemes (such as the one Richard had begun at McDonald's). Two-thirds of all recruits on to modern apprenticeship schemes, for example, failed to complete the course. These failures were attributed to both the quality of the recruits and to poor provision. Providers failed to diagnose skill deficits adequately among school leavers who (as the Inspector noted in section 3 of his report 'Diagnosing the problem' [no page numbers]) 'have neither done well at school, nor enjoyed it' and often were unable to 'read, write or handle numbers fluently'. But as well as the quality of the participants, the provision was also often poor, as providers were unable to cope both with 'years of reduction in Government funding and increased demands imposed by the introduction of modern apprenticeship frameworks'. The net result was participants who were unable to meet the academic requirements of the apprenticeship schemes and providers who had little idea of how to deliver what was demanded. 'On the face of it poor achievement rates, poor grades, the inconstancy of standard from area-to-area, place to place, paint a depressing picture' ('Into the second round'). In his conclusion the Inspector argued that

embedded within our modern apprenticeship systems are some false premises, some misunderstandings of modern businesses, and some mistaken
attempts to meld academic and vocational traditions ... We must not make
modern apprenticeships a soft option, or betray the young people and their
parents who see an apprenticeship as a preparation for a career, not just a
job, but we do need to be realistic in tackling things that do not work.

This stinging indictment of current provision is, nevertheless, part of the
final section of the report ironically headed 'Grounds for optimism'! In
the following section I look at some of the lessons from US-based
schemes that might be adopted in the UK.

Labour market policies

As the economy continues to shift towards the domination of employment in the service sector, new policies are required to improve not only
the terms and conditions of jobs at the bottom end of the service-sector
service, but also the prospects for promotion and career progression for
young people who find themselves in entry-level 'McJobs'. It is clear that
as well as the sorts of policies, such as the Connexions Service just
discussed and the New Deal for Young People, which focus on improving the credentials and skills of potential employees by raising their
human capital through additional training and so forth, attention also
needs to be focused on the labour market itself and the terms and
conditions of the jobs on offer. As Hodkinson, Sparkes and Hodkinson
(1996: 156) argued, it is important to 'recognize that inequalities will
not be lessened by paying attention to the young people themselves.
Changes are needed to job availability, employer recruitment patterns,
workplace cultures and labour market structures.' Rhetorical reliance on
the development of a 'learning culture', or insistence on the diversity of
available options as 'individualization' increases has little to offer poorly
educated young working class men. As Ball, Maguire and Macrae (2000:
22) aptly noted, 'reflexivity will get you only so far if you leave school
without qualifications'.

   This is not to suggest that post-school training is without value. It
clearly is important for all young people currently deciding to leave
school as soon as possible. Although there is relatively little difference
in the levels of ability of the young men in this study, it is clear that the
future working lives of those who are successful in obtaining job-related
training, especially forms of apprenticeship with the prospect of future

employment, are much more certain than those who go into poorly paid, often casual, employment straight from school. While McDonald's may have disadvantages as an employer in that it recruits in the main young workers who seldom become permanent long-term employees, it is a good example in the sense that it pays all its employees (in Sheffield at least) the basic minimum wage and also encourages shop-floor workers to study for vocational qualifications. Other service and retail organizations might adopt these policies.

Employers in the service sector might also be encouraged to develop consortia not only to provide training but also to construct links between organizations dominated by entry-level jobs and those with higher paid positions. The former employers might then introduce schemes whereby reliable, punctual and hardworking employees enter a special 'pool' of workers who become eligible for referral to employers with better jobs on offer and who agree to provide training and educational opportunities for those who are successfully selected. Such a scheme would improve the commitment of workers and perhaps reduce the turnover rates in entry-level jobs, and perhaps also improve the success of appointment procedures for higher-level firms, as workers would come to them with a good recommendation from their previous employer as vetted and tested workers. Other employer-based initiatives might include savings schemes through the wage package for young workers. However, given the exploitative wages paid to many under-18-year-olds, an additional requirement would be the extension of the basic minimum wage to all employees, whatever their age, involving both the inclusion of 16- and 17-year-olds and the abolition of the 'youth' rate for 18- to 21-year-olds.

Finally, the trade unions might become involved in some of these schemes and in recruiting young people as members. It was noticeable that none of the young men already in work belonged to a union, nor indeed did most of them have a contract of employment, eligibility for paid holidays or membership of a pension scheme – or at least if they had they were not aware of it. Young workers are as a group particularly vulnerable to exploitation. At present, labour markets are tight, especially in the South-East and East Anglia. But even in a deindustrializing city such as Sheffield, there are many vacancies at the bottom end of the service sector and low-wage employment is easy to find. But it unlikely that this boom will be indefinite. If interest rates rise and levels of consumer spending drop then youth unemployment rates will start to rise. As was evident in the recession in the early 1990s, young workers, especially poorly qualified ones, are extremely vulnerable in a recession. In 2002 the Trades Union Congress included in its campaign against low pay a resolution to extend the minimum wage to 16- and 17-year-olds and to abolish the young persons' rate for 18- to 21-year-olds. But other actions are needed. Trade unions might perhaps initiate special campaigns in different sectors to improve the working conditions for young people, especially in fast food and the rest of the retail sector. In the USA in the last few years there has, for example, been a deliberate strategy of organizing bottom-end jobs in hotels and hospitals to try to provide higher wages and something resembling a career structure. On both the east and west coasts union organizers in a number of cities have developed successful policies. For example, the Cape Cod Hospital and Hospital Workers Union developed the Career Ladder Program to provide clearer job grades within departments and scope to progress, linked to specific requirements related to skills and qualifications, often acquired through on-the-job training.

In San Francisco, the Hotels Partnership Project also aims to provide opportunities for upward mobility for a largely unskilled workforce, enhancing skills through on-the-job training including language skills, as well as providing opportunities for workers in different jobs and positions across the participating hotel groups to meet each other and exchange their experiences. In Los Angeles a labour-community coalition, building on an initiative by a Latina-led service union, persuaded the city council to adopt an ordinance that introduced a mandatory living-wage for all employees in firms who had subcontracts form the city (Pastor 2001). In the 1990s the Tourism and Industry Development Council in LA was also a key player in the Living Wage Campaign, a movement that is increasingly common in US cities (Pollin and Luce 1998) and which has begun to have an impact in Britain. These initiatives are not restricted to service-sector workers. The Centre on Wisconsin Strategy, for example, started a scheme for the metal trades forming the Wisconsin Regional Training Partnership, in which 40 participating firms agreed to provide training and promotion opportunities in a common scheme. These place-based and sectorally specific schemes might be copied by British trade unions and workers' organizations, to supplement the current efforts of the living wage campaigns that have also drawn on US experience. In Britain the dominant emphasis on the labour supply, through schemes to enhance the skills of poorly qualified workers and potential workers, that informs both the Connexions service and the New Deal, needs complementing by an equal focus on labour demand, improving both the number of jobs, especially in the northern regions and, particularly, their terms and conditions. Despite, the recent range of area-based programmes in Britain, such as the Excellence in Cities initiative, for example, active local labour market policies that recognize and challenge the stubborn geographical variations in employment opportunities must become a key component of schemes to redress inequalities among young school leavers.

Sex education and counselling, personal counselling, equal opportunities policies

Finally, some improvements might be made to services that address personal issues and problems that loom large in young people's lives. While these young men may not have expressed explicit anxieties about the construction and achievement of an acceptable version of masculinity, they did talk about issues and problems in their personal lives. In particular, it became clear that many of them were extremely dissatisfied with the nature of sex education in schools, and indeed more generally with the type of personal help and support that is available to adolescents in general in their final years of compulsory schooling. To some extent the Personal Advisors proposed in the Connexions strategy may meet their anxieties, although the skills needed to counsel, *inter alia*, depressed young men and potential suicides, are both particular and demanding. Difficult questions about confidentiality arise too, for example in cases of known substance abuse, which the new service will have to address.

In the arena of sex education, however, all the young men were clear that what they wanted was extensive and practical advice from an impersonal source. They reported that the information given at school was, in their view, completely inadequate and also too technical. Given the rising rates of teenage pregnancies, especially in localities were youth unemployment rates are high, it is clear that new strategies are essential. All the young men to whom I talked personally knew at least one young woman of their age who was pregnant or who had had a child recently. Young men need help and advice to ensure that they are familiar with contraception and that they use it. In an interesting project with young men aged 17 and 18 initiated in 1999 by the Family Planning Association in Wales and undertaken in youth-work settings, it was found that young men wanted to talk about a wide range of issues including stereotypes, masculinity, friendship, homophobia, cancer and fatherhood (Wallace 1999). Initiatives like this one (FPA 1999) need to be made more widely available.

A small number of the men whom I interviewed wanted more help in dealing with issues about violence and abuse in the home. A survey of young adults aged between 18 and 24 carried out by the NSPCC in 2000 found that one in sixteen of the respondents had been subjected to various forms of abuse in the home. Clearly, family intervention services and child protection measures are vital both to prevent harm and to assist families who are struggling to parent adequately. Forms of independent and confidential advice and assistance for young people are also an important part of campaigns to improve the quality of life for adolescents.

Conclusions

As I have shown in the preceding chapters, waged work is still the central element in the development of an acceptable and respected masculine identity. It is vital to ensure that working class young men do not become the victims of economic change that constructs them as an increasingly disposable labour force, unskilled and stigmatized, with almost no prospects of occupational or social mobility. The 24 young men at the heart of this study may have been identified as low achievers at school and too-often stereotyped as yobbish louts by the general public, but they are also committed to the conventional values of a society that increasingly designates social worth and citizenship rights through labour market participation. These young men are, in the main, including the more disaffected among them, convinced of the necessity of participation in waged work. They adhere to mainstream communal values and are aiming for adult independence. Yet for many of them the sorts of low-level entry jobs that they have at present may be all they are able to achieve. It is hard to see how those with no skills or qualifications will progress and be able to attain adult independence. Many of them are doing the sorts of McJobs that are regarded as dead end by the majority of the population, and it is a tribute to their tenacity that these young men slog it out day to day, believing they are on the way to something better.

I came both to respect and admire the tenacity of the men whose voices dominate the preceding pages, and to regret deeply their limited horizons and potential prospects. It seems to me that most of them have far more personal and social skills than their examination performances suggest and that they certainly do not conform to commonly held stereotypical views about low-ability working class youths. While I have no desire to romanticize these youths as stoical working class heroes, rather than the cheeky, macho 'lads' of earlier academic studies, I believe that it is important to give them credit for the efforts they are making to hold together educational and/or labour market participation, a continuing input into family life, often including relatively substantial financial contributions given their low incomes, and to construct an independent social life, in the context of economic change and restructuring that is reducing their chance of the successful transition to adult independence and the prospects of the kind of life they desire. The type of young men represented in the pages of this book has tended to be invisible in much of the youth research literature that is typically more interested in the more spectacular aspects of youth culture. These men are neither rebels nor yobs, neither failures nor successes, but instead they lead careful, constrained local lives in their attempts to construct a version of acceptable working class masculinity in the face of economic circumstances that militate against their efforts. A longer study, continuing to follow these or similar young men as they move from the teenage years into their twenties, is needed to assess my gloomy prognosis of their future lives. Indeed, youth programmes and youth research in general would benefit from a longer temporal perspective in the future. As Williamson (1997: 75) has consistently argued, it is important not to become 'over-preoccupied with the acute anxieties of adolescence to the detriment of the chronic crisis of young adulthood'.

As recent research in both the UK (Aldridge 2001; Dearden, Machin and Reed 1997; Johnson and Reed 1996) and in the USA (Finnegan 1998) has demonstrated, the rise of poor work and the halt to the intergenerational social and occupational mobility that characterized both economies in the post-1945 decades is a worrying new feature of the post-millennium. Indeed, Roberts (1993) noted a decade earlier that social mobility was becoming a mirage for working class youths in contemporary Britain. As well as the declining prospects facing new labour market entrants among working class school leavers, an expanding number of adults are also being forced to accept 'poor work'. This type of work, largely in the service sector, provides insufficient income to support the sort of family life desired by the young men here, a way of life that still lies at the heart of many moral pronouncements and social policies in contemporary Britain, despite the absence of the economic conditions necessary to support it. The 'brave new world of work' identified by Beck (2000) might more accurately be designated, as Finnegan (1998) labelled US society, a 'cold new world'. In this cold climate, the typical attributes of working class masculinities – that complex and variable negotiation between a traditional streetwise laddish or macho protest masculinity and a respectable working class version of manhood described here – are increasingly undervalued, even redundant in a service-based economy in which jobs for the unskilled and unqualified demand a quite other set of personal attributes. And in their personal lives too the domestic conformity and often conservative assumptions about future relationships and family life of these young men may lead to their growing redundancy in a world in which older gender relations and power structures are increasingly being challenged by young women's growing success and new aspirations in the labour market and at home.

Postscript: Two Years Later

In September 2002 I attempted to contact the 21 young men who had participated in all three stages of my research to see how they were faring and whether my categorization of their labour market orientations two years previously was reflected in their current position. Despite letters and phone calls, it proved impossible to contact Michael in Cambridge and Gareth and Paul in Sheffield as their home phone numbers were no longer in use and letters were returned.

Table 9.1 The employment and housing position of the remaining 18 young men in autumn 2002

In Cambridge	
Andrew	Working as a cleaner in a Cambridge nursing home. Living with girlfriend in a local authority flat; problems with drink and drugs.
Chris	Finished his automotive mechanics course, with level 1 and level 2 GNVQ and a tyre-fitting certificate and now working at a tyre and auto centre in a large village near Cambridge; living with parents.
Damian	Completed only the first year of his college mechanics course and joined Parcel Force full-time as a collection driver; living with his parents.
Daniel	Finished a foundation GNVQ in IT but left college half way through the second year to start work as a computer engineer for Marshall Aerospace in Cambridge; still living with his parents.
Guy	Numerous jobs over the past two years as well as spells of unemployment but currently employed in telesales, selling advertising space. Living at home with his parents.
John	After a period of unemployment, working full-time as a pedal-cycle mechanic in Cambridge Market and still living at home.

Table 9.1   (*Continued*)

In Cambridge	
Kurt	Now working full-time for Debenhams in the in-store canteen – the same department store he had worked for part-time when a student. His college art Foundation course and extra GCSE had not gone well – 'I wasn't really interested' – and his final grades were poor. He was still living with his father but had a serious girlfriend and they were saving up to live together independently. He was also job-hunting and told me that 'at the moment I'd take just about anything'.
Lee	Left his IT course to go to college and do A levels, which he successfully completed. Starting a university course in September. Still living with his mother, although will live in campus accommodation in term time.
Wayne	Dropped out of his apprenticeship, although has the option to return in September 2002. Found it hard to get work as a bricklayer and has been working on a temporary basis as a painter and decorator for his girlfriend's father. Still living with his parents.

In Sheffield	
Craig	Still an optical technician; finished training at local college on a day-release basis; left home after an argument and living locally with a friend and his mother.
Darren	He had stuck with the mould-makers until four months earlier (May 2002) but left as 'it got boring' and had been unemployed since then. He was signing on and looking for work, in the main though the jobcentre and said, 'I'd take owt, anything what comes up,' although he told me that he would ideally like to find work in the steel industry 'a smelting job or summat'. He was living at home 'on and off' and also staying at his girlfriend's parents several nights a week.
Greg	Had previously been working at McDonald's in Meadowhall, but for the past year was a warehouseman 'just moving general stock, order rotation and that'; still living at home but planning to move out in about a year's time to live with his girlfriend.
Matthew	Left Sheffield Wednesday FC 12 months earlier and currently working as a glass collector in a Sheffield nightclub; living with his mother but also has a 4-month-old daughter whom he had not yet seen, as the mother, his ex-girlfriend, had moved away from Sheffield.
Richard	He had held a range of retail jobs, all in Meadowhall, but for the last few months had been working locally as a window cleaner with a

Table 9.1 (*Continued*)

In Sheffield	
	small local independent firm. His parents had moved and left the tenancy of the house to their son and he was living there with his girlfriend, as well as with his sibling.
Rick	Working for a steel company in Sheffield, doing general engineering and studying part-time for an NVQ in engineering, having already gained an NVQ in production engineering; engaged to be married but still living with his parents.
Shaun	Working as a warehouseman for Sheffield Kitchen Appliances; living with parents.
Simon	Still at Crosby Kitchens but hoping to move to a small joinery firm run by a friend and to be trained by him; living with parents; engaged to the same young woman that he was going out with two years previously but not intending to get married 'for a good long time, though she don't know that'.
Steve	Successfully completed his modern apprenticeship with Vauxhall and now working as a mechanic for a Vauxhall dealership in Sheffield; living with his father.

The lives of most of these young men as they left their teens thus remained remarkably similar to the way they had been two years earlier. Apart from Lee's notable success in gaining a university place (and as I emphasized in the main text, although he was a disaffected and difficult school student, he was incorrectly identified as a low achiever), these young men continue to be employed in low-wage, often casualized work with few prospects for advancement. Their lives and employment patterns two years after the final interview I carried out with them largely confirmed the categories into which I had placed them, although disappointingly the committed workers had not on the whole fulfilled their prospects. Only Steve of the group of three whom I identified as committed had completed his training on time. Wayne had taken a year out and had not yet decided in September 2002 whether to return to college and complete his apprenticeship, and Damian had dropped out of his course, defeated by the difficulties of obtaining a placement. However, in Cambridge, Chris, who had begun a somewhat similar course to Damian, had successfully completed the course and was now employed in a related job. What is noticeable, however, is the tendency of those who had begun some form of further education in Cambridge to abandon the course partway though. While this confirms my conclusion that these young men were not completely committed to their lives as students but rather were focused on labour market participation, it has worrying implications for the provision of further education and for upgrading the skill-levels of poorly educated young people. In Sheffield, as I explained in the main text, few of the participants had even registered for or begun basic-level NVQ courses after completing their compulsory secondary education.

On the optimistic side, however, many of these young men continued to work hard. Rick in Sheffield, for example, after a period of temporary casual work in Meadowhall, had given up all idea of joining the army and was now pleased to be settled in an engineering-related job and to be studying while he was employed. Richard, who was among the hardest working of all the young men, was still doing his best to stay in work and was earning a living as a window cleaner. Craig and Simon, also among the committed-worker category (but whose full story was not included in the main text) were also still in employment. In both cases they were working in the same job they had been in when I last saw them in the summer of 2000, although Simon was hoping to change jobs in the near future. But others were drifting between different types of low-wage employment and, in Darren's case, into unemployment.

A small number of these young men were also dogged by difficult personal problems. Matthew in Sheffield was struggling to come to terms with fathering a daughter whom he had never seen and Andrew was living with an older partner whose involvement in drugs and heavy drinking had led to his expulsion from home. His mother had eventually thrown him out because of his persistent theft of money from her and her partner to support the bad habits of his girlfriend and himself. But many of the others remained optimistic. A considerable proportion of them were in committed relationships and were planning to set up home independently in the next year or so. Significantly, however, only two of these 18 had yet left their family home on a permanent basis and both because of familial disputes. As I noted in the main text, the prospects of independent living for young men in low-wage employment are not hopeful, although perhaps with the additional income from a wage-earning partner their options might be rosier, especially in Sheffield where rental housing is both more widely available and less expensive than in Cambridge. Overall, then, two years later, the lives of these men continue to show how changing economic circumstances have trapped young men with little educational and social capital in poor work. Their labour market position provides few opportunities for them to benefit from, in most cases, their dogged commitment to the values of a working class Protestant ethic that has less and less meaning in modern Britain.

Appendix 1
Research Methodology

In this brief appendix I extend the discussion in chapter 4 about the method I used to identify school leavers who were prepared to participate in the project. I also address some of the ethical issues that were raised by the interview strategy.

As with many researchers interested in the transitions commonly negotiated throughout adolescence, I initially identified the young men I planned to interview with the assistance of their school. With the co-operation of the schools, a list was compiled of all the white boys in their final year of compulsory education who were regarded as low achievers. Each boy on the list was sent a letter from me to his home address in which I explained the nature of the research I hoped to do. I provided letters and stamped envelopes which were then addressed in the school as the data protection act forbids schools to release pupils' addresses to third persons. The letters, however, came from my university address. With each letter, I enclosed a prepaid reply card, asking the recipient to return it to me if he was interested in taking part in the study. I explained that it would involve meeting me three times over the next 12 to 18 months and also that I would pay them a small sum (£10) at each meeting. I strongly believe that it is important to be able to recompense the individuals who are prepared to answer what must often seem like intrusive questions from social scientists. As these young men were all from relatively low-income households and many of them held casual jobs while still at school, a small sum for participation seemed both an adequate reward and, I hoped, a way of encouraging their participation over the course of the year or so. Other researchers engaged in youth work have 'paid' their participants in kind, using vouchers for popular stores, for example, but I felt that cash was more appropriate and the Joseph Rowntree Foundation, which funded the research, agreed to my request.

By writing to each boy at home and enclosing a reply card I was able to ensure confidentiality. Just as I had no list of the young men initially identified, the school had no record of those who replied to me. Whereas the school is often the site for research about children and young people and their significant life-course events, several issues are raised by interviewing there which seemed to me to be particularly problematic for older students and for the less committed among them. Participants might feel that they have little option but to participate if they are 'volunteered' by their class teacher. Further, if the interviews and conversations actually take place in the classroom, then students might be reluctant to reveal opinions of which they suspect their teacher might disapprove.

I felt it was crucial to the nature of the interaction between us that the young men were assured of both privacy and confidentiality and so able, if they wished, to talk openly about their lives. I wanted to make it absolutely clear that I was not a teacher, nor connected in any way to their school or the educational authority. I also wanted to be clear that the school did not know who had agreed to participate and who had not, just as I did not know which students had initially been identified as possible participants. It also seemed important to me that I interview the young men on 'neutral' ground if I hoped that they would talk openly and honestly to me about their aspirations and feelings and their everyday experiences, including their involvement in illegal activities. I was clear, therefore, that neither their schools nor their homes were the place to interview. As I explained in chapter 4, the interviews in Sheffield were undertaken in a range of public spaces, as were some of the Cambridge ones. However, in Cambridge I also interviewed in both my own home and, during stages 2 and 3, in the homes of some of the participants. When interviewing in my own home, I ensured that in each case the young man in question was already 16 years old, that I had the permission of his parent or guardian to see him at a time that I had agreed with them and that there were also other people in the house. I decided in these cases to interview in my kitchen, as it is a room that is visible from the street outside (and incidentally opposite the Cambridge main police station) and I hoped that it would provide an informal and non-intimidating atmosphere. I offered each young man a drink initially and we also chatted informally before I began to tape the conversation. The young men who came to my house seemed to feel relaxed, but interviewing there rather than in a public space altered the dynamics of the interaction, as I was on home territory. However, there was little apparent difference between the topics broached when I compared the transcripts from interviews in different locations.

Before I met any of the young men involved, I ensured that I had spoken by telephone both to each of them and to an adult in their household, as a number of them were not quite 16 years old at the time of the first interview. I did not, however, ask their parents or guardian for written consent for them to visit my private address. In retrospect I think I should have done so. As the research progressed and the participants came to feel more relaxed and to know me better, a number of them invited me to interview them in their own homes when they knew that we could have a room to ourselves and that we would not be interrupted. I always accepted these invitations, but ensured that their parents or guardian knew of my planned visit and that someone knew where I was going. A recent code of practice for British social researchers, drawn up by the Social Research Association, recommends researchers avoid 'the risk of being in a compromising situation, in which there might be accusations of improper behaviour' (Craig, Corden and Thornton 2000: 1). Further, in all studies that involve interviews with minors, interviewers should be cleared by the local police and must take scrupulous care to avoid situations that are open to the possibilities of abusive behaviour. When the interviewees are aged 16 or over, the legal requirement is waived. I did not register but perhaps I should have, and in future I think I would be more cautious about undertaking one-to-one interviews in a private space.

Participating in the Research

A key issue in youth research is the problem of how to ensure participation from the range of young people who have been identified as possible participants. I received almost 50 responses in total to my letters and clearly some of the most disaffected young people might not have been reached because of residential instability, for example, and literacy problems, as well as a general unwillingness to participate. It might be, therefore, that among the 24 eventual participants, the 'less reliable' were excluded. This issue potentially is magnified when a strategy of repeat interviews is adopted as I was reliant not only on the young men turning up initially to meet a woman whom they had never seen but also on their continuing participation. It is often assumed that young men, especially 'lads', are feckless and unreliable and hard to involve in social research. However, as Howard Williamson (1997: 7) has asked, if this is the case, 'how has so much well-organized and unflawed research been conducted with them?' In his own work with young people, both as a researcher and a youth worker, Williamson found that 'that young men, like young people generally, know their minds, have their reasons for their orientations towards their lives but, when it comes to research, may well appear to be nihilistic and unco-operative; after all research is hardly at the top of their priority list or planning agenda' (1997: 7).

Forewarned, I expected to have to spend time waiting around, to be prepared to rearrange meetings and perhaps to have a high dropout rate between interviews. I recognized that for the young men whom I hoped to meet three times over a year, significant changes would take place in their lives as they left school and they might have neither the time, inclination nor, perhaps, the confidence to explain these changes to a university researcher whose own life probably seemed remote to them. As I expected, there were times when appointments were missed and had to be rearranged, but in general most of the young men who turned up the first time were remarkably consistent in returning for the second and third interview at the time previously arranged, although I always phoned the day before as a reminder. The growing ownership of mobile phones proved a lifeline as I was often able to contact a missing inter-viewee, remind him that I was waiting and sometimes talk him into coming to meet me there and then. Apart from two young men who moved between stages 2 and 3 and one who sadly died, all the others – 21 in total – participated in all three stages.

In each stage the conversation ranged across a number of issues and aspects of the daily lives of those involved. The first stage, however, was focused more on collecting biographical information and establishing a relationship and rapport than with detailed explorations of attitudes and opinions. In the two later stages, the conversation was more open-ended and branched out from work and education choices to cover a range of topics including family life, relationships, sexuality, leisure, finance, health and prospects. I used a simple list of topics as an aid during the interviews, a version of which I gave to the participants to reassure them about what might be coming. I also used a number of newspaper headlines, about teenage pregnancy for example, to help in discussions about sexuality.

All the interviews were transcribed and I have presented relevant extracts here in ways that I hope capture the vernacular speech patterns of the participants and the evident regional differences between them, retaining comprehensibility for the reader without, I hope, seeming condescending in any way.

Appendix 2
The Participants

Cambridge Ten

Name	Born	Family	Parents' occupations
Andrew	12/82	Mother and older sister; father in prison	M: care worker, OAP home
Chris	5/83	Shared weekly with mother and stepfather, own father and stepmother; brother and sister live with mother	F: plumber M: childminder SF: mechanic
Daniel	12/82	Both parents and younger brother	F: police constable M: part-time retail assistant
Damian	2/83	Both parents, 2 older sibs left home	F: Post Office (collections manager) M: part-time elder care
Guy	11/82	Both parents, 2 older sibs left home	F: security work M: part-time elder care
John	8/83	Both parents and one sister living at home; grandmother near neighbour	F: odd jobs M: nursery assistant
Kurt	4/83	Mother and stepfather separated; spends time with both; 2 sisters, 2 brothers, of whom 3 live with his stepfather	SF: unemployed initially, then insurance salesman M: nursery assistant
Lee	11/83	Mother (divorced); two older stepsibs (mother's first marriage) and two younger (father's second marriage)	M: care worker, OAP home

Michael4/83		Lives with mother and stepfather; one older sister at home	F: unemployed and disabled SF: retraining course M: part-time care worker
Wayne	7/83	Both parents and younger brother	F: industrial cleaner M: part-time care worker

Sheffield Fourteen

Name	Born	Family	Parents' occupations
Craig	12/82	Both parents	F: unemployed M: unemployed (previously a cleaner)
Darren	9/82	Parents, 2 brothers and one sister all at home	F: car mechanic M: hospital cleaner (works evenings)
Gareth	4/83	Parents divorced; lives with mother and younger sister	F: no contact M: several cleaning jobs
Greg	4/83	Both parents and 2 older brothers still at home	F: machine operator M: retail sales assistant
Kevin	5/83	Mother, stepfather, 7 older sibs not at home, one younger stepsister at home	F: cleaner M: housewife
Paul	6/83	Parents and older brother at home	F: forklift truck driver M: aerobics instructor
Pauly	11/82	Parents separated; lives with mother and two younger brothers	F: taxi driver M: unemployed
Matt	7/83	Mother and sister; three stepsisters living away	F: deceased M: housewife
Richard	4/83	Both parents and older brother at home	F: unemployed M: hospital nurse
Rick	4/83	Both parents, one sister, at home; one living away	F: hospital porter M: personal carer
Shaun	7/83	Both parents and four younger brothers at home	F: machine shift-worker in bakery M: housewife
Simon	4/83	Parents, older brother and younger sister at home	F: clerical work for local authority M: part-time cleaner

| Steve | 4/83 | Parents separated; lives with father and younger sister | F: local authoirty surveyor
M: care worker for old people |
| Vince | 7//83 | Adoptive parents, three sibs; only one at home | F: self-employed mechanic
M: foster-mother |

Notes

Chapter 2 The Rise of Poor Work: Employment Restructuring and Changing Class and Gender Identities

1 'Poor' means living in a household where total income, adjusted for family size, children's ages and housing costs falls at or below 60 per cent of the median income for all households.

Chapter 4 Living on the Edge: Marginal Lives in Cambridge and Sheffield

1 School inspections are carried out by the Office for Standards in Education (Ofsted) at approximately 5-year intervals. 'Fenland' had been inspected in 1994 and 1999 and Park Edge in 1996 and 2001. I have not attributed the school descriptions as their identity would then no longer be confidential. However, as far as possible I have provided portraits of the schools at the end of the school year 1999. Reports for all state schools are available on the Ofsted web site: <www.ofsted.gov.uk>.
2 This is a commonly used indicator of educational disadvantage, although it more accurately reflects familial circumstances – especially low income.
3 The gender reversal at Fenland Community College in 1999 would not of course have been known about at the time of the first interview, which was carried out before these boys sat their school-leaving examinations. In previous years Fenland conformed to the emerging pattern of female superiority, at least in examination achievement at the age of 16.
4 As this was in Sheffield, Richard is referring to industrial premises and not the retail sector.

Chapter 5 Leaving School: Pathways to Employment and Further Education

1   South Yorkshire Training Group.

Chapter 6 Actively Seeking Employment: Committed Workers and Reluctant Learners

1   'Slogging' (playing truant) rather than 'slacking' or 'wagging off' (the local term for skipping class) was the term Richard used more than once, but his meaning was clear.
2   Richard took only four subjects – Maths, Religious Education, English Literature and English Language and achieved only low grades (two Es and two Fs) which are too low to qualify him to move on to A level courses or further education.
3   Although Richard did not elaborate, one of his friends, in an unsolicited comment, said to me that Richard was from 'a rough family, a real rough dad but he [Richard] is such a hard worker'.

Chapter 7 Uncertain Transitions: Accidental and Incidental Workers, the Excluded and Escape Attempts

1   The year his father died, although Matthew said it was not because of that.
2   'Dissing', from disrespect, means that one of Vince's co-workers was insulting his mother by calling her names that impugned her morals.
3   Kevin set himself on fire in summer 1999 after an argument with his girlfriend and sadly died from third-degree burns.

Chapter 8 Performing Identity: Protest and Domestic Masculinities

1   A notorious inner-area estate in Sheffield, which ranks high on all common indicators of socio-economic deprivation.
2   The term 'poof' is used as a general term of disparagement and not to refer directly to (homo)sexuality. It does, however, as one of the Steering Group pointed out, speak volumes about this respondent's attitude to the lifestyle and prospects of someone such as Beckham. And as I noted earlier, there was evidence of homophobic behaviour among this group of men.

Bibliography

Abbott, E. and Breckenridge, S. 1912: *The Delinquent Child and the Home*. Charities Publication Committee, New York.

Abbott, E. and Breckenridge, S. 1916: *Truancy and Non-attendance in the Chicago Schools*. University of Chicago Press, Chicago.

Abrams, F. 1998: Classroom rescue for Britain's lost boys. *Independent*, 5 January.

Adkins, L. 2000: Objects of innovation: Post-occupational reflexivity and re-traditionalisation of gender. In S. Ahmed, J. Kilby, C. Lury, M. McNeil and B. Skeggs (eds), *Transformations: Thinking Through Feminism*. Routledge, London, 259–72.

Adonis, A. and Pollard, S. 1998: *A Class Act*. Penguin, London.

Ahmed, K. and Hinsliff, G. 2002: Blair launches attack on Britain's 'sick note' culture. *Observer*, 10 June.

Aitken, S. 1994: *Children's Geographies*. Association of America Geographers, Washington, DC.

Aldridge, S. 2001: *Social Mobility: A Discussion Paper*. Performance and Innovation Unit, the Cabinet Office, available from www.cabinet-office/innovation/whatsnew/socialmobility.shtm.

Alexander, C. 2000: *The Asian Gang*. Berg, Oxford.

ALI (Adult Learning Inspectorate) 2002: *Chief Inspector's Annual Report 2001–2*. HMSO, London (available on www.ali.gov.uk).

Allatt, P. and Yeandle, S. 1986: 'It's not fair, is it?' Youth unemployment, family relations and the social contract. In S. Allen, K. Purcell, A. Watson and S. Wood (eds), *The Experience of Unemployment*, Macmillan, London, 98–115.

Allatt, P. and Yeandle, S. 1992: *Youth Employment and the Family: Voices of Disordered Times*. Routledge, London.

Allen, J. 1992: *The Nature of a Growth Region: The Peculiarity of the South East*. South East Programme Occasional Paper 1, Faculty of Social Sciences, Open University.

Allen, J. 1999: Worlds within cities. In D. Massey, J. Allen and S. Pile (eds), *City Worlds*. Routledge, London, 53–98.

Allen, J. and du Gay, P. 1994: Industry and the rest: The economic identity of services. *Work, Employment and Society*, 5, 195–206.

Allen, J. and Henry, N. 1997: Ulrich Beck's risk society at work: Labour and employment in the contract services industry. *Transactions, Institute of British Geographers*, 22, 180–96.

Alvesson, M. and Billing, Y. 1997: *Understanding Gender and Organisations*. Sage, London.

Amit-Talai, V. and Wulff, H. 1995: *Youth Cultures: A Cross-cultural Perspective*. Routledge, London.

Ardlidge, J. 1999: Sad culture kills 12 'lads' a week. *Observer*, 17 October.

Aries, P. 1962: *Centuries of Childhood: A Social History of the Family*. Alfred A. Knopf, New York.

Arnot, M., David, M. and Weiner, G. 1996: *Educational Reforms and Gender Inequality in Schools*. Equal Opportunities Commission, Manchester.

Arnot, M., David, M. and Weiner, G. 1999: *Closing the Gender Gap: Postwar Education and Social Change*. Polity, Cambridge.

Ashton, D. and Green, F. 1996: *Education, Training and the Global Economy*. Edward Elgar, Cheltenham.

Ashton, D., Maguire, M., and Spilsbury, M. 1990: *Restructuring the Labour Market: The Implications for Youth*. Macmillan, London.

Askew, G. and Ross, C. 1988: *Boys Don't Cry*. Open University Press, Milton Keynes.

Back, L. 1996: *New Ethnicities and Urban Culture: Racisms and Multiculture in Young Lives*. UCL Press, London.

Ball, M., Gray, F. and McDowell, L. 1989: *The Transformation of Britain: Social and Economic Change*. Collins, London.

Ball, S., Macrae, S. and Maguire, M. 1999: Young lives at risk in the 'futures' market: Some policy concerns from on-going research. In F. Coffield (ed.), *Speaking Truth to Power: Research and Policy on Lifelong Leaning*, Policy Press, Bristol, 32–47.

Ball, S., Maguire, M. and Macrae, S. 2000: *Choice, Pathways and Transitions Post-16: New Youth, New Economies in the Global City*. Routledge, London.

Banks, M., Bates, I., Breakwell, G., Bynnes, J., Emler, N., Jameson, L. and Roberts, K. 1992: *Careers and Identities*. Open University Press, Buckingham.

Banton, M. 1970: The concept of racism. In S. Zubaida (ed.), *Race and Racialism*, Tavistock, London, 17–34.

Barker, M. 1981: *The New Racism*. Junction, London.

Barrett, F. 1996: The organisational construction of hegemonic masculinity: The case of the U.S. navy. *Gender, Work and Organisation*, 3, 129–42.

Baty, P. 2002: Bring lost boys back from neverland, comment on a National Audit Office report on university access. *Times Higher Educational Supplement*, 26 July.

Baumann, G. 1996: *Contesting Culture: Discourse and Identity in Multi-ethnic London*. Cambridge University Press, Cambridge.

Bauman, Z. 1982: *Memories of Class*. Routledge, London.

Bauman, Z. 1998: *Work, Consumerism and the New Poor*. Open University Press, Buckingham.

Beatson, M. 1995: Progress towards a flexible labour market. *Employment Gazette*, February, 55–66.

Beck, U. 1992: *Risk Society: Towards a New Modernity*. Sage London.

Beck, U. 1994: The reinvention of politics: Towards a theory of reflexive modernisation. In U. Beck, A. Giddens and S. Lash (eds), *Reflexive Modernisation: Politics, Tradition and Aesthetics in the Modern Social Order*, Polity, Cambridge, 1–54.

Beck, U. 2000: *The Brave New World of Work*. Polity, Cambridge.

Beck, U. and Beck-Gernsheim, E. 1995: *The Normal Chaos of Love*. Polity, Cambridge.

Beck, U. and Beck-Gernsheim, E. 1996: 'Individualisation' and 'precarious freedoms': Perspectives and controversies of a subject-oriented sociology. In P. Heelas, S. Lash and P. Morris (eds), *Detraditionalisation: Critical Reflections on Authority and Identity*, Blackwell, Oxford, 23–48.

Beck, U., Giddens, A. and Lash, S. (eds) 1994: *Reflexive Modernisation: Politics, Tradition and Aesthetics in the Modern Social Order*. Polity, Cambridge.

Beder, S. 2000: *Selling the Work Ethic: From Puritan Pulpit to Corporate PR*. Zed, London.

Benedict, R. 1983: *Race and Racism*. Routledge and Kegan Paul, London.

Bennett, C. 1996: The boys with the wrong stuff. *Independent*, 5 November.

Bentley, T. and Oakley, K. 1999: *The Real Deal: What Young People Think about Government, Politics and Social Exclusion*. Demos, London.

Berger, M., Wallis, B. and Watson, S. (eds) 1995: *Constructing Masculinity*. Routledge, London.

Berliner, W. 2002: The race is over. *Guardian Education*, 12 March.

Bernstein, B. 1971: *Class, Codes and Control*, vol. 1. Routledge and Kegan Paul, London.

Bernstein, B. 1996: *Pedagogy, Symbolic Control and Identity: Theory, Research and Critique*. Taylor and Francis, London.

Besson, P. 1993: Reputation and respectability reconsidered: A new perspective on Afro-Caribbean peasant women. In J. Momsen (ed.), *Women and Change in the Caribbean*, Indiana University Press, Bloomington, 70–87.

Beveridge, W. 1944: *Full Employment in a Free Society*. Allen and Unwin, London.

Bhabha, H. 1990: Interrogating identity: The postcolonial prerogative. In D. Goldberg (ed.), *Anatomy of Racism*, Unversity of Minnesota Press, Minnesota, 183–209.

Biddulph, S. 1994: *Manhood: A Book about Setting Men Free*. Finch, Sydney.

Bly, R. 1990: *Iron John: A Book about Men*. Addison-Wesley, Reading, Mass.

Bonnett, A. 1997: Geography, 'race' and whiteness: Invisible traditions and current challenges. *Area*, 29, 193–9.

Bonnett, A. 2000: *White Identities: Historical and International Perspectives*. Prentice Hall, Harlow.

Bordo, S. 1993: *Unbearable Weight*. University of California Press, Berkeley, California.

Bottero, W. 2000: Gender and the labour market at the turn of the century: complexity, ambiguity and change. *Work, Employment and Society*, 14, 781–91.

Bourdieu, P. 1984: *Distinction*. Routledge, London.

Bourdieu, P. 1990: *In Other Words*. Polity, Cambridge.

Bourdieu, P. 1991: *Language and Symbolic Power*. Polity, Cambridge.

Bourdieu, P. 1999: *The Weight of the World*. Polity, Cambridge.

Bourdieu, P. and Wacquant, L. 1992: *An Invitation to Reflexive Sociology*. Polity, Cambridge.

Bourgois, P. 1995: *In Search of Respect: Selling Crack in El Barrio*. Cambridge University Press, Cambridge.

Bowlby, S. and Lloyd-Evans, S. 2000: Crossing boundaries: Racialised gendering and the labour market experiences of Pakistani migrant women in Britain. *Women's Studies International Forum*, 23, 461–74.

Bowlby, S. R, Lloyd Evans, S. and Mohammad, R. 1998: Becoming a paid worker: Images and identity. In T. Skelton and G. Valentine (eds), *Cool Places: Geographies of Youth Culture*, Routledge, London, 229–48.

Bradley, H. 1999: *Gender and Power in the Workplace: Analysing the Impact of Economic Change*. Macmillan, Basingstoke.

Bradley, H., Erickson, M., Stephenson, C. and Williams, S. 2000: *Myths at Work*. Polity, Cambridge.

Bradley, H. and Fenton, S. 1999: Reconciling culture and economy: Ways forward in the analysis of gender and ethnicity. In L. Ray and S. Sayer (eds), *Culture and Economy*, Sage, London.

Brake, M. 1987: *Comparative Youth Culture*. Routledge, London.

Brittan, A. 1989: *Masculinity and Power*. Basil Blackwell, Oxford.

Brod, H. and Kaufman, M. (eds) 1994: *Theorizing Masculinities*. Sage, Thousand Oaks, Calif..

Brown, D. 2000: Policing yob culture. *Guardian*, 3 July.

Brown, L. and Gilligan, C. 1992: *Meeting at the Crossroads: Women's Psychology and Girls' Development*. Harvard University Press, Cambridge, Mass.

Brush, L. 1999: Gender, work, who cares? Production, reproduction, deindustrialisation and business as usual. In M. Marx Ferre, J. Lorber and B. Hess (eds) *Revisioning Gender*, Sage, Thousand Oaks, Calif., 161–89.

Budd, L. and Whimster, S. (eds) 1992: *Global Finance and Urban Living*. Routledge, London.

Butler, J. 1990: *Gender Trouble: Feminism and the Subversion of Identity.* Routledge, London.

Bynner, J. and Parsons, S. 1997: *It Doesn't Get Any Better: The Impact of Poor Basic Skill Attainment on the Lives of 37-year-olds.* Basic Skills Agency, London.

Byrne, D. 1997: Social exclusion and capitalism: The reserve army across time and space. *Critical Social Policy,* 17, 27–51.

Callaghan, G. 1992: Locality and localism: The spatial orientation of young adults in Sunderland. *Youth and Policy,* 39, 23–33.

Campbell, A. 1984: *The Girls in the Gang.* Basil Blackwell, New York.

Campbell, B. 1993: *Goliath: Britain's Dangerous Places.* Methuen, London.

Canaan, J. 1996: Drinking, fighting and working class masculinities. In M. Mac an Ghaill (ed.), *Understanding Masculinities,* Open University Press, Buckingham, 114–25.

Carnoy, M. 2000: *Sustaining the New Economy: Work, Family and Community in the Information Age.* Russell Sage Foundation, New York; Harvard University Press, Cambridge Mass.

Carrigan, T., Connell, R. and Lee, J. 1985: Towards a new sociology of masculinity. *Theory and Society,* 14, 551–604.

Castells, M. 1996: *The Rise of the Network Society.* Blackwell, Oxford.

Castells, M. 1997: *The Power of Identity.* Blackwell, Oxford.

Castells, M. 1998: *End of Millennium.* Blackwell, Oxford.

Castells, M. 2000: Materials for an exploratory theory of the network society. *British Journal of Sociology,* 51, 5–22.

Chapman, R. and Rutherford, J. (eds) 1988: *Male Power: Unwrapping Masculinity.* Lawrence and Wishart, London.

Charlesworth, S. 2000: *A Phenomenology of Working Class Experience.* Cambridge University Press, Cambridge.

Chatterton, P. and Hollands, R. 2002: Theorizing urban playscapes: Producing, regulating and consuming youthful nightlife cityscapes. *Urban Studies,* 39, 95–116.

Christian, H. 1994: *The Making of Anti-sexist Men.* Routledge, London.

Christie, H. and Munro, M. 2000: Working all the time? Students in the labour market. Paper presented at the Youth Research 2000 conference, Keele University, 4–5 September, funded by the Joseph Rowntree Foundation and the Economic and Social Research Council (available from the authors, Heriot-Watt University, Edinburgh).

Clare, A. 2000: *On Men: Masculinity in Crisis.* Chatto and Windus, London.

Clare, J. 2000: Schools told to root out 'lad' culture. *Daily Telegraph,* 18 August, 1.

Clatterbaugh, K. 1990: *Contemporary Perspectives on Masculinity: Men, Women and Politics in Modern Society.* Westview, Oxford.

Coffield, F., Borrill, C. and Marshall, S. 1986: *Growing up at the Margins.* Open University Press, Buckingham.

Cohen, P. 1992: It's racism what dunnit: Hidden narratives in theories of racism. In J. Donald and A. Rattansi (eds), *Race, Culture and Difference*, Sage London, 62–103.

Cohen, P. 1997a: Labouring under whiteness. In R. Frankenberg (ed.), *Displacing Whiteness: Essays in Social and Cultural Criticism*, Duke University Press, Durham, NC, 244–82.

Cohen, P. 1997b: *Rethinking the Youth Question*. Macmillan, London.

Cohen, S. 1973: *Folk Devils and Moral Panics*. Paladin, St Albans.

Coles, B. 1995: *Youth and Social Policy: Youth Citizenship and Young Careers*. UCL Press, London.

Coles, B. 2000: Retheorising the transition. Plenary paper presented at the Youth Research 2000 conference, Keele University, 4–5 September, funded by the Joseph Rowntree Foundation and the Economic and Social Research Council (available from the author at the Department of Social Policy, University of York).

Collinson, D. and Hearn, J. 1994: Naming men as men: Implications for work, organisation and management. *Gender, Work and Organisation*, 1, 2–22.

Connell, R. W. 1987: *Gender and Power*. Basil Blackwell, Oxford.

Connell, R. W. 1989: Cool guys, swots and wimps: The interplay of masculinity and education. *Oxford Review of Education*, 15, 291–303.

Connell, R. W. 1990a: Reply to a symposium on R. W. Connell's *Masculinities*. *Gender and Society*, 12, 474–7.

Connell, R. W. 1990b: A whole new world: Remaking masculinity in the context of the environmental movement. *Gender and Society*, 4, 452–78.

Connell, R. W. 1991: Live fast and die young: The construction of masculinity among young working class men on the margin of the labour market. *Australia and New Zealand Journal of Sociology*, 27, 141–71.

Connell, R. W. 1993: The big picture: Masculinities in recent world history. *Theory and Society*, 22, 597–624.

Connell, R. W. 1994: Knowing about masculinity, teaching boys: Educational implications of the new sociology of masculinity. Paper presented at the Pacific Sociological Conference, San Diego, April.

Connell, R. W. 1995: *Masculinities*. Polity, Cambridge.

Connell, R. W. 2000: *The Men and the Boys*. Polity, Cambridge.

Cornwall, A. and Lindisfarne, N. (eds) 1994: *Dislocating Masculinity: Comparative Ethnographies*. Routledge, London.

Corrigan, P. 1979: *Schooling the Smash Street Kids*. Macmillan, London.

Coward, R. 1994: Whipping boys. *Guardian Weekend*, 3 September.

Coward, R. 2000: Slurring the proles. *Guardian*, 4 July.

Craig, G., Corden, A. and Thornton, P. 2000: A code of practice for the safety of social researchers. Social Research Association, draft, March, available for the first author at the University of Hull.

Crang, P. and Martin, R. 1991: Mrs Thatcher's Britain or, the other side of the Cambridge phenomenon. *Environment and Planning D: Society and Space*, 9, 91–116.

Craig, S. (ed.) 1992: *Men, Masculinity and the Media*. Sage, London.

Crompton, R. 1999: *Restructuring Gender Relations and Employment: The Decline of the Male Breadwinner*. Oxford University Press, Oxford.

Davies, B. 1982: *Life in the Classroom and Playground*. Routledge and Kegan Paul, London.

Deacon, A. 2000: Learning from the US? The influence of American ideas upon 'New Labour' thinking on welfare reform. *Policy and Politics*, 28, 5–18.

Dearden, L., Machin, S. and Reed, H. 1997: Intergenerational mobility in Britain. *Economic Journal*, 107, 47–64.

De Beauvoir, S. 1972: *The Second Sex*. Penguin, Harmondsworth (originally published in French in 1947).

Delamont, S. 1980: *Sex Roles in Schools*. Methuen, London.

Delamont, S. 2000: The anomalous beasts: Hooligans and the sociology of education. *Sociology*, 34, 95–111.

Department for Education and Employment (DfEE) 1997a: *Design of the New Deal for 18 to 24 Year Olds*. London.

Department for Education and Employment 1997b: *New Deal: Operational Vision*. London.

Department for Education and Skills (DfES) 2001: *Youth Cohort Study: The Activities and Experiences of 17 Year Olds, England and Wales 2000*. London.

Department of the Environment, Transport and the Regions (DETR) 1998: *1998 Index of Local Deprivation: A Summary of Results*. London.

Department of Social Security 1998: *New Ambitions for our Country: A New Contract for Welfare*. Green Paper on Welfare Reform, Cmnd 3805, HMSO London.

Department for Education and Employment (DfEE) 2000: Connexions: The best start in life for every young person <http://www.connexions.gov.uk>.

Dicken, P. 1998: *Global Shift*. 3rd ed. Guildford, London.

Dickens, R., Wadsworth, J. and Gregg, P. 2001: What happens to the employment prospects of disadvantaged workers as the labour market tightens? In R. Dickens, J. Wadsworth and P. Gregg (eds), *The State of Working Britain: Update 2001*, Centre for Economic Performance, London School of Economics, York Publishing Services, York, 55–60.

Dixon, C. 1997: Pete's tool: Identity and sex-play in the design and technology of the classroom. *Gender and Education*, 9, 89–104.

Dollimore, J. 1991: *Sexual Dissidence: Augustine to Wilde, Freud to Foucault*. Clarendon, Oxford.

Dolowitz, D. P. 1997: British employment policy in the 1980s: Learning from the American experience. *Governance*, 10, 23–42.

Dolowitz, D. P. 1998: *Learning from America: Policy Transference and the Development of the British Workfare State*. Academic, Brighton.

Dolton, P. and O'Neil, D. 1996: Unemployment duration and the restart effect. *Economic Journal*, 106, 387–400.

Doogan, K. 2001: Insecurity and long-term employment. *Work, Employment and Society*, 15, 419–41.

du Gay, P. 1996: *Consumption and Identity at Work*. Sage, London.

du Gay, P. and Pryke, M. (eds) 2002: *Cultural Economy*. Sage, London.

Duneier, M. 1992: *Slim's Table: Race, Respectability and Masculinity*. University of Chicago Press, Chicago.

Duster, T. 1995: Postindustrialisation and youth employment. In K. McFate, R. Lawson and W. Wilson (eds), *Poverty, Inequality and the Future of Social Policy: Western States in the New World Order*, Russell Sage Foundation, New York.

Dyer, R. 1997: *White*. Routledge, London.

Edley, N. and Wetherell, M. 1995: *Men in Perspective: Practice, Power and Identity*. Prentice Hall, London.

Edley, N. and Wetherell, M. 1996: Masculinity, power and identity. In M. Mac An Ghaill (ed.), *Understanding Masculinities*, Open University Press, Buckingham, 97–113.

Edwards, T. 1994: *Erotics and Politics: Male Sexuality, Masculinity and Feminism*. Routledge London.

Egerton, M. and Savage, M. 2000: Age stratification and class formation: A longitudinal study on the social mobility of young men and women, 1971–1991. *Work, Employment and Society*, 14, 23–49.

Ehrenreich, B. 2001: *Nickel and Dimed: On (Not) Getting by in America*. Metropolitan Books, New York.

Ekinsymth, C. and Bynner, J. 1994: *The Basic Skills of Young Adults*. Basic Skills Agency, London.

Elliott, L. and Atkinson, D. 1999: *The Age of Insecurity*. Verso, London.

Epstein, D. 1993: Practising heterosexuality. *Curriculum Studies*, 1, 275–86.

Epstein, D. 1997: Boyz own stories: Masculinities and sexualities in schools. *Gender and Education*, 9, 105–15.

Epstein, P., Ellwood, D., Hey, V. and Maw, J. (eds) 1998: *Failing Boys?* Open University Press, Buckingham.

Erdem, E. and Glyn, A. 2001: Job deficits in UK regions. In R. Dickens, J. Wadsworth and P. Gregg (eds), *The State of Working Britain: Update 2001*, Centre for Economic Performance, London School of Economics, York Publishing Services, York, 34–41.

Evans, M. 1997: *Introducing Contemporary Feminist Thought*. Polity, Cambridge.

Fainstein, S., Gordon, I. and Harloe, M. (eds) 1992: *Divided City: New York and London in the Contemporary World*. Basil Blackwell, Oxford.

Faludi, S. 2000: *Stiffed: The Betrayal of Modern Man*. Random House, London.

Family Planning Association (FPA) 1999: *Strides: A Practical Guide to Sex and Relationships Education with Young Men*, available from the FPA, 2–12 Pentonville Rd, London N1 9FP.

Faux, J. and Mishel, L. 2001: Inequality and the global economy. In Hutton, W. and Giddens, A. (eds), *On the Edge: Living with Global Capitalism*, Vintage, London, 93–111.

Fenkel, S., Tam, M., Korczynski, M. and Shire, K. 1999: *On the Front-line: Organisation of Work in the Information Economy*. Cornell University Press, Ithaca.

Fernandez Kelly, P. 1994: Towanda's triumph: Social and cultural capital in the transition to adulthood in the urban ghetto. *International Journal of Urban and Regional Research*, 18, 88–111.

Finch, J. and Mason, J. 1993: *Negotiating Family Responsibilities*. Routledge, London.

Fine, G. A. and Sandstrom, K. L. 1988: *Knowing Children: Participant Observation with Minors*. Sage, Newbury Park, Calif.

Fine, M. and Weiss, L. 1998: *The Unknown City: The Lives of Poor and Working Class Young Adults*. Beacon, Boston.

Fine, M., Weiss, L., Addelstone, J. and Marusza, J. 1997: (In)secure times: constructing white working class masculinities in the late twentieth century. *Gender and Society*, 11, 52–68.

Finnegan, W. 1998: *Cold New World: Growing up in a Harder Country*. Picador, London.

Ford, N. 1991: *The Socio-sexual Lifestyles of Young People in the South-West of England*. South-West Regional Health Authority, King Square House, 26–27 King Square, Bristol BS2 8EF.

Foucault, M. 1977: *Discipline and Punish*. Allen Lane, London.

Frankenberg, R. 1993: *White Women, Race Matters: The Social Construction of Whiteness*. Routledge, London.

Frankenberg, R. (ed.) 1997: *Displacing Whiteness: Essays in Social and Cultural Criticism*. Duke University Press, Durham, NC.

Fraser, N. 1997: *Justice Interruptus: Critical Reflections on the 'Post-socialist' Condition*. Routledge, London.

Freeman, C. 2000: *High Tech and High Heels in the Global Economy*. Duke University Press, Durham, NC.

Friedman, S. S. 1998: *Mappings: Feminism and the Cultural Geographies of Encounter*. Princeton University Press, Princeton.

Frosh, S. 1995: Unpacking masculinity: From rationality to fragmentation. In C. Burck and B. Speed (eds), *Gender, Power and Relationships*, Routledge, London, 218–31.

Frosh, S., Phoenix, A. and Pattman, R. 2002: *Young Masculinities: Understanding Boys in Contemporary Societies*. Palgrave, Basingstoke.

Fryer, D. and Ullah, P. (eds) 1987: *Unemployed People: Social and Psychological Perspectives*. Open University Press, Milton Keynes.

Furlong, A. 1992: *Growing up in a Classless Society? School to Work Transition*. Edinburgh University Press, Edinburgh.

Furlong, A. and Cartmel, F. 1997: *Young People and Social Change: Individualisation and Risk in Late Modernity*. Open University Press, Buckingham.

Gabriel, Y. 1988: *Working Lives in Catering*. Routledge, London.

Gallie, D., White, M., Cheng, Y. and Tomlinson, M. 1998: *Restructuring the Employment Relationship*. Oxford University Press, Oxford.

Gamble, A. 1994: *Free Economy and the Strong State: The Politics of Thatcherism*. Macmillan, London.

Gamble, A. and Kelly, G. 1996: The new politics of ownership. *New Left Review*, 220, 62–97.

Giddens, A. 1991: *Modernity and Self-Identity: Self and Society in the Late Modern Age*. Polity, Cambridge.

Giddens, A. 1992: *The Transformation of Intimacy*. Polity, Cambridge.

Giddens, A. 1998: *The Third Way: The Renewal of Social Democracy*. Polity, Cambridge.

Gillborn, D. 2002: *Education and Institutional Racism*. Institute of Education, London.

Gillis, J. R. 1981: *Youth and History: Transition and Change in European Age Relations 1770–Present*. Academic, New York.

Gilmore, D. 1993: *Manhood in the Making: Cultural Concepts of Masculinity*. Yale University Press, New Haven.

Gilroy, P. 1987: *There Ain't No Black in the Union Jack: The Cultural Politics of Race and Nation*. Hutchinson, London.

Gilroy, P. 1990: 'One nation under a groove': The cultural politics of 'race' and racism in Britain. In D. Goldberg (ed.), *Anatomy of Racism*, University of Minnesota Press, Minnesota, 263–82.

Gilroy, P. 1993: *Black Atlantic: Modernity and Double Consciousness*. Verso, London.

Glennester, H. 1999: *Poverty, Social Exclusion and the Neighbourhood: Studying the Area Bases of Social Exclusion*, Centre for the Analysis of Social Exclusion, London School of Economics, London.

Gofton, L. 1990: On the town: Drink and the 'new lawlessness'. *Youth and Policy*, 29, 33–9.

Gorz, A. 1999: *Reclaiming Work: Beyond the Wage-Based Society*. Polity, Cambridge (originally published in French in 1997).

Gosling, A., Johnson, P., McCrae, J. and Paull, G. 1997: *The Dynamics of Low Pay and Unemployment in Early 1990s Britain*. Institute for Fiscal Studies, London.

Government Statistical Service 1995: *Family Spending*. HMSO, London.

Granovetter, M. 1996: *Getting a Job*. Harvard University Press, Cambridge, Mass.

Gray, J. 1998: A strained rebirth of liberal Britain. *New Statesman*, 21 August, 28–9.

Green, A. and Owen, D. 1998: *Where Are the Jobless? Changing Unemployment and Non-employment in Cities and Regions.* Policy Press, Bristol.

Greg, P. and Wadsworth, J. 2000: Mind the gap please: The changing nature of entry level jobs in Britain. *Economica*, 67, 499–524.

Gregg, P. and Wadsworth, J. (eds) 1999: *The State of Working Britain.* Manchester University Press, Manchester.

Griffin, C. 1993: *Representation of Youth: The Study of Youth and Adolescence in Britain and America.* Polity, Cambridge.

Griffin, C. 2000: Discourses of crisis and loss: Analysing the boys' underachievement debate. *Journal of Youth Studies*, 3, 197–8.

Griffin, C. and Lees, S. 1997: Editorial, special issue on Masculinities in Education. *Youth and Education*, 9, 5–8.

Grosz, E. 1994: *Volatile Bodies.* Indiana University Press, Bloomington.

Hall, S. 1978: Racism and reaction. In Commission for Racial Equality (ed.), *Five Views of Multi-racial Britain*, Commission for Racial Equality, London.

Hall, S. 1988: *Thatcherism and the Crisis of the Left: The Hard Road to Renewal.* Verso, London.

Hall, S. 1991: Old and new identities, old and new ethnicities. In A. King (ed.), *Culture, Globalisation and the World System*, Macmillan, London.

Hall, S. 1992: The question of cultural identity. In S. Hall, D. Held and T. McGrew (eds), *Modernity and its Futures*, Polity, Cambridge.

Hall, S. and Jefferson, T. (eds) 1976: *Resistance Through Rituals: Youth Subcultures in Post-war Britain.* Hutchinson, London.

Hall, S., Critcher, C., Jefferson, T. and Roberts, B. 1978: *Policing the Crisis: Mugging, the State and Law and Order.* Macmillan, London.

Hall, S. and Martin, J. (eds) 1983: *The Politics of Thatcherism.* Lawrence and Wishart, London.

Hammersley, M. and Woods, P. (eds) 1984: *Life in School.* Open University Press, Milton Keynes.

Hanson, S. and Pratt, G. 1995: *Gender, Work and Space.* Routledge, London.

Harding, S. 1987: *Feminism and Methodology.* Indiana University Press, Bloomington.

Hargreaves, D. 1967: *Social Relations in a Secondary School.* Routledge and Kegan Paul, London.

Harvey, D. 1989: *The Condition of Postmodernity.* Blackwell, Oxford.

Harvey, D. 2001: *Spaces of Capital: Towards a Critical Geography.* Routledge, London.

Haylett, C. 2001: Illegitimate subjects? Abject whites, neoliberal modernisation and middle-class multiculturalism. *Environment and Planning D: Society and Space*, 19, 351–79.

Haywood, C. and Mac an Ghaill, M. 1995: The sexual politics of the curriculum: Contesting values. *International Studies in the Sociology of Education*, 5, 221–36.

Hearn, J. 1992: *Men in the Public Eye: The Construction and Deconstruction of Public Men and Public Masculinities*. Routledge, London.

Hearn, J. and Morgan, D. 1990: *Men: Masculinites and Social Theory*. Unwin Hyman, London.

Hebdige, D. 1988: *Hiding in the Light*. Comedia, London.

Henson, K. and Rogers, J. K. 2001: 'Why Marcia, you've changed!' Male clerical temporary workers doing masculinity in a feminized occupation. *Gender and Society*, 15, 218–38.

Hill, D. 1997: *The Future of Men*. Weidenfeld and Nicholson, London.

Hills, J., Le Grand, J. and Paichaud, D. (eds) 2002: *Understanding Social Exclusion*. Oxford University Press, Oxford.

Hobcraft, J. 1998: *Intergenerational and Life-Course Transmission of Social Exclusion: Influences of Childhood Poverty, Family Disruption and Contact with the Police*. Center for the Analysis of Social Exclusion, Paper 15, London School of Economics, London.

Hochschild, A. 1983: *The Managed Heart: The Commercialisation of Human Feeling*. University of California Press, Berkeley.

Hodkinson, P., Sparkes, A. and Hodkinson, C. 1996: *Triumphs and Tears: Young People, Markets and the Transition from School to Work*. David Fulton, London.

Holland, J., Ramazanoglu, C. and Sharpe, S. 1993: *Wimp or Gladiator: Contradictions in Acquiring Male Sexuality*. Tufnell, London.

Holland, J., Ramazanoglu, C., Sharpe, S. and Thomson, R. 1998: *The Male in the Head: Young People, Heterosexuality and Power*. Tufnell, London.

Hollands, R. 1995: *Friday Night, Saturday Night: Youth Cultural Identification in the Post-industrial City*. Newcastle University Press, Newcastle.

Holloway, S., Valentine, G. and Bingham, N. 1999: Institutionalising technologies: Masculinities, femininities and the heterosexual economy of the classroom. *Environment and Planning A*, 32, 617–33.

Hollway, W. 1984: Gender difference and the production subjectivity. In J. Henriques, W. Hollway, C. Urwin, C. Venn and V. Walkerdine (eds), *Changing the Subject: Psychology, Social Regulation and Subjectivity*, Methuen, London, 26–59.

Home Office 2002: *Secure Borders, Safe Haven: Integration with Diversity in Modern Britain*. Cm 5387. HMSO, London

hooks, b. 1992: *Black Looks: Race and Representation*. Turnaround, London.

hooks, b. 2000: *Where we Stand: Class Matters*. Routledge, London.

House of Commons Social Security Committee 1998: *Social Security Reforms: Lessons from the United States of America*. HC 552. HMSO, London.

Hudson, R. and Williams, A. 1995: *Divided Britain*. 2nd ed. Wiley, Chichester.

Hutton, W. 1996: *The State we're in*. Vintage, London.

Iacovou, M. and Berthoud, R. 2001: *Young People's Lives: A Map of Europe*. University of Essex, Institute of Social and Economic Research, Essex.

Irwin, S. 1995: *Rights of Passage: Social Change and the Transition from Youth to Adulthood*. UCL Press, London.

Jackman, R. and Savouri, S. 1999: Has Britain solved the 'regional problem'? In P. Gregg and J. Wadsworth (eds), *The State of Working Britain*, Manchester University Press, Manchester, 29–46.

Jackson, D. 1990: *Unmasking Masculinity*. Unwin Hyman, London.

Jackson, P. 1991: The cultural politics of masculinity: Towards a social geography. *Transactions of the Institute of British Geographers*, 16, 199–213.

Jackson, P. 1998: Constructions of 'whiteness' in the geographical imagination. *Area*, 30, 99–106.

James, A., Jenks, C. and Prout, A. 1998: *Theorizing Childhood*. Polity, Cambridge.

Jarvis, H., Pratt, A. and Wu, P. 2001: *The Secret Life of Cities: The Social Reproduction of Everyday Life*. Prentice Hall, London.

Jefferson, T. 1994: Theorising masculine subjectivity. In T. Newburn and E. Stanko (eds), *Just Boys Doing Business? Men, Masculinities and Crime*, Routledge, London.

Johnson, A., Wadsworth, J., Wellings, K. and Field, J. 1994: *Sexual Attitudes and Lifestyles*. Blackwell, Oxford.

Johnson, P. and Reed, H. 1996: Intergenerational mobility among the rich and poor: Results from the National Child Development Survey. *Oxford Review of Economic Policy*, 7, 127–42.

Johnston, L., MacDonald, R., Mason, P., Ridley, L. and Webster, C. 2000: *Snakes and Ladders: Young People, Transitions and Social Exclusion*. Policy Press and the Joseph Rowntree Foundation, York.

Jones, G. 1987: Leaving the parental home: An analysis of early housing careers. *Journal of Social Policy*, 16, 49–74.

Jones, G. 1995: *Leaving Home*. Open University Press, Buckingham.

Jones, G. 2002: *The Youth Divide: Diverging Paths to Adulthood*. York Publishing Services, York.

Jones, G. and Wallace, C. 1992: *Youth, Family and Citizenship*. Open University Press, Buckingham.

Jones, M. 1996: Full steam ahead to a workfare state? Analysing the UK Employment Department's abolition. *Policy and Politics*, 24, 137–57.

Jordan, E. 1995: Fighting boys and fantasy play: The construction of masculinity in the early years of school. *Gender and Education*, 7, 69–86.

Kanter, R. 1977: *Men and Women of the Organisation*. Basic Books, New York.

Katz, C. 1991: Sow what you know: The struggle for social reproduction in rural Sudan. *Annals of the Association of American Geographers*, 81, 488–514.

Katz, C. 1993: Growing girls/closing circles: Limits on the spaces of knowing in rural Sudan and US cities. In C. Katz and J. Monk (eds), *Full Circle: Geographies of Women Over the Life Course*, Routledge, London, 88–106.

Kehily, M. and Nayak, A. 1997: 'Lads and laughter': Humour and the production of heterosexual hierarchies. *Gender and Education*, 9, 69–88.

Kenway, J. and Willis, S. with Blackmore, J. and Rennie, L. 1998: *Answering Back: Girls, Boys and Feminism in Schools*. Routledge, London.

Kerfoot, D. 1999: The organisation of intimacy. In S. Whitehead and R. Moodley (eds), *Transforming Managers: Gendering Change in the Public Sector*, UCL Press, London, 184–98.

Kett, J. 1977: *Rites of Passage*. Basic Books, New York.

Kiernan, K. 1985: *A Demographic Analysis of First Marriages in England and Wales 1950–1985*, CPS Research Paper 85–1. Centre for Population Studies, London.

Kiernan, K. 1995: *Transition to Parenthood: Young Mothers, Young Fathers – Associated Factors and Later Life Experiences* STICER Welfare Sate Programme Discussion Paper WSP/113. London School of Economics, London.

King, D. S. 1995: *Actively Seeking Work? The Politics of Unemployment and Welfare Policy in the United States and Britain*. University of Chicago Press, Chicago.

Kobayashi, A. and Peake, L. 1994: Unnatural discourse: 'race' and gender in geography. *Gender, Place and Culture*, 1, 225–43.

Kondo, D. 1990: *Crafting Selves: Power, Gender and Discourses of Identity in a Japanese Workplace*. University of Chicago Press, Chicago.

Krahn, H. and Lowe, G. 1991: Transitions to work: Findings from a longitudinal study of high school and university students in three Canadian cities. In D. Ashton and G. Lowe (eds), *Making their Way: Education, Training and the Labour Market in Canada and Britain*, University of Toronto Press, Toronto, 23–39.

Kuhn, A. 1995: *Family Secrets: Acts of Memory and Imagination*. Verso, London.

Lash, S. 1994: Reflexivity and its doubles: Structure, aesthetics, community. In U. Beck, A. Giddens and S. Lash (eds), *Reflexive Modernisation*, Polity, Cambridge, 110–73.

Lash, S. and Urry, J. 1987: *The End of Organised Capitalism*. Polity, Cambridge.

Lash, S. and Urry, J. 1994: *Economies of Signs and Space*. Sage, London.

Laslett, P. 1971: *The World we Have Lost*. Metheun, London.

Leadbeater, C. 1999: *Living on Thin Air*. Viking, London.

Lee, R. 1995: Look after the pounds and the people will look after themselves. *Environment and Planning A*, 27, 1577–94.

Leidner, R. 1991: Selling hamburgers, selling insurance: Gender, work and identity. *Gender and Society*, 5, 154–77.

Leidner, R. 1993: *Fast Food, Fast Talk: Service Work and the Routinisation of Everyday Life*. University of California Press, Berkeley.

Leslie, D. 2002: Gender, retail employment and the clothing commodity chain. *Gender, Place and Culture*, 9, 61–76.

Lewis, M. 1989: *Liar's Poker: Two Cities, True Greed*. Hodder and Stoughton, London.

Lewis, O. 1961: *The Children of Sanchez*. Methuen, London.

Lewis, O. 1966: The culture of poverty. *Scientific American*, 215, 4.

Llewelyn Lewis, E. 1924: *The Children of the Unskilled*. Publisher unknown, London.

Lloyd, T. 1999: *Young Men, the Job Market and Gendered Work*. Work and Opportunity Series 8, Joseph Rowntree Foundation, York.

Lowe, G. and Krahn, H. 2000: Work aspirations and attitudes in an era of labour market restructuring: A comparison of two Canadian youth cohorts. *Work, Employment and Society*, 14, 1–22.

Mac an Ghaill, M. 1994: *The Making of Men: Masculinities, Sexualities and Schooling*. Open University Press, Buckingham

Mac an Ghaill, M. 1996a: Irish Masculinities and sexualities. In England in L. Adkins and V. Merchant (eds), *Sexualising the Social: Power and the Organisation of Sexuality*, Macmillan, London, 122–44.

Mac an Ghaill, M. (ed.) 1996b: *Understanding Masculinities: Social Relations and Cultural Arenas*. Open University Press, Buckingham.

Macdonald, C. L. and Sirianni, C. (eds) 1996: *Working in the Service Society*. Temple University Press, Philadelphia.

MacDonald, R. 1998: Youth transitions and social exclusion: Some issues for youth research in the U.K. *Journal of Youth Studies*, 1, 163–76.

MacDonald, R. (ed.) 1997: *Youth, the 'Underclass' and Social Exclusion*. Routledge, London.

McClintock, A. 1995: *Imperial Leather: Race, Gender and Sexuality in the Colonial Context*. Routledge, New York.

McConville, B. 1998: *The State they're in: Young People in Britain Today*. Youth Press, Leicester.

MacDonald, R. 1994: Fiddly jobs, undeclared working and the 'something for nothing' society. *Work, Employment and Society*, 8, 507–30.

Machin, S. 1998: Childhood disadvantage and intergenerational transmissions in economic status. In A. B. Atkinson and J. Hills (eds), *Exclusion, Employment and Opportunity*, CASE Paper 4. London School of Economics, London, 55–64.

MacLennan, E., Fitz, J. and Sullivan, J. 1985: *Working Children*, Pamphlet 34. Low Pay Unit, London.

Majors, R. 1990: Cool pose: Black masculinity and sports. In M. Messner and D. Sabo (eds), *Men and the Gender Order*, Human Kinetics, New York, 109–14.

Majors, R. and Billson, J. 1992: *Cool Pose: The Dilemmas of Black Manhood in America*. Lexington, New York.

Makeham, P. 1980: *Youth Unemployment*, Research paper 11. Department of Employment, London.

Marshall, A. 1920: *Principles of Economics*. Macmillan, London.

Martin, R. and Townroe, P. 1992: *Regional Development in the 1990s: The British Isles in Transition*. Jessica Kingsley, London.

Massey, D. 1984: *Spatial Divisions of Labour*. Macmillan, London (revised edition 1994).

Massey, D. 1995: Masculinity, dualisms and high technology. *Transactions, Institute of British Geographers*, 20, 487–99.

Massey, D. 1997: Economic/non-economic. In R. Lee and J. Wills (eds), *Geographies of Economies*. Edward Arnold, London, 27–36.

Massey, D. and Allen, J. (eds) 1984: *Geography Matters*. Cambridge University Press Cambridge.

Massey, D. S. and Denton, N. A. 1993: *American Apartheid: Segregation and the Making of the Underclass*. Harvard University Press, Cambridge, Mass.

Matthews, H. and Limb, M. 1999: Defining and agenda for the geography of children: Review and prospect. *Progress in Human Geography*, 23, 61–90.

McDowell, L. 1991: Life without father and Ford: The new gender order of postFordism. *Transactions, Institute of British Geographers*, 16, 400–19.

McDowell, L. 1997a: *Capital Culture: Gender at Work in the City*. Blackwell, Oxford.

McDowell, L. 1997b: *Undoing Place? A Geographical Reader*. Edward Arnold, London.

McDowell, L. 2000: The trouble with men? *International Journal of Urban and Regional Research*, 24, 201–9.

McDowell, L. 2001a: Men, management and multiple masculinities in organisations. *Geoforum*, 32, 2, 181–98.

McDowell, L. 2001b: Father and Ford revisited: Gender, class and employment change in the new millenium. *Transactions of the Institute of British Geographers*, 24, 448–64.

McDowell, L. 2001c: It's that Linda again: Ethical and practical issues in research with young men. *Ethics, Place and Environment*, 4, 88–100.

McDowell, L. 2002: Working with young men. *Geographical Review*, 91, 201–14.

McInnes, J. 1997: *The End of Masculinity*. Open University Press, Buckingham.

McRobbie, A. 1980: Settling accounts with subcultures: A feminist critique. *Screen Education*, 34, 37–49.

McRobbie, A. 1991: *Feminism and Youth Culture*. Macmillan, Basingstoke.

McRobbie, A. 2002: From Holloway to Hollywood: Happiness at work in the new cultural economy? In P. du Gay and M. Pryke (eds), *Cultural Economy*, Sage, London, 97–114.

Middleton, P. 1992: *The Inward Gaze: Masculinity, Subjectivity and Modern Culture*. Routledge, London.

Miles, R. 1991: *The Rites of Man: Love, Sex and Death in the Making of the Male*. Grafton, London.

Miles, S. 2000: *Youth Lifestyle in a Changing World*. Open University Press, Buckingham.

Millar, J. 2000: *Keeping track of Welfare Reform: The New Deal Programmes.* Joseph Rowntree Foundation, York.

Miller, D. 1994: *Modernity: An Ethnographic Approach: Dualism and Mass Consumption in Trinidad.* Berg, Oxford.

Miller, J. and Glassner, B. 1997: The 'inside' and the 'outside': Finding realities in interviews. In D. Silverman (ed.), *Qualitative Research: Theory, Method and Practice*, Sage, London, 99–112.

Mitos, E. and Browne, K. 1998: Gender differences in education: The under-achievement of boys. *Sociology Review*, September, 27–31.

Mitterauer, M. 1992: *A History of Youth.* Blackwell, Oxford (originally published in German in 1986).

Mizen, P., Bolton, A. and Pole, C. 1999: School-age workers: The paid employment of children in Britain. *Work, Employment and Society*, 13, 423–38.

Mohan, J. 1999: *A United Kingdom: Economic, Social and Political Geographies.* Edward Arnold, London.

Morgan, D. 1992: *Discovering Men.* Routledge, London.

Morgan, D. 1996: *Family Connections.* Polity, Cambridge.

Morgan, D. 2002: Private Men. In S. Whitehead (ed.), *Men and Maculinities*, Polity, Cambridge, 146–80.

Morrison, T. 1992: *Playing in the Dark: Whiteness and the Literary Imagination.* Harvard University Press, Cambridge, Mass.

Mortimore, P. and Whitty, G. 1997: *Can School Improvement Overcome the Effect of Disadvantage?* Institute of Education, London.

Mungham, G. and Pearson, G. (eds) 1976: *Working Class Youth Culture.* Routledge and Kegan Paul, London.

Musterd, S. and Ostendorf, W. 1998: *Urban Segregation and the Welfare State: Inequality and Exclusion in Western Cities.* Routledge, London.

Nardi, P. 1999: *Gay Men's Friendships: Invincible Communities.* University of Chicago Press, Chicago.

Negus, K. 2002: Identities and industries: The cultural formation of aesthetic economies. In P. du Gay and M. Pryke (eds), *Cultural Economy*, Sage, London, 115–31.

Newman, K. 1999: *There's No Shame in my Game: The Working Poor in the Inner City.* Vintage and Russell Sage Foundation, New York.

Nickson, D., Warhurst, A., Witz, A. and Cullen, A. 2001: The importance of being aesthetic: Work, employment and service organisation. In A. Sturdy, I. Grugulis and H. Willmott (eds), *Customer Service: Empowerment and Entrapment*, Palgrave, London, 170–90.

Nilan, P. 1995: Masculinity as social practice and cultural 'becoming'. *Journal of Interdisciplinary Gender Studies*, 1, 57–69.

O'Byrne, D. 1997: Working class culture: Local community and global conditions. In J. Eade (ed.), *Living the Global City*, Routledge, London, 73–89.

O'Donnell, M. and Sharpe, S. 2000: *Uncertain Masculinities: Youth, Ethnicity and Class in Contemporary Britain*. Routledge, London.

Offe, C. 1985: 'Work' – a central sociological concept? In C. Offe, *Disorganised Capitalism*, Polity, Cambridge, 129–50.

Oppenheim, C. 1998: *An Inclusive Society: Strategies for tackling Poverty*. Institute of Public Policy Research, London.

O'Regan, K. and Quigley, J. 1993: Family networks and youth access to jobs. *Journal of Urban Economics*, 34, 230–48.

Ortner, S. 1974: Is female as to male as nature is to culture? In M. Z. Rosaldo and L. Lamphere (eds), *Woman, Culture and Society*, Stanford University Press, California, 67–88.

Paechter, C. 1998: *Educating the Other: Gender, Power and Schooling*. Falmer Press, Brighton.

Panitch, L. and Leys, C. 2000: *Working Class: Global Realities*. Merlin, London.

Pastor, M., Jr 2001: Common ground at ground zero: The new economy and the new organizing in Los Angeles. *Antipode*, 33, 260–89.

Pateman, C. 1989: *The Disorder of Women*. Polity, Cambridge.

Payne, J. 1995: Routes beyond compulsory schooling. *Youth Cohort*, 31. Department of Employment, London.

Pearce, J. 1996: Urban Youth Cultures: Gender and spatial forms. *Youth and Policy*, 52, 1–11.

Pearson, G. 1983: *Hooligan: A History of Respectable Fears*. Macmillan, London.

Peck, J. 1996: *Work-Place: The Social Regulation of Labour Markets*. Guilford Press, New York.

Peck, 1998a: Workfare: A geopolitical etymology. *Environment and Planning D: Society and Space*, 16, 133–61.

Peck, J. 1998b: Workfare in the sun: Politics, representation and method in the US welfare-to-work strategies. *Political Geography*, 17, 535–66.

Peck, J. 1999: New Labourers: Making a New Deal for the 'workless class'. *Environment and Planning C: Government and Planning*, 17, 345–72.

Peck, J. 2001: *Workfare States*. Guilford Press, New York.

Peck, J. and Theodore, N. 1998: The limits of policy transfer: innovation and emulation in welfare-to-work. Paper presented at the annual conference of the Association for Public Policy Analysis and Management, New York, October (available from the first author at the School of Geography, University of Wisconsin).

Peck, J. and Theodore, N. 2000: 'Work first': Workfare and the regulation of contingent labour markets. *Cambridge Journal of Economics*, 24, 119–38.

Peck, J. and Tickell, A. 2002: Neoliberalizing space. *Antipode*, 34, 380–404.

Perrons, D. 2000: Care, paid work and leisure: Rounding the triangle. *Feminist Economics*, 6, 105–14.

Phillips, A. 1993: *The Trouble with Boys: Parenting the Men of the Future.* Pandora, London.

Phillips, A. 1999: *Which Equalities Matter?* Polity, Cambridge.

Philo, C. (ed.) 1995: *Off the Map: Poverty in Britain.* Child Poverty Action Group, London.

Piatt, W. 2001: A school sweetener. *Guardian*, 13 April.

Platt, A. 1969: *The Child-Savers: The Invention of Delinquency.* University of Chicago Press, Chicago.

Pollard, A. 1985: *The Social World of the Primary School.* Holt, Rhinehart and Winston, London.

Pollin, R. and Luce, S. 1998: *The Living Wage: Building a Fair Economy.* New Press, New York.

Poynter, C. 2000: *Restructuring in the Service Industries: Management Reform and Workplace Relations in the UK Service Sector.* Mansell, London.

Poynting, S., Noble, G. and Tabar, P. 1998: If anybody called me a wog, they wouldn't be speaking to me alone: Protest masculinity and Lebanese youth in Western Sydney. *Journal of Interdisciplinary Gender Studies*, 3, 76–94.

President's Commission on Law Enforcement and Administration of Justice. 1967: *The Challenge of Crime in a Free Society.* US Dept. of Justice, Washington, DC.

Pringle, R. 1998: *Sex and Medicine: Gender, Power and Authority in the Medical Profession.* Cambridge University Press, Cambridge.

Putnam, R. 1995: *Making Democracy Work: Civic Traditions in Modern Italy.* Princeton University Press, Princeton.

Quah, D. 1996: *The Invisible Hand and the Weightless Economy.* Centre for Economic Performance, London School of Economics, London.

Quah, D. 1999: *The Weightless Economy in Economic Development.* Centre for Economic Performance, London School of Economics, London.

Raffe, D. 1985: *Youth Employment in the UK, 1979–84.* Centre for Educational Sociology, Edinburgh.

Raffe, D. 1988: *Education and the Youth Labour Market.* Falmer Press, Brighton.

Raffe, D. and Willms, J. 1989: Schooling the discouraged worker: Local labour market effects on educational participation. *Sociology*, 23, 559–81.

Ray, L. and Sayer, S. (eds) 1999: *Culture and Economy.* Sage, London.

Reay, D. 1997: Feminist theory, habitus and social class: Disrupting notions of classlessness. *Women's Studies International Forum*, 20, 225–33.

Reay, D. 1998: *Class Work: Mothers' Involvement in their Children's Primary Schooling.* UCL Press, London.

Regional Trends 1999: National Office of Statistics, HMSO, London.

Rifkin, J. 2000: *The End of Work.* Penguin, London.

Ritzer, G. 1998: *The McDonaldisation Thesis.* Sage, London.

Roberts, K. 1993: Career trajectories and the mirage of increased social mobility. In I. Bates and G. Riseborough (eds), *Youth and Inequality*, Open University Press Buckingham, 229–45.

Roberts, K. 1995: *Youth and Employment in Modern Britain*. Oxford University Press, Oxford.

Robinson, P. 1998: Education, Training and the youth labour market. In P. Gregg and J. Wadsworth (eds), *The State of Working Britain*, Manchester University Press, Manchester, 147–67.

Robinson, P. and Oppenheim, C. 1998: *Social Exclusion Indicators: A Submission to the Social Exclusion Unit*. Institute for Public Policy Research, London.

Roche, J. and Tucker, S. 1996: *Youth in Society: Contemporary Theory, Policy and Practice*. Sage, London.

Rodgers, G. and Rodgers, J. 1990: *Precarious Jobs in Labour Market Regulation: The Growth of Atypical Employment in Western Europe*. International Institute of Labour Studies, Geneva.

Roediger, D. 1994: *The Wages of Whiteness: Race and the Making of the American Working Class*. Verso, New York.

Rotundo, E. A. 1993: *American Manhood: Transformations in Masculinity from the Revolution to the Modern Era*. Basic Books, New York.

Rubery, J. 1996: The labour market outlook and the outlook for labour market analysis. In R. Crompton, D. Gallie and K. Purcall (eds), *Changing Forms of Employment: Organisations, Skills and Gender*, Routledge, London, 23–39.

Rubery, J., Smith, M. and Fagan, C. 1999: *Women's Employment in Europe: Trends and Prospects*. Routledge, London.

Ruddick, S. 1996: *Young and Homeless in Hollywood*. Routledge, London.

Runnymede Commission 2000: *Report on the Future of Multi-ethnic Britain*. Profile, London

Rutter, M. 1979: *Fifteen Thousand Hours: Secondary Schools and their Effects on Children*. Open Books, London.

Salisbury, J. and Jackson, D. 1996: *Challenging Macho Values: Practical Ways of Working with Adolescent Boys*. Falmer Press, London.

Sassen, S. 2001: *The Global City*. 2nd ed. Princeton University Press, Princeton (new edition published 2001).

Sayer, A. 2001: What are you worth? Why class is an embarrassing subject. Paper presented at the British Sociological Association Annual Conference, Manchester, April (available from the author at the University of Lancaster).

Sayer, A. and Walker, R. 1992: *The New Social Economy: Reworking the Division of Labour*. Basil Blackwell, Oxford.

Schill, M. 1993: Race, the underclass and public policy. *Law and Social Enquiry*, 19, 433–56.

Schlosser, E. 2001: *Fast Food Nation: What the All-American Meal Is Doing to the World*. Allen Lane, London.

Schneider, E. 1999: *Vampires, Dragons and Egyptian Kings: Gangs in Postwar New York*. Princeton University Press, Princeton.

Sedgwick, E. K. 1994: *Epistemology of the Closet*. Penguin, London.

Segal, A. 2000: Masculinity, school and self in Sweden and the Netherlands. *Journal of Men's Studies*, 8, 171–94.

Segal, L. 1990: *Slow Motion: Changing Masculinities, Changing Men*. Virago, London.

Segal, L. 1999: *Why Feminism? Gender, Psychology, Politics*. Polity, Cambridge.

Sennett, R. 1966: *The Uses of Disorder: Personal Identity and City Life*. Faber, London.

Sennett, R. 1998: *The Corrosion of Character: The Personal Characteristics of Work in the New Capitalism*. W. W. Norton, New York.

Sewell, T. 1997: *Black Masculinities and Schooling: How Black Boys Survive Modern Schooling*. Trentham Books, Stoke on Trent.

Shilling, C. 1991: Social space, gender inequalities and educational differentiation. *British Journal of the Sociology of Education*, 12, 127–39.

Showalter, E. 1990: *Sexual Anarchy: Gender and Culture at the Fin de Siecle*. Penguin, London.

Sibley, D. 1995: *Geographies of Exclusion*. Routledge London.

Signs 1998: Special Issue on feminisms and Youth Culture. *Signs: A Journal of Feminist Culture*, 23.

Siltanen, J. 1986: Domestic Responsibilities and the structuring of employment. In R. Crompton and M. Mann (eds), *Gender and Stratification*, Polity, Cambridge, 23–38.

Siltanen, J. 1995: *Locating Gender: Occupational Segregation, Wages and Domestic Responsibilities*. UCL Press, London.

Silva, E. and Smart, C. (eds) 1999: *The New Family?* Sage, London.

Simpson, M. 1994: *Male Impersonators: Men Performing Masculinity*. Cassel, London.

Sinfield, Adrian 1998: *Gay and After*. Serpent's Tail, London.

Skeggs, B. 1992: Challenging masculinity and using sexuality. *British Journal of the Sociology of Education*, 12, 127–39.

Skeggs, B. 1997: *Formations of Class and Gender*. Sage, London.

Skelton, C. 1998: Feminism and research into masculinities and schooling. *Gender and Education*, 10, 217–27.

Skelton, T. and Valentine, G. (eds) 1998: *Cool Places: Geographies of Youth Cultures*. Routledge, London.

Smith, N. 2000: What happened to class? *Environment and Planning A*, 32, 1011–32.

Somers, M. 1994: The narrative constitution of identity: A relational and network approach. *Theory and Society*, 23, 605–49.

Sparkes, J. and Glennester, H. 2002: Preventing social exclusion: Education's contribution. In J. Hills, J. Le Grand and D. Paichaud (eds), *Understanding Social Exclusion*, Oxford University Press, Oxford, 178–201.

Stafford, B., Heaver, C., Ashworth, K., Bates, C., Walker, R., McKay, S. and Trickey, H. 1999: *Work and Young Men*. Joseph Rowtree Foundation, York.

Steedman, H. and Green, A. 1996: *Widening Participation in Further Education and Training: A Survey of the Issues.* Centre for Economic Performance, London School of Economics, London.

Storper, M. and Walker, R. 1989: *The Capitalist Imperative: Territory, Technology and Industrial Growth.* Basil Blackwell, Oxford.

Sturdy, A., Grugulis, I. and Willmott, H. (eds) 2001: *Customer Service: Power and Entrapment.* Palgrave, London.

Sunley, P., Martin, R. and Nativel, C. 2001: Mapping the New Deal: Local disparities in the performance of Welfare-to-Work. *Transactions, Institute of British Geographers*, 26, 484–512.

Sutton, C. 1974: Cultural duality in the Caribbean. *Caribbean Studies*, 14, 96–101.

Sweetman, C. (ed.) 1997: *Men and Masculinity.* Oxfam, Oxford.

Taylor, I., Evans, K. and Fraser, P. 1996: *A Tale of Two Cities: Global Change, Local Feeling and Everyday Life in the North of England. A Study in Manchester and Sheffield.* Routledge, London.

Taylor, I. and Jamieson, R. 1997: 'Proper little mesters': Nostalgia and protest masculinity in de-industrialised Sheffield. In S. Westwood and J. Williams (eds), *Imagining Cities: Scripts, Signs, Memories*, Routledge, London, 152–78.

Teese, R., Davies, M., Charlton, M. and Polesel, J. 1995: *Who Wins at School? Boys and Girls in Australian Secondary Education.* Department of Education Policy and Management, University of Melbourne, Melbourne.

Theodore, N. 1998: Wefare to what? Job availability and welfare reform in the US. *Working Brief*, February, 18–20.

Theodore, N. and Peck, J. 1998: Between work and welfare: workfare and the re-regulation of contingent labour markets. Paper presented at the twentieth annual meeting of the International Working Party on Labour Market segmentation, Trento, Italy, July (available from the second author at the School of Geography, University of Wisconsin, Madison).

Thorne, B. 1993: *Gender Play: Girls and Boys in School.* Rutgers University Press, New Brunswick, NJ.

Thrasher, F. 1927: *The Gang.* University of Chicago Press, Chicago.

Tilly, C. 1999: *Durable Inequality.* University of California Press, Berkeley.

Tolson, A. 1977: *The Limits of Masculinity.* Tavistock, London.

Training and Enterprise Council 1998: *TECS and CCTEs Working Towards Achieving Social and Economic Inclusion.* Training and Enterprise Council and Department for Education and Employment, Sheffield.

Turok, I. and Edge, N. 1999: *The Jobs Gap in Britain's Cities.* Joseph Rowntree and Policy Press, Bristol.

Turok, I. and Webster, D. 1998: The New Deal: Jeopardised by the geography of unemployment. *Local Economy*, 13, 309–28.

Valentine, C. 1968: *Culture and Poverty.* University of Chicago Press, Chicago.

Valentine, G. 1996: Angels and devils: Moral landscapes of childhood. *Environment and Planning D: Society and Space*, 14, 581–99.

Valentine, G. 1999: Being seen and heard? The ethical complexities of working with children and young people at home and at school. *Ethics, Place and Environment*, 2, 141–55.

Valentine, G. 2000: Exploring childhood and young people's narratives of identity. *Geoforum*, 31, 257–68.

Van Reenen, J. 2001: No more scivvy schemes? Active labour market policies and the British new deal for the young unemployed in context. In D. Card and R. Freeman (eds), *Seeking a Premier League Economy*, University of Chicago Press, Chicago.

Wajcman, J. 1998: *Managing Like a Man: Women and Men in Corporate Management*. Polity, Cambridge.

Walby, S. 1997: *Gender Transformations*. Routledge, London.

Walker, A. and Walker, C. (eds) 1997: *Britain Divided: The Growth of Social Exclusion in the 1980s and 1990s*. Child Poverty Action Group, London.

Walker, D. 2001: Getting to the top of the class. *Guardian*, 30 April.

Walker, J. 1986: Romanticising resistance, romanticising culture: Problems in Willis' theory of cultural production. *British Journal of Sociology of Education*, 7, 59–80.

Walker, L. 1998: Chivalrous masculinity among juvenile offenders in western Sydney: A new perspective on young working class men and crime. *Current Issues in Criminal Justice*, 9, 279–93.

Walker, R. 1998: The Americanisation of British welfare: A case study of policy transfer. *Focus*, 19, 32–40.

Walkowitz, C. 2002: The social relations of body work. *Work, Employment and Society*, 16, 497–510.

Wallace, C. 1987: *For Richer, for Poorer: Growing up in and out of Work*. Tavistock, London.

Wallace, W. 1999: Boy's own torment. *Guardian: Society*, 14 April.

Walter, B. 2001: *Outsiders inside: Whiteness, Place and Irish Women*. Routledge, London.

Ward, L. 2001: CRE to pay more heed to young white men. *Guardian*, 17 December.

Ware, V. 1992: *Beyond the Pale: White Women, Racism and History*. Verso, London.

Warhurst, C. and Thompson, P. 1998: Hands, hearts and minds: Changing work and workers at the end of the century. In P. Thompson and C. Warhurst (eds), *Workplaces of the Future*, Macmillan, London.

Watson, G. 1994: The flexible labour force. *Employment Gazette*, July, 239–47.

Watt, P. 1998: Youth, 'race' and place in the South East of England. *Environment and Planning D: Society and Space*, 16, 687–703.

Webb, S. 1996: *Poverty Dynamics in Great Britain*. Institute for Fiscal Studies, London.

Webster, C. 1996: Local heroes: Violent racism, localism and spacism among Asian and white young people. *Youth and Policy*, 53, 15–27.

Weeks, J. 1991: *Sexuality and its Discontents: Meanings, Myths and Modern Sexualities*. Routledge, London.

Weeks, J. 1995: *Invented Moralities: Sexual Values in an Age of Uncertainty*. Polity, Cambridge.

Weeks, J. 2000: *Making Sexual History*. Polity, Cambridge.

West, C. and Zimmerman, D. 1987: Doing gender. *Gender and Society*, 1, 125–51.

West, P., Wight, D. and Macintyre, S. 1993: Heterosexual behaviour of Eighteen-year olds in the Glasgow area. *Journal of Adolescence*, 16, 367–96.

Westwood, S. 1990: Racism, black masculinity and the politics of space. In J. Hearn and D. Morgan (eds), *Men, Masculinities and Social Theory*, Unwin Hyman, London.

Wexler, P. 1992: *Becoming Somebody: Toward a Social Psychology of School*. Falmer Press, London.

Whitehead, S. 2002: *Men and Masculinities: Key themes and New Directions*. Polity, Cambridge.

Whitehead, S. and Barrett, F. (eds) 2001: *The Masculinities Reader*. Polity, Cambridge.

Whyte, J. 1983: *Beyond the Wendy House*. Longman, London.

Wight, D. 1994: Boys' thoughts and talk about sex in a working class locality of Glasgow. *Sociological Review*, 42, 703–37.

Wight, D. 1996: Beyond the predatory male: The diversity of young Glaswegian men's discourses to describe heterosexual relationships. In L. Adkins and V. Merchant (eds), *Sexualizing the Social: Power and the Organisation of Sexuality*, Macmillan, London, 145–70.

Wilkinson, S. and Kitzinger, C. (eds) 1995: *Feminism and Discourse*. Sage, London.

Willetts, D. 1998: *Welfare to Work*. Social Market Foundation, London.

Williamson, H. 1997: *Youth and Policy: Contexts and Consequences – Young Men, Transition and Social Exclusion*. Ashgate, Aldershot.

Willis, P. 1977: *Learning to Labour: How Working Class Kids Get Working Class Jobs*. Hutchinson, London.

Willis, P. 1984: Youth unemployment: Thinking the unthinkable. *Youth and Policy*, 2, 17–36.

Wilson, P. 1969: Reputation and respectability: A suggestion for Caribbean ethnography. *Man* 4, 70–84.

Wilson, W. J. 1997: *When Work Disappears: The New World of the Urban Poor*. Vintage, New York.

Winchester, H. and Costello, L. 1995: Living on the street: Social organisation and gender relations of Australian street kids. *Environment and Planning D: Society and Space*, 13, 329–48.

Woods, P. and Hammersley, M. (eds) 1993: *Gender and Ethnicity in Schools: Ethnographic Accounts*. Routledge, London.

Woodward, W. 2000: Single sex lessons to counter lad culture. *Guardian*, 21 August.

Wright, S. (ed.) 1994: *Anthropology of Organisations*. Routledge, London.

Young, I. M. 1990: *Justice and the Politics of Difference*. Princeton University Press, Princeton.

Young, L. 1996: *Fear of the Dark: 'Race', Gender and Sexuality in the Cinema*. Routledge, London.

Zukin, S. 1995: *Cultures of Cities*. Blackwell, Oxford.

Index